The Political Web
of American Schools

The Political Web
of American Schools

FREDERICK M. WIRT
University of California, Berkeley

MICHAEL W. KIRST
Stanford University

Little, Brown and Company   *Boston*

LIBRARY OF CONGRESS CATALOG CARD NUMBER: 79-188158

FIRST PRINTING

*Published simultaneously in Canada
by Little, Brown & Company (Canada) Limited*

PRINTED IN THE UNITED STATES OF AMERICA

Copyrights and Acknowledgments

The authors thank the following publishers and copyright holders for permission to use material reprinted in this book:

AMERICAN POLITICAL SCIENCE ASSOCIATION. For Table 6.3 on page 102, from James Q. Wilson and Edward C. Banfield, "Public Regardingness as a Value Premise in Voting Behavior," *American Political Science Review,* 58 (1964), 833.

CENTER FOR APPLIED RESEARCH IN EDUCATION, INC. For Table 7.4 on page 127, from Laurence Iannaccone, *Politics in Education* (New York, 1967), p. 57.

DAEDALUS. For Figure 9.2 on page 188, from Paul B. Sheatsley, "White Attitudes Toward the Negro," *Daedalus,* 95 (1966), 219.

D. C. HEATH & COMPANY. For quotations on pages 227, 236, and 238, from Sheldon S. Wolin, "Politics, Education, and Theory," in Michael W. Kirst (ed.), *State, School, and Politics: Research Directions.* Copyright © 1972 by D. C. Heath & Company.

NATIONAL SCHOOL BOARDS ASSOCIATION. For a quotation on pages 6 and 7, from David B. Tyack, "Needed: The Reform of a Reform," in NSBA, *New Dimensions of School Board Leadership,* pp. 30–31. Copyright © 1969 by National School Boards Association.

PRENTICE-HALL, INC. For Figure 1.2 on page 18, from David Easton, *A Framework for Political Analysis,* diagram 2, p. 110. Copyright © 1965 by Prentice-Hall, Inc., Englewood Cliffs, N.J.

For Wendy, Chip, and Anne,
who must endure or enjoy the schools of which we write

Preface

This book is an effort to talk to political scientists and educators about what is happening to American schools. The diversity of these audiences, even though they provide most of our concepts, makes difficult the writing of a book that will reach both. Their disciplines seem to have a common focus in the school and its relationship to the community. Yet, oddly enough, recent political science has had little to say about schools, even though classical political theory did deal with them. Rather, for reasons not altogether clear, political scientists, although they have applied their concepts and methods of research to every other institution, have avoided applying them to this one. We notice the oddity of a political discipline's ignoring governing units and electoral contests more numerous than any others in America.

In addition, scholars of education who did focus upon the schools applied perspectives and methods different from those used by the political scientist. Among the social sciences, sociology and (to a lesser degree) economics have shaped most of these scholars' analytical approaches. Aside from a stray item, most of what political science was doing, particularly after the post–World War II behavioral refocus, did not cross over to these scholars. This studied ignorance of each other's work was unbroken even occasionally by a scholar's calling the other discipline to pay attention.

Typically, the ever present course in Social Foundations, designed to inculcate the teacher- and administrator-initiate with the school's connectivity with society, was heavy on sociology and skimpy — hence superficial — on political science. Also typically, political science courses on state and local government or policy analysis, designed to cause laymen or apprentice public administrators to think politically, were heavy on urban government or policies of business or labor but skimpy — hence superficial — on school politics.

This mutual blindness or indifference was reinforced by a popular notion that schools had somehow been sanitized against politics. After the successful Progressive revolt against party and boss control of urban schools following the turn of this century, schools were seen as "above politics," or apolitical. Being "professionally" motivated, administrators and teachers had been made antiseptic against the corruption of politics. Schools were not thought of as "political" in the old sense; educational scholars were unfamiliar with political scientists' concept of "political" in its new sense; and the latter accepted the Progressives' vision as a full statement of the reality of schools.

These two houses of scholarship were not, like those of Capulet and Montague, opposed. They did not know one another well enough for hate. They were just indifferent. The classical realization that the two were intrinsically paired was thus lost. After Charles Merriam wrote on citizenship training in 1931, no major political scientist did a study of schools until David Easton and Thomas Eliot wrote trumpet-call articles in the late 1950's. Even then, the call was little noted. On the other side, not until the educational conflict over community-power studies broke into education journals in the early 1960's did professional educators receive notice of useful concepts.

By the late 1960's, however, the two houses were increasingly calling back and forth, although the sound level was weak and specialized. Political scientists took up socialization studies, while educational scholars wrote of power structures and, increasingly, wrestled with the applicability to their discipline of concepts such as systems analysis. By 1971, the American Educational Research Association had an affiliated "interest group" on the politics of education numbering under one hundred. AERA meetings regularly conducted panels for research papers under this rubric, and educational journals now accepted articles under this title. In political science, on the other hand, acceptance was slower, convention papers on the subject few, and journal articles even fewer — almost all restricted to socialization studies. But compared to a decade earlier, this interchange was an impressive step toward uniting the ancient houses that had once been jointly tended by Plato and Aristotle. Our work, then, is a contribution to the joint venture of scholarship on the School and the State.

In this effort, we are indebted even more than is usual to many other scholars. Their names and ideas fill the pages that follow, particularly those whose writings we have judged important for use in text or note. Not all will appreciate their inclusion within the systems framework we employ, but we hope they will accept our belief that we sought to judge their work fairly.

Some have given us an opportunity to try out our ideas on their journals or institutions. We thank William G. Walker, editor of *Australian Journal of Educational Administration,* the Rand Corporation Seminar

Series, the National Academy of Sciences, and the *Review of Educational Research*. Financial assistance of considerable size makes this book sponsored in part by the Institute of Governmental Studies of the University of California at Berkeley, with the support of its patient director, Eugene C. Lee. Other financial assistance for clerical expenses was provided by our two Schools of Education at Berkeley and Stanford, which had the courage to hire political scientists. An impressive typing job done from the illegible writing of the two authors was provided by Jane Burton.

We wish also to acknowledge the intellectual inspiration and encouragement provided us by two groups of scholars. The first consists of two men, David Easton, of the University of Chicago, and James Guthrie, of the University of California at Berkeley. Easton reviewed an early draft of an article and of this book, gently assisting us in understanding his ideas and suggesting spinoff ideas that we have used here. Although his ideas frame this entire book, we do not accept all their components, as we say in our conclusions. A good teacher, Easton does not expect his students to mirror him. Guthrie encouraged one author's first steps in the field of the politics of education and later provided a most helpful review of the manuscript. He has another special quality of the good teacher: making the student feel he knows more than he does. It is appropriate, given the nature of this book, that one is a scholar of political science and the other of educational administration. Both, however, are eclectic students of this particular brand of politics.

The second group we wish to acknowledge is composed of our graduate students, particularly Les Pacheco. Through a year of preparation and another of evaluation, they have assisted us in clarifying ambiguities and in searching for the significant questions. No experience is more useful for a teacher or writer than having his beautifully phrased sentence bounced back as too general, contradictory, or empirically nonsensical. As scholars know, students like these provide the first barrier of peer evaluation. We thank them for their encouragement.

En fin, we bow to our wives for their part in this. "They also serve who stand and wait" originated as a naval tradition, but academics know it really applies to their wives.

F.M.W.
M.W.K.

Contents

xiii

The Political Web
of American Schools

PART ONE

The Political Elements
of the School System

A major purpose of this book is the hope of increasing the once-interrupted interchange between scholars of the State and the School, who are what one denomination refers to as its "temporarily separated brethren." One difficulty of this translation task is that the political scientist and the educational scholar each possess different degrees of knowledge about the other's field. To stop to explain or define every technical concept or methodology known in one field so the other could grasp it would bore the initiated, and so we could wend our way through the book boring each discipline. Instead, we have sought to keep the technical language to a minimum while maintaining the rich concepts the language symbolizes. We know that we have not been fully successful in this effort, but as with advertising programs, we can't be sure which portion is wasted. Readers, we suspect, will let us know. However, we have provided a full set of bibliographic notes as part of this translation effort. This is designed to provide the student new to the cited topic a start on the literature relevant and valuable for his further understanding.

We have tried to curb the tendency to overstress the wide-open research possibilities in the politics of education. We have deleted many statements to the effect that "more research is badly needed here," because, frankly, they were repetitive. At various places we have provided some of our own research efforts currently underway in order to demonstrate research utilities or methods not yet developed.

Thus we have written a book that is textbook, research project, bibliographic essay, and statement of research directions. No textbook exists on the politics of education, for only a score or so of universities now offer such a course, although the number is due to increase dramatically during the 1970's. Nor is this a narrow monograph of limited research design and purpose. We believe the subject traverses the fields of normative, behavioral, and prescriptive analysis, requires some understanding of all the social sciences, and offers a rich opportunity for students interested in research. Thus, we use doctoral dissertation findings here, one sign of the newness of the concepts under analysis.

We use wherever possible comparative, aggregate data rather than a case study. The latter, we believe firmly, has been overused in schools of education to the detriment of the state of systematic knowledge about the politics of education. It is not that the case study is devoid of uses but that it is too often not used in a systematic fashion. A little anecdote about how a bond issue was successfully adopted in Round Bottom, Ohio, is not scholarship but vanity; it performs a function for one's vita that a filler about a six-legged dog does at the bottom of a newspaper column. The future of this field, we are agreed, lies rather in comparative studies, in research designs employing directed hypotheses, and in systematic knowledge about regularities in the interactions of school, government, and citizens. Only in this fashion can we learn something beyond the specific, time-bound event. Only in this way can we test policy recommendations against norms of what should be, what could be, and what is.

The foregoing suggests some of the problems and our answers in the task of addressing ourselves to two disciplines. But the major difficulty this purpose imposes is conceptual. What perspective could we employ that might be familiar to the two? For this reason, among others we shall later note, we have set this book within a systems framework of analysis, relying heavily upon David Easton's formulation. Its main utility lies in organizing in a simple fashion some perceptions that permit us to understand a bit more clearly James's "buzzing, booming confusion of reality." But it is also as familiar as any concept now available for crossing the two disciplines.

The first eight chapters of this book lay out the elements of systems analysis as we believe they apply to elements of the school system. Chapter 1 notes the myth of apolitical schools in America as an introduction to presenting the systems analysis concept of "political." The root causes of the myth are treated throughout the book, but particularly in Chapter 3. Chapter 2 treats system support, an important input to the State that the School provides, and analyzes models of political socialization currently operative in American schools.

Chapter 3 initiates consideration of the local and state levels of school policy making by pointing out the values in our history that give rise to conflict in the social system, which then gets transmitted into the school system through the transfer agents of interest groups. Chapters 4–6 focus upon this process at the local level, treating access channels (such as board elections and community power structures), the formal policy-making structure and political authorities of the schools, and the special significance of the tax and bond referenda for school policy making. Chapter 7 analyzes similar policy-making features and authorities at the state level, with special attention to the impact of political culture upon policy.

The second part of the book turns from analysis of levels to analysis of interlevel actions in the policy process, focusing upon three major areas of policy. The last part returns to examine the utilities of the conceptual framework of systems analysis.

Throughout this book, then, we are concerned with this task of addressing two scholarly disciplines. But we are also concerned to develop the reality of the politicalness of school policy making, which makes that institution's operations share much with other — more overtly recognized — political institutions that are also authorized to distribute resources and values in American society. Much of the current complaint against the insensitivity and rigidity of the school system is that it fails to act in response to politically expressed demands put upon it, a failure thought incompatible with democratic control of the uses of power. Those dominant in the school system, however, resist such notions of "accountability" on grounds of their responsibility to professional requirements, hence of their being "above politics." In short, because this is a clash over the uses of public power, we believe there is a political controversy afoot, and the failure of the antagonists to perceive this is so may make difficult the resolution of their conflict.

The struggle to make power responsive and responsible was the crux of the struggle for democracy wherever it arose. That struggle did not succeed totally at Yorktown or Appomattox, it was not realized for all time at Philadelphia in 1787, and it is not guaranteed by any presidential election or Supreme Court decision. That struggle is always with us, as it is today in the current conflict over the methods and results of our schools. Why this struggle is political, then, is a major thread throughout this book. What difference that perception makes for the struggle's outcome we touch upon only occasionally, but at a minimum it affects the kind of strategies one employs to change or defend the political system of the American school.

1   Schools and the Political System

The purpose of this book is to trace the ways in which American schools can be viewed as political. This view arises in part from the school's connection to the recognizable political system of state and national government. It arises also from the way in which schools act like miniature political systems. However, many schoolmen and lay participants have regarded both parts of this view as not merely untrue but also misleading, if not pernicious, for the "apolitical" institution they know and operate. An indirect purpose of this volume, therefore, is to assist in the task of revealing the extent of the intersect between politics and education and to demonstrate that even "professional" tasks such as curriculum decisions are highly political.

Much of this misunderstanding, of course, stems from different conceptions of what constitutes a "political" act. Traditionally, it has meant that schools had nothing to do with political parties, whose characteristic interactions with the citizenry have been regarded as "dirty," whereas the schools were sanitized products, untouched by party hands. For political scientists, however, parties are only one facet of political life. For them, the essence of the political act is the struggle of men and groups to secure the authoritative support of government for their values. Under this rubric, then, much of what schoolmen regard as apolitical is highly political indeed.

Let us be clear on our focus. We do not wish to discuss *how* schools should be run nor *what* they should teach and *why*. The literature abounds with such critiques, and we have our own ideas on that, of course — but that is the subject of another book. Rather our focus is upon *how the process of policy making in schools has certain characteristics that can be termed "political"* in a way we seek to demonstrate. We wish to indicate

4

how this process is becoming increasingly and more overtly politicized because of major changes in the relationship to the school system of state and local governments and of the citizens themselves. New definitions of school purposes, new claims on school resources, new efforts to make the schools responsive to certain groups and their values — all are giving rise to a larger, more web-like set of political relationships surrounding the local school.

Although the basic political quality of school policy making will be our concern throughout the book, we will deal only at certain places with the *new* politicization of schools. Part of it is seen below in conditions in urban education around the turn of the century that separated party politics from schools. Elsewhere we shall return to the current scene and the new politics of schools; our last chapter collects these occasional discussions into a more organized theme. This seemingly haphazard reference to the new politics reflects only our wish not to be repetitious, for almost every element of schools could be shown to be caught up currently in political controversy. Rather, we selected several phases of this development we think most interesting. However, it would be well first to deal with the popular notion of a divorce between schools and politics.

THE MYTH OF APOLITICAL EDUCATION

By a mutual but unspoken and long-standing agreement, American citizens and scholars have contended for many years that the world of education is and should be kept separate from the world of politics. Although *elections* and *referenda* concerning other policies were viewed as "political," these words did not connote "politics" when used for educational policy. Two reasons for attempting to preserve the folklore that "politics and education do not mix" were the risk to the schoolmen who were overt players of politics and the relative benefits to schoolmen who preserved the image of the public schools as a unique, nonpolitical function of government.[1]

Before these advantages are explored, it is useful to review the political environment of urban schools at the turn of the century. Changes in this period established the basic administrative structure and pattern of school policy making we have today. This era also reinforced the norm of separation of education and politics. The underlying roots of this separation, however, lie deep in some basic American values, which we will treat throughout this volume, particularly in the next two chapters.

However, at the turn of the century, a nationwide interlocking director-ate of "progressive" university presidents, school superintendents, and lay allies emerged from the business and professional elites in the cities. One of the aims of its members was to emancipate the schools from parti-san politics and excessive decentralization. They saw political corruption as the prime cause of the inefficiency of education in large cities. Indeed, many politicians at that time regarded the schools as a useful support for the spoils systems and awarded jobs and contracts as political favors. Lincoln Steffens and other muckrakers revealed how textbook publishers and contractors allied with corrupt school trustees for common boodle in the common school.[2] Tyack has put together a number of direct quotations from leaders concerned about such practices in urban education during 1890–1910. Some views of these educational spoils are:

> *D.T.*   I believe that you have with you a number of letters from school administrators across the country which refer to this problem of political corruption. Would you kindly share some of these with us?
>
> *Jones.*   A superintendent in one of the Eastern States writes: "Nearly all the teachers in our schools get their positions by political 'pull.' If they secure a place and are not backed by political influence, they are likely to be turned out. Our drawing teacher recently lost her position for this reason." One writes from the South: "Most places depend on politics. The lowest motives are frequently used to influence ends." A faint wail comes from the far West: "Positions are secured and held by the lowest principles of corrupt politicians." "Politicians wage a war of extermination against all teachers who are not their vassals," comes from the Rocky Mountains.
>
> *D.T.*   Mr. Wetmore, you have been a school committeeman in Boston. Have you had similar experience?
>
> *S. A. Wetmore.*   The teachership is still a spoil of office. It is more difficult, at the present time, for a Catholic than for a Protestant young woman to get a place, but, nevertheless, some Catholics secure appointments, for "trading" may always be done, while each side has a wholesome fear of the other assailing it in the open board. A member said one day, in my hearing: "I must have my quota of teachers."
>
> *D.T.*   Mr. Cubberley, from your vantage point as a professor at Stanford, how does San Francisco fare?
>
> *Ellwood P. Cubberley.*   The worst kind of boss rule has prevailed in San Francisco, and the board of education gradually became a place sought by those who wished to use the position for political preferment or for personal ends. Once every six or eight years there would be an effort at reform, and a few good men were elected; but they were usually in a minority, and the majority, held together by "the cohesive force of plunder," ruled things with a high hand.
>
> *D.T.*   Probably most of you could tell similar stories of corruption. How do you explain this problem?
>
> *Cubberley.*   These Southern and Eastern Europeans [in our cities are] of a very different type from the North and West Europeans who preceded them. Largely illiterate, docile, often lacking in initiative, and almost wholly without the Anglo-Saxon conceptions of righteousness,

liberty, law, order, public decency, and government, their coming has served to dilute tremendously our national stock and to weaken and corrupt our political life.[3]

A decentralized, ward-based committee system for administering the public schools provided the opportunities for this political influence. In 1905, Philadelphia had forty-three elected district school boards consisting of 559 members. There were only seven members on the Minneapolis board, while Hartford, with only a third as many people, had thirty-nine school visitors and committeemen.[4] While there were great variations, at the turn of the century sixteen of twenty-eight cities of more than 100,000 population had boards of twenty members or more.

The reformers contended that the board members elected by wards advanced parochial and special interests at the expense of the needs of the school district as a whole. What was needed to counter this atomization of interest was election at large. Professional expertise rested upon the assumption that scientific ways to administer schools existed and were independent of the particular values of particular groups. A good school system is good for everyone, not just a part of the community. This unitary-community idea would help protect the schools from the local political processes. The reformers charged, moreover, that, since the larger school boards worked through numerous subcommittees, their executive authority was splintered. No topic was too trivial for a separate subcommittee, ranging from ways of teaching reading to the purchase of doorknobs. At one time, Chicago had seventy-nine subcommittees and Cincinnati seventy-four.[5] The primary prerequisite for better management was thought to be centralization of power in a chief executive who had considerable delegated authority from the board. Only under such a system could someone make large-scale improvements and be held accountable.

By 1910, a conventional educational wisdom had evolved among the schoolmen and leading business and professional men who spearheaded the reforms. The watchwords of reform became *centralization, expertise, professionalization, nonpolitical control,* and *efficiency.* The governance structure needed to be revised so that school boards would be small, elected at large, and purged of all connections with political parties and general government officials, such as mayors and councilmen. It was sometimes a very small group of patricians who secured new charters from state legislatures and thereby reorganized the urban schools without a popular vote in the cities.[6]

In all these reform concepts the most attractive model for organization and governance was that of the large-scale industrial bureaucracies rapidly emerging in the turn-of-the-century economy. A school board elected from the city as a whole would reflect a unitary-community perspective rather than partial-special interests. Divorced from the city political leaders, such a board would be less susceptible to graft and job favoritism. Further, centralizing power in the superintendent would overcome the bureaucratic tangle and inefficiency of the board subcommittees. Given the administrative trivia which the boards then processed, subcommittees were the only feasible means of conducting business. These reform concepts, spreading rapidly from the large cities to the small cities and towns, found their major forum and vehicle in the National Education Association.[7]

Urban school reform was part of a broader pattern of elite municipal change at the turn of the century. Although the surface rhetoric pitted the corrupt politician against the community-oriented citizen, the reformers' underlying motives have been questioned by several historians. For instance, Hays has emphasized that the financial and professional leaders deplored the decentralized ward system in large part because it empowered members of the lower and lower middle classes (many of whom were recent immigrants). Reformers wanted "not simply to replace bad men with good; they proposed to change the occupational and class origins of decision makers."[8] Tyack expresses this viewpoint in stronger language:

> Underlying much of the reform movement was an elitist assumption that prosperous, native born Protestant Anglo-Saxons were superior to other groups and thus should determine the curriculum and the allocation of jobs. It was the mission of the schools to imbue children of the immigrants and the poor with uniformly WASP ideals.[9]

Counts's classic study in 1927 demonstrated that it was the upper-class professionals and business people who made up the centralized boards of education.[10] For instance, in St. Louis after the centralization reforms in 1897, professional men on the board had jumped from 4.8 percent to 58.3 percent, big businessmen from 9.0 percent to 25 percent; small businessmen dropped from 47.6 percent to 16.7 percent and wage-earning employees from 28.6 percent to none (10 percent were of unknown earlier occupation).[11] These board members in turn delegated much of their formal powers to professionals who had the flexibility to shape the schools to the needs of industrial society — as defined by only one segment of that society.

The "no-politics" doctrine of public education has demonstrated impressive popularity and longevity among the general public. But there have been advantages for the professional in the maintenance of this folklore, summarized by one school superintendent in this manner:

> 1. "politics" per se, because it is popularly conceived as a sordid business conducted by amoral men bent on furthering their own ends, has an image not appealing to school men and seen as detrimental to their position lest the public tar them with the same brush;

2. the higher social status and salary generally accorded school people by the public is better maintained and somewhat dependent upon a situation where the schools are seen as unique rather than where schools are seen as merely an extension of the same local government that provides dog catchers and sanitation departments;

3. that, in a moral sense, the interests of public schools really are better served by keeping politicians "out" and high-minded professional educators "in," serving the best interest of children;

4. in maintaining a tighter hold on control over the public school system, the image of "unique function" allows greater leverage for control by the professional school administrator than an image acknowledging that schools are "ripe for picking" by dilettante and professional politicians; and

5. that the "unique function" image provides the schools with a stronger competitive position for tax funds wherever voters are allowed to express a choice of priorities among government agencies.[12]

The outcome of this nonpolitical ideology was summed up by Martin as a massive irony in the American political system. To be sure, the situation is somewhat different today, but this historic ideology has deeply affected the entire range of school politics.

> Thus is the circle closed and the paradox completed. Thus does the public school, heralded by its champions as the cornerstone of democracy, reject the political world in which democratic institutions operate. Thus is historical identification with local government accompanied by insistence on complete independence of any agency . . . of local government, lip service to general citizen activity attended by mortal fear of general politics, the logical and legitimate companion of citizen action.[13]

The Force of Politicization

In the past decade, several national trends have made the public schools more overtly political, challenging severely the governance tenets of the turn-of-the-century reformers. Perhaps most current is the call for "community participation" in public agencies of all types that has become widely accepted among social critics and reformers. This ideology stresses the belief that citizens have to be more than "involved" or "consulted" if government is to gain their active consent. Rather, they have to "participate" in their democracy, even though this might in some circumstances imply social conflict, such as picketing and strikes.[14] The federal school aid legislation of the 1960's encouraged these trends by creating a number of watchdog, citizens' advisory commissions and by requiring consultation by school authorities with community groups. Whatever the moral urgency of this effort to expand political participation in school policy making, little evidence existed by 1971 that many citizens were heeding the call, even under programs explicitly providing it. Thus, turnout for elections to locally controlled school boards was very small. Thus, the national advisory councils on education policy turned out to be staffed with relatively few blacks; those appointed were mostly supportive of administrators' policy views.[15]

Part of this failure to participate as fully and independently as possible may well lie with the schools. If, as we shall show later, schools do little to teach the means and values of participation in political conflict, if they teach instead that "politics" is dirty, then part of the fault for this inaction is theirs. Note, though, that such lack of involvement by the groups currently being entreated to participate runs through a wide gamut of their lives; few from this stratum of life, white or black, have an organizational life that extends their resources outside the self. For this condition, many other institutions and features of society than the school are responsible. This sense of inefficacy, not merely in political processes but in any effort to shape one's destiny, stems from a complex of factors that schools do not cause but contribute to. Yet, even if only a few of this group are being currently politicized, they form a cadre of activists that is putting new and forcefully expressed demands upon the school. And it may well be that they are representative of many of the inarticulate and privatized others whose self-image precludes social action.

Many other forces for politicizing the schools were also at work. The prodigious post–World War II demand for all kinds of domestic public services resulted in intensive competition for fiscal support among public programs and their supporters. Legislators and public who were caught in the crossfire were no longer willing to accept educators' open-ended cost estimates of their needs. Demands arose for accountability by educators to the layman and for evaluations of the results of formal schooling that citizens would understand. After many years of increases, the burden of the property tax as the prime source of school finance has generated greatly increased taxpayer resistance. The trend is toward increased reliance on federal and state aid — but with the funds have come both controls from higher levels and an emerging school politics of intergovernmental relations.

In short, the era of the hegemony of professional educators supported by the norm of professionally neutral competence is under assault from those who feel that the present mode of educational policy making is inadequate. Community groups, students, mayors, and interest groups, all of whom press for special political values, are now more visible and more clamorous. Teachers, repudiating turn-of-the-century doctrine stressing the harmony of the profession, are using collective bargaining to wring concessions from boards and administrators. Controversial issues, such as the war in Southeast Asia, are finding a place in the curriculum, and many more teachers now participate in political campaigns. One senses that the politicization of school policy making in all its dimensions is becoming much more apparent and is accelerating. The result will be significant changes in the school governance model institutionalized by early reformers. Just as we cannot return to the one-room school house, so we can no longer accept the professional educators' claim that they are apolitical experts.

THE ANALYTIC SCHEME OF SYSTEMS THEORY

The Need for Theory

The mass of data about the school's outreach into the community, as well as data of schools' internal politics, invites political analysis. By 1970 there were about 19,300 school districts — half the 1962 level — and every year board elections and referenda take place in many of these. But what is needed is an organization of concepts and data in some analytic scheme that makes sense of the variety and similarity of American schools. If, as we have argued, there is much about school policy which is political and if data are available for testing some propositions about this condition, it becomes imperative to develop an analytical framework to unite these components.

Some of this framework has been provided by educational scholars — most of it by professional educators, a little by sociologists, and even less by political scientists. Such frameworks, however, differ in their objectives. Educational journals are filled with *descriptions* — of the operations of school systems and subsystems, of their actors and agents, and of their laws and regulations. Further, this purported reality is invariably accompanied by normative *evaluations*. These are value judgments about whether the object described is worthwhile or not, often accompanied by recommendations to change or retain the observed reality. Further, description and evaluation merge indefinably into *prescription* — recommendations on how to change reality so as to achieve normative objectives, how to close the gap between the real and the ideal. What is least found is *explanation* — suppositions and supporting evidence about the causes, consequences, and interrelationships of that which is found in reality. Causal theory of this kind is found frequently in the psychology of education, sometimes in the sociology of education, but seldom in educational administration.[16]

When, however, we ask what causal theory is found in the study of the politics of education, the answer must be very little. The reasons lie in the myth of apolitical schools and in the lack of a theory to direct and channel our research. This is less true in 1971 than before, as the myth is being discarded and theory sought. But these two factors were related. If school policy is regarded as "above" politics, policy study using standard, political, analytic frameworks is regarded as misguided, and consequently theoretical statements of explanatory power are unlikely to develop. Accepted theories of childbirth that emphasize the stork make it difficult to think of other explanations.

Iannaccone has explained how the profession has inculcated this orientation by asserting that education is a "closed system" isolated from politics. Its leaders are therefore free from external control. Also, by controlling what comes in from the outside environment, they reduce change within their system. Such effort is clearly functional for professional educators, freeing them from many external constraints and from the unsettling demands of internal change that characterize other social — and "more political" — institutions.[17] In the past, so skilled were educators that they moved the community to adopt their apolitical myth. As Eliot wryly noted, a successful superintendent was one adept in "community relations," but, "why not say frankly that he must be a good politician?"[18] Yet most political scientists unquestioningly accepted the closed-system definition of the educators. Only recently, seeing here similarities to other policies, have they recalled that "Rosy O'Grady and the Colonel's lady are sisters under the skin."

But the most significant reason for the meager scholarly analysis of educational politics may be the lack of an applicable theoretical orientation and methodology. As Kirst and Mosher have shown, it is clear that no single theory, simple or complex, presently guides such research, nor is there agreement on the appropriate methodology.[19] Political scientists have been severely split between traditional studies of institutional and legal analysis and those which utilize statistical and other quantitative methods. Among the behavioralists, another complication is the existence of a number of partial theories of political behavior. In short, no over-arching general theory generates hypotheses that can be tested by accepted methods in the crucible of political experiences. There exists instead a grab bag of partial theories and contrasting methods. That this is typical in the early stages of any scholarship is nonetheless frustrating for those concerned to make some order out of the confusion. This is certainly no field for those who prefer their scholarship to take the form of explicating established truths, but it will be exciting to those who prefer to innovate in the development of theory and hypothesis.

How can we proceed, then, in the absence of established theory for organizing knowledge? Theory in its traditional sense is directed toward explanation and prediction by means of "a set of . . . related propositions which include among them some law-like generalizations, and which can be assigned specific truth value via empirical tests."[20] Because scholarship, like life, is always imperfect and because all research involves some compromise with ideal requirements, we turn instead to another form of theory: *heuristic. Heuristic theory is not so much a predictive scheme as a method*

of analytically separating and categorizing items in experience. As Gregor
has shown, much of what parades in political science as theory of the first
type — predictive — is really heuristic, providing at best a "framework
for political analysis." We agree with Easton that "the appropriate question to ask about a theoretical analysis today is not: does this fully explain
the functioning . . . or does it offer a fire-proof set of concepts toward
that end? . . . The appropriate question is: does this approach help us to
take a small step in the right direction?" [21]

Easton's comment is appropriate, for it is his heuristic scheme or "framework for political analysis" that we employ in developing the concepts and
data around which this book is organized. The framework is most often
termed "systems analysis," although as indicated by the words in the last
paragraph, Easton de-emphasizes "theory" in the classical sense and pre-
fers, instead, to discuss a "conceptual framework," or "categories for the
systems analysis of politics." [22] In short, the utility of systems theory is
that of all heuristic schemes — it enables us at least to order existing
knowledge or hunches and thereby to determine what portions of the
scheme are clearly untenable, which ones have at least some support, and
which need to be further studied. Its use has limits, as we shall note in our
conclusions. But the categorization of the state of knowledge in the politics
of education is our major purpose in this volume, and, for this, systems
analysis provides at least an organizing principle. Only in this fashion do
we believe we can "take a small step in the right direction."

Components of Systems Analysis

Easton's framework contains the familiar perspective of a society composed of major institutions — the economy, the school, the church, and so
on. Individuals interact with one another and with these institutions, and
the institutions interact with one another in patterned ways of belief and
action that constitute a distinctive culture. One of these social components
is "the political system," different from others because it alone is the source
of "authoritative allocation of values, [i.e.,] those interactions through
which values are authoritatively allocated for society." The political system
is the social subsystem whose decisions, about how private members and
groups will be allocated the limited objects that are valued in a society, are
generally accepted as authoritative (that is, are *legitimate*). The values
allocated by the system may be *material* — a textbook, defense contract,
free land for constructing railroads or "dropout" schools. They may also
be *symbolic* by conferring status and deference upon favored groups of
persons — making Christmas or Martin Luther King's birthday a school
holiday. In every society such an allocative mechanism exists and persists,
although its exact form, inherent values, and public policies may differ
with place and time.

The linkage between the political system and other social subsystems is a key element in this framework of analysis, because Easton is reaching for a general statement of the conditions under which other subsystems reciprocally interact with the political system. In highly simplified terms, this relationship is one in which *stress* in other subsystems of the social environment generates *inputs* of *demands* and *supports* upon the *political system,* which then reduces or *converts* these inputs into public decisions or *outputs,* which in turn *feed back* allocated values into the society whence the process began. Figure 1.1 is a preliminary sketch of this set of interactions.[23] These concepts seek to describe components of a dynamic, interactive, political system which may or may not *persist* in the society in which it is embedded. Easton's concern is not merely with how the political system operates, then, but with how it persists through time by adapting itself to the host of demands made on it.

A somewhat fuller statement of systems analysis is appropriate here, although what we offer is a gross reduction of the expanded interpretation found in Easton's writings.[24] It is appropriate to begin with that environment of subsystems lying outside the political system. This environment is of two parts, that within and that outside the society itself. The former (such as the economy, culture, social structure, and personalities) represent potential sources of inputs for the political system. The environment outside society is the international world, a "suprasystem of which any single society is part," the international political, economic, and cultural systems.

Within either environment, disturbances arise from changes in existing interactions, although not all disturbances need stimulate or strain the political system. But some are in the form of *stress,* which critically im-

Figure 1.1   A Simplified Model of a Political System

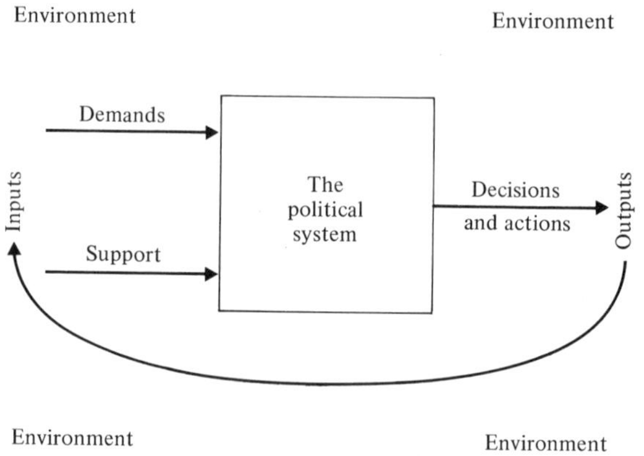

Source: David Easton, *A Systems Analysis of Political Life* (New York: Wiley, 1965), p. 32.

pinges upon the basic capacities of any political system — the ability to allocate values for a society and to induce most members to accept such decisions as binding. Such stress could be a defeat in war or a major depression for a nation or a new consciousness of ethnic frustration in a school district. The Greek city-states and the empires of the Romans and Aztecs, as well as various tribal clusters, may be illustrations of political systems that failed to reduce stress and consequently disappeared. As long as the stress is maintained within a critical range, however, the system as such persists. At some point, however, a disturbance becomes a stress that moves from the external environment as *exchanges* or *transactions* to penetrate the political system's *boundaries.* These stress-generated influences, *outputs* of the environment and hence *inputs* to the political system, "concentrate and mirror everything in the environment that is relevant to political stress." These inputs are of two kinds, *demands* and *supports,* "key indicators of the way in which environmental influences and conditions modify and shape the operations of the political system."

Demands are associated most often with the pressures upon the government, the requests for justice or help, for reward or recognition. Behind these diverse demands lies the common presence of wants, the human condition of longing for that which is in short supply. The shortage may be not only material but also symbolic — the lack of money or of prestige. But in all societies these wanted objects are never plentiful enough to match the claims upon them — a phenomenon of tremendous importance to all aspects of society. Particularly is this so for the political system, for without such wants there would be no demands, and without demands (not all of which can be met) society would not need to authorize an agent to meet them — that is, to "authoritatively allocate resources and values."

Those making demands mobilize resources in order to affect other private groups and so influence the disposition of the political system. The issues that develop and the way in which demands penetrate the political system will vary among cultures, economies, and political systems.

Supports, on the other hand, take the form of a willingness to accept the decisions of the system or the system itself. A steady flow of supports is necessary if any political system is long to maintain its legitimacy (the accepted sense that the system has the right to do what it is doing). So vital is this input that all societies indoctrinate their young to support the system, a task that is part of the school's work, shared with family and peers.

School desegregation demands, for example, arose from a racially based stress, long endured — but more lately unendurable — by blacks. Moving from private rancor across the political boundary to public challenge, this race mobilized its limited resources, first in demands upon courts and later upon Congress, but continually upon local school boards. Counterdemands of segregationists mobilized other resources to block and delay this challenge. In the process, both those seeing too much and those seeing too little change arising from this specific conflict began to decrease their support for the Supreme Court's authority to allocate values generally.

The political system processes these inputs, sometimes combining or reducing them, sometimes absorbing them without any reaction, but sometimes converting them into public policies — or outputs. Clearly, not all demands are converted into policy, for the political system evidences sensitivity to certain values, those dominant in the *conversion* machinery and its personnel, and in the larger society. In short, what gets through depends upon which values the conversion process reinforces and which it frustrates, and upon the values of the political authorities as they operate in this flow of inputs.

Some schoolmen insist, for example, that "maintaining discipline" is a prime value of classwork, while others rate this of little importance, preferring to elevate the value of achieving "intellectual excitement." Which of these values gets reinforced by state authority is the end result of a political struggle. That is, eventually, one of these values will be "authorized," and the school system and its personnel will allocate their resources to that successful value. This struggle to have resources allocated authoritatively for one's own educational value is "political," sharing much with the process in other policy fields.

The authorities, responsible for the daily running of the system, constantly interact in the conversion process, with either those outside or those inside the political system. The pattern of their interactions stems in part from role definitions often imposed by the political system itself. Such interactions generate inside the political system certain pressures, or *within-puts,* that shape the conversion process and its products.

Desegregation demands, for example, were ignored much longer by Congress and some presidents than by the Supreme Court and other presidents. Border states desegregated more quickly than Southern states, and Mississippi school boards resisted most of all. This differential reaction reflected varying combinations of power and values in each of these political subsystems. It also reflected varying role definitions thrust upon different political authorities. The role definition for a Congressman or a school board member who represented Atlanta or Holmes County, Mississippi, was different from the role definition of an official who spoke for Kentuckians. Each used his resources in the political system to advance his demands, of course, and the resulting conflicts generated the conversion process — which continues at this moment.

The outputs of the political subsystem in turn become inputs to the other social subsystems that originated them as stresses. The administration of outputs in the larger community, however, even though its major purpose is to cope with stress, always has a differential impact. Policy administration always acts to enhance the safety, income, and status of some persons and groups while detracting from others. The resulting structure of public policy, while varying with culture and time, always mirrors the structure of power and privilege, telling us much about the allocation of values by the political system.

Moreover, the built-in intent of the output gets meaning only in the reality of *feedback* — the interaction of output with administration — on the way to becoming an *outcome*. The Supreme Court, for example, requires desegregation at "all deliberate speed," but district courts define that output differently for innumerable school districts. Congress authorizes school aid for *poor* children, but the *outcome,* in the United States Office of Education's administration of that law, is aid for *all* schools. It is clear that the gap between output and outcome is a major forum for policy making, perhaps the real one for the lives of most citizens affected by the "authoritative allocation of values."

The action of the political system may not have concluded with outcomes. Outputs, in influencing the society, can generate another set of inputs to the political system through a *feedback loop*. This term designates one way in which the system copes with stress — that is, (1) dealing with stress causes a response in the system, (2) the response creates new stress, and (3) the new stress is communicated to the political authorities as a new round begins.

The essential elements of systems analysis are summarized in Figure 1.2.[25] This diagram bears a certain resemblance to a wide number of explanations of human behavior, such as tension reduction, conditioned responses, and information theory. More important, however, it offers a first approximation of a highly complex interrelationship of societal components. Note that this analytical framework presents the political system as something other than just an allocative process, a feature of many partial theories in political science. More than that, this framework is an attempt to comprehend the larger question of how any allocative process acts to persist through time, an inquiry strengthened by Easton's concern to understand how the political system copes with stress. Thus he notes:

> we give new content and meaning to the ideas so familiar in political research, that of political process. The study of political systems embraces an understanding of the processes through which authoritative allocations take place. But it does more. It needs to be extended to the analysis of the processes underlying system persistence through time. And persistence . . . is intricately connected with the capacity of a political system, as an open, self-regulating, and goal-setting system, to

Figure 1.2   A Dynamic Response Model of a Political System

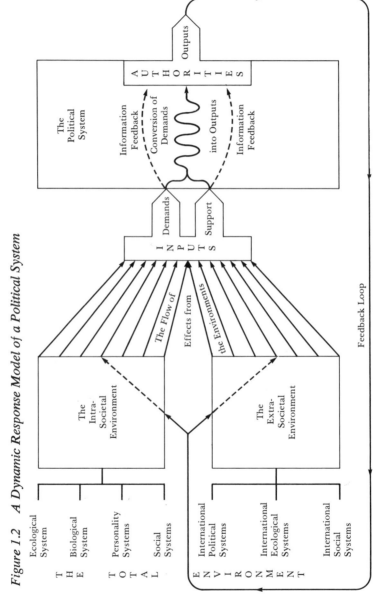

Source: David Easton, *A Framework for Political Analysis* (Englewood Cliffs, N.J.: Prentice-Hall, 1965), p. 110.

change itself. The puzzle of how a system manages to persist through change if necessary, forms a central problem of the analysis of political life.[26]

SYSTEMS ANALYSIS AND
THE POLITICS OF EDUCATION

It is now appropriate to consider the relationship of this general framework to the study at hand, the politics of education. Recall that we urged it as a method useful primarily for organizing knowledge and suggesting areas of needed research. The belief that schools are embedded in society and responsive to its demands is a truism, perhaps the oldest in the study of education. We believe systems analysis can help the student to see this relationship more clearly through such specific conceptual terms as *wants, demands,* and *support.* We believe that considerable explanation can result from observing the school systems as converting inputs from subsystems of society and doing so in response to group-defined stresses. Further, it seems to us that schools exhibit conversion processes similar to those in other subsystems more clearly recognized as political. That political authorities in schools seek to maximize support through use of appropriate outputs also seems demonstrable. And certainly a central question to be explored in this book is the degree to which the feedback loop operates between schools and society.

In this effort to apply systems analysis, we follow Easton's suggestion that "it is perfectly feasible — more than that, I would argue that it is necessary and revealing — to apply the present mode of analysis to any specific class of systems." We raise the basic questions in applying systems analysis to schools that he raises in applying it to the class of systems called "democracies." Substituting "schools" for democracy, we ask:

> How do [school] systems, as defined, manage to persist under conditions of stability and change? Over and above the normal kinds of stresses to which all political systems are subjected, are there any special kinds that impinge upon [school] systems? Have [schools] devised typical ways, other than those described for most systems in general, for coping with the kinds of stresses to which they are exposed? Is there anything special about the feedback processes in a [school system] that impairs or improves the chances of such a system for coping with normal or system-specific types of stress? [27]

In answering such basic questions, we say with Easton that we are seeking to "elaborate a conceptual structure and suggest, where possible, some theoretical propositions. . . . In the outcome, we shall not have a theory in the full-blown sense of the term [but] a conceptual structure which . . . is the most that we can expect in the area of general theory today." [28]

But in this work we seek something more. We wish to know how valid such a general concept is in explaining the structure and processes of American public education in its time of increasing stress. Old forms and ideas in education are everywhere challenged, not merely by new interest groups seeking a reallocation of traditional resources. Widespread and increasing resistance to school tax referenda in recent years (about two in three failed during 1969) suggests disappointment, frustration, or malaise about what our schools are or are not doing. Stress, then, is not merely an abstract, academic concern. It is a quality of contemporary education that permeates the school boards, classrooms, administrators' offices, and professionals' conventions, as well as decision-making forums at state and national levels. The four questions about schools and their stress problems that we have adapted from Easton are the kinds of questions asked by authorities and administrators in the school system today.

To answer these basic questions, we offer a contour study designed to stimulate thinking and research by scholar and layman alike. We explore knowledge based on existing research and provide some of our own. But this is not merely to show its relevance to the conceptual orientation we employ, but to suggest where more needs to be done. We later explore three major national educational policies of present times, not only because systems analysis seems to explain them well, but because of what they suggest about stress adaptation by all those interested in the survival of their schools.

The precise labels used for these concepts are not the important thing, of course. What is relevant is whether the concepts provide an insight into what is transpiring and some guide to what may be done. If so, our contribution ironically must be classified as feedback, which Wiener defined as "the property of being able to adjust future conduct by past performances." [29]

2 Schools and System Support

The concern of the political theorist for the tie between the school and the political system reflects their reciprocal importance. In one sense, this book deals with that relationship; yet it must be kept clear that we view as political both the larger system, which articulates all of society, and the smaller one of the schools. For the purpose of clarity, in this chapter we shall use a shorthand term for each of these political systems: *State* and *School*. We wish to examine the two as analytically separate entities in order to determine the essentials of their bonds. More specifically, we focus upon one of these bonds, the process of political socialization, in this chapter. Other factors tie State and School, particularly programs of finance and regulation, but these will concern us in later chapters. Yet, before we focus on the child at the intersection of the two systems, we must first clarify some of the theoretical problems with which we deal.

STATE-SCHOOL LINKAGES IN DEMOCRATIC THOUGHT

The previous chapter's delineation of the apolitical myth of the schools needs recasting in terms of broader perspectives on the State-School relationship. Three views of this linkage are found in classical political theory, democratic theory, and systems analysis.

The Classical Question: Which Is the Independent Variable?

As Eulau has noted, Western political philosophy concerning the State-School relationship centers around one basic query: Should the State shape the School's function and purpose, or should the School shape and guide

21

the State's? [1] In behavioral terms, which is the independent and which the dependent variable? In any period of our history, much of the controversy over schooling is rooted in one's answer to this question.

The Greek tradition was most explicit in its belief on the matter. The two were one, concerned with producing the good State (*polis*). Schooling shaped the citizen to fulfill himself in terms of the interests of a polis, which ensured that the school did that job well. There is about all this what Eulau has termed "the utopian scent — education can create the perfect political order." More important, this orientation assumed that education was subordinate to, indeed the servant of, the political order.

While Plato and Aristotle wrote about a culture, now twenty-five centuries dead, in which a good society was sought by integration of all institutions and values, their insistence on the State-School relationship has echoes today. We hear it from contemporary School critics on the right who insist that teacher, student, and curriculum should uphold the ends of the national government. They demand an uncritical acceptance of a patriotic and generalized presentation of history. The individual must be subordinated to the State and School so that they may shape his values. Only by having School support State and State support School can society be preserved. On the left, meanwhile, one hears assertions that the School creates and reinforces that "establishment" that controls all American life. These charges are followed by demands that the School be reformed because of its submission to false values that are producing a conformist and corrupt population.

Both sides are alike in many ways, however. Both wish subordination of School to State. Both agree that the State can be upheld only by the School's instruction in the moral life. Both believe that the State can be only what the School lets it be. In short, the potential independent effect the School can have on the State makes it the potentially dominant institution in society — and hence it must be controlled. In such a formulation, the collectivity is more important than the individual, so the individual must be shaped to the larger end. The Athenians would agree.

The harnessing of education to shape the political — and religious — order was a dominant feature of States until quite recently. Education for the pursuit of other than prescribed and approved ends, political and religious, was unknown. Indeed, the development of private education in this country, with an implied sense of freedom from the dictates of the State, originated in the desire to be free — free, that is, to inculcate the right religion. Not even that development, however, was allowed to be unpatriotic or politically heretical.

In the last century, however, another possibility emerged from this State-School union. After all, it would be hard to find, as Eulau has observed, a "political order in the real world which, even if we could agree on its being close to perfection, has been created out of or by an educational system." Might it not be the reverse, that the condition of the political order shaped the nature of the educational system? That the State is not what the School makes it, but, quite the opposite, that the State is the independent variable? If so, political problems are not basically traceable to the School but to the State.

The argument here is something more than that all schools have to be patriotic in their teaching so as not to undermine the State. It is, rather, that from society to society the basic School philosophy and accompanying practices and structures may be shaped by the State more often than the reverse. Note two examples of this possibility. First, conceive of a State whose political premise is exclusive, unchallengeable, and immutable. School philosophy there will take as its first duty the shaping of the child to understand, accept, and glorify that premise. Behind this duty is the belief that when one knows the Truth, it is foolish at best, and sinful at worst, to permit the malleable young to have equal access to Error. However, the case is different if the premise of the State is that political Truth is either not known or not knowable, that there is not Truth but truths. Then the School may more easily entertain instruction admitting of plural truths — from which men may choose as befits their individual values.

The second case underlies the rise of the liberal, democratic state in the Western world, no matter how it may have been eroded in practice. Its pluralist premise, its doubt about ascertaining moral certitudes, and its separation from the absolutist framework that provided guidance to those who did not question — all are familiar elements of English and American thinking in the last century or more.

Eulau reminds us that John Stuart Mill's essay *On Liberty* could well be an expression of this philosophy just as Plato's *Republic* could be of the other. Writing before universal education, Mill argued against "State education" and for "enforcement of education by the State" in a statement that directly urges breaking the State-School linkage from its old mold:

> All that has been said of the importance of individuality, character, and diversity in opinions and modes of conduct, involves, as of the same unspeakable importance, diversity of education. A general State education is a mere contrivance for moulding people to be exactly like one another; and as the mould in which it casts them is that which pleases the predominant power in the government, whether this be a monarch, a priesthood, an aristocracy, or the majority of the existing generation; in proportion as it is efficient and successful, it establishes a despotism over the mind, leading by natural tendency to one over body.

The possibility that school systems may vary with political systems suggests the independent quality of the latter. A major research question would be to determine whether new School concepts change old State programs or whether State changes School. One testing field lies in the new nations. The importance of education as a preceding factor in the development of new states has been studied closely in the post–World War II era. Yet there has not been enough comparative research to determine whether or how school systems are shaped by distinctive elements in new and old political systems.*

In the United States, which of the two institutions is independent and which dependent? Is the union a closed one, wherein Truth is known and each system reinforces the other in its impact on the young? Or is the union an open one, where doubt prompts a search by School and State for answers to fit a varied population? Empirical indicators of the State-School ties, then, tell us much about the conflict of values rooted in traditional political thought.

Problems of Education in a Democracy

An additional conflict arises because our study focuses upon a democratic system where the School must manage tensions between opposing values. Two paradoxes underlie these tensions. First, the School must teach not only support of the State but also the virtues of individualism. However, the latter value can lead to opposition to the State, as the American history of civil rights — as well as violence — attests. The line between support and opposition is never clear. This is an always new and yet ever old dilemma haunting the sensitive intellect from *Antigone* to today's conscientious objector.

A second paradox arises because the breadth of plural values is narrowed by the institutional demands of State and School for controlling the environment where they exercise authority. This is seen in the School, which praises the American ideal of freedom but seeks to regularize every aspect of the student's life. The familiar ringing of bells in American high schools is a reflection of this trend toward standardization and regularity. The conflict of these norms of freedom and regulation created a major crisis in the 1960's among American youth, who challenged rote learning, reality descriptions at odds with their own experience, and the whole effort to impose uniformity in the name of diversity. Here the School shared a common problem with the State. Liberty has never been total, for individuals' pursuit of their diverse definitions of freedom creates social conflict; this has caused authoritative institutions to define it so as to avoid disorder and injustice. Each definition is a constraint for some and a shield

---

* Comparative education as a subdiscipline seems to consist mostly of country-by-country analyses, in which the potential explanatory power of diverse influences in the political order is not comparatively assessed.

for others. Against this narrowing experience, there are always some who will rebel, decrying the "hypocrisy" of an institution that says one thing but does another.

These paradoxes are related, of course. The breadth of democratic values provides convenient justification for any narrowing act of State and School. As we shall see in a later chapter, local control of the School has been a dominant value in our history, but so also has been the concept of equality. These two have collided head-on over segregation since 1954, as Washington's actions in the name of equality have restricted the school district's in the name of local control. In short, then, the potential for value conflict exists because of our pluralism, and the reality of the conflict exists because of selective emphasis on certain of those values by those with power to enforce it.[3]

In a totalitarian State, such value disjunction rarely exists; there, all values and their institutions are designed to achieve monolithic results.[4] In a democracy, however, values are diverse and value conflict is frequent, all to be worked out within the system's emphasis upon majority decision making. In both systems, however, the School is assigned prime responsibility for instruction of the young in civic virtue. When such virtue is basically defined under totalitarianism as obedience to the State, all other civic values can be aligned to this central command. In democracies, however, where individualism is stressed as the central virtue and where individuals differ about what that entails, the lack of value congruence places an inordinate, perhaps impossible, burden on the School.

We can illustrate these tensions by reference to the value of equality in the American creed.[5] One of the norms of citizenship in our society is egalitarianism, yet we exist in a system of unequal social status. The School acts not only to socialize norms such as equality, but also to select the persons who will get most and least of society's rewards. In important ways, to be "educated" is to be sorted into groups that vary widely in skills, self-esteem, influence, and social status. Parsons' formulation poses the dual functions:

> Our main interest, then, is in a dual problem: first, of how the school class functions to internalize in its pupils both the commitments and capacities for successful performance of their future adult roles, and second, of how it functions to allocate these human resources within the role-structure of the adult society.[6]

How then is one to handle the contradictions impressed upon the young? On the one hand, Schools are selective in distributing rewards or allocating values, whether in "grading on a curve" or in differential admission requirements. School structures provide an important means of legitimating a whole system of inequalities both in the eyes of students as well as of business and governmental leaders. At the end of high school, grades and other performance records determine in large part whether a student goes on to a prestige college or begins low-skilled work. At the same time, the School teaches a vague "equality" as desirable behavior expected of apprentice citizens. Against this it also teaches the inequalities of society, even only if offered as something to be corrected. This conflict of function produces a parallel conflict in the young, a form of cognitive dissonance that is resolved by possessing and acting on contradictory notions of equality.[7] The School, in short, handles these conflicting demands of reward differentiation, as well as of political socialization, by leaving it up to the young to sort out the contradictions. Such uncoordinated socialization, a direct result of the value contradiction of a democracy, is bound to be repeated across the range of our plural values.

handling plural values

Political Socialization and Systems Analysis

Systems analysis, particularly in its definition of the relationship between School and State, provides an additional theoretical perspective. Whether writers use systems terms or not, all agree that the primary relationship of the two is close in every nation. Further, while the School is everywhere subordinate to the State, it engages in a trade-off of needs and advantages. Thus, the School inculcates obedience to the law and the legitimacy of the State, while the latter provides the former with funds, some protection from outsiders, and a growing monopoly in educating.[8]

This broadly stated interrelationship is familiar in systems terms. The School is one of the agents that provides the State with *diffuse support,* defined by Easton as "broad political good will that a system generates through various means over the years . . . that helps members to accept or tolerate outputs to which they are opposed or the effect of which they see as damaging to their wants." [9] The securing of such support takes place as a result of *political socialization,* "those developmental processes through which persons acquire political orientations and patterns of behavior." [10] These processes orient the young to appropriate political values, attitudes, and behaviors.[11] To Easton, diffuse support provides a theoretical explanation for the political system's ability to handle stress when its specific outputs fail to meet all demands.

But political socialization not only affects what happens to the system's outputs but also has consequences for the input side. The young are taught what can be properly presented as demands and what roles can be properly performed by citizens in policy conversion. Such instruction helps limit demands to those the system can normally and usefully handle. For example, the fact that the political authorities were never a source of assistance in the bank crises before 1900 was clearly accepted then; by the 1930's crisis, their intervention had become marginally proper, and in our own time unquestionably appropriate — indeed, demanded. In the earlier era, a restricted view of proper demands eased the task of political authorities, but in later periods an expansive view overwhelmed it. Similarly, political socialization defines proper role behavior for citizens. Inculcation of the view that in policy conversion the act of voting is proper, whereas bomb-throwing is not, helps keep down the number of schoolhouses the political authorities must rebuild. Such role instruction also helps recruit and train political leaders attracted to political power and its uses.

In this fashion, the political system's persistence can be enhanced by the School's political socialization functions. System-citizen interactions are regularized, citizen expectations about outputs made realistic, their input demands shaped, and leaders attracted.[12] School operations among different States show considerable uniformity in the general functions of system-induced political socialization. But the specific content of such functions — the teaching of role expectations, for example — can vary with time and cultures. As Litt asked:

> Is this model student to be a member of a mass who does not question the rule of a superior and ordained elite, an industrial worker who needs the skill and understanding to know his role in modern society, or a child of the Enlightenment expected to participate in the voluntary mosaic of parties, interest groups, and informal circles of political opinion-formation?[13]

What variation and uniformity exist in political socialization patterns and what forces account for them are basic research questions for which there are few state and national cross-analyses.[14]

THE INSTRUMENTS OF POLITICAL SOCIALIZATION

We wish now to bring together these philosophical, democratic, and systems perspectives as they bear upon political socialization. They provide frameworks for the analysis, both normative and empirical, of two basic queries: What is attempted and what is the result in the effort to socialize the young to the American political system? Little empirical analysis bearing currently on these questions exists prior to the middle third of this century, but probably studies of earlier periods would not show much different patterns. For when scholars did turn to the content of what was attempted in socialization, they consistently found highly similar qualities in the instruments of curriculum, textbook, and teacher.

Models of Political Learning

There is no one necessary way these instruments must interact. Indeed, it is possible to argue, as Litt has, that two distinctive models of civic learning have operated at different stages in our history, that a third may be emerging now, and that these reflect social changes and produce political learning changes.[15] He argues that a *rational-activist* model of individual citizen political action dominated an earlier period, emphasizing a nineteenth-century, liberal ethos of the individual citizen's "mastery of the political environment [through] reasoned, voluntary effort" and the search for "harmony and political compromise." Instruction emphasized man's "rights, duties, and obligations"; that is, a citizen was to participate out of a sense of moral duty and be responsible for his use of power. Policy making was predicated on "rational deliberation . . . an open exchange of opinion in face-to-face meetings, and strong confidence in the ability of self-governing men to decide for the good of the community." The preparatory schools and strong liberal arts colleges generated this set of norms and infused it into public civic instruction through secondary textbooks and teacher training.

Changes in society, however, produced a new concept of civic education, which Litt calls the *integrative-consensual* model. The new urban immigrant masses threatened national consensus with their passionately different views of the nature of the State and its uses of power. Where earlier civic instruction was absorbed from shared, peer-group values, now civic education took the form of Americanization textbooks and courses to integrate aliens into an allegiant consensus. The immigrant was to be turned away from "dirty" parties, patronage, and ethnic group conflict to accept nonpartisanship, the merit system, and "a harmony of community interests." In short, the immigrant who sought to use the schools to gain social and political respectability had to change his political values, perspectives, and behavior — even change his definition of "political."

This model, generated through the comprehensive high school and public university, may not have changed the style of city politics greatly. But it did develop a consensus by using "conventional information about American history and institutions as a damper to 'dysfunctional' radical political ideologies and intense subcultural loyalties." Such diffuse support was functionally related not only to the arrival of new ethnic groups with different civic values, but also to the development of a national political and economic system and to the emergence of major social conflicts over the uses of political power.

A third model has not yet loomed large in civic instruction. Termed *segmented-organizational* by Litt, this seeks to develop skills of technical intellectual analysis, such as political management, and technical concepts and analytical tools that are highly abstract and impersonal — such as "models." The generating institution is the research group, which transmits its ideas to the large public universities. Such instruction is adaptive to and reflective of the segmented organizations that dominate the national scene, including the dominant bureaucratic and scientific political elites.

The instruments of political socialization, then, may be woven into three instructional models. One emphasizes civic duties and obligations, rational deliberation, and compromise in policy making. A second emphasizes allegiance to a common culture, social harmony, and distaste for political agencies whose conflict threatens such allegiant harmony. The third emphasizes the technical ability to understand the nature of the political world in order that one may manage it. Our task now is to determine which model best describes what is attempted in American schools by curriculum, textbooks, and teachers, as School seeks to support State.

Curriculum Content

We begin the task of specifying the diffuse support function by asking what is known of the actual content of the curriculum. The answer can be brief, as the findings generally agree. What is offered in American public school is formalistically descriptive, weakly linked to reality, devoid of analytical concepts except legalistic ones, highly prescriptive in tone — and, as a direct consequence of all this, noncontroversial. Smith recently found few changes in a half-century of social studies offerings: civics in the ninth grade, world history in the tenth, American history in the eleventh, and some government or social problems in the senior year.[16] The curriculum contains little of the recent behavioral developments, comparative analysis, or international studies, and almost no sociology, anthropology, or psychology.[17]

From elementary to secondary education, the instruction proceeds from emphasis on indirect and symbolic patriotism to explicit but shaded use of facts about American history and government. In the elementary school child's world, Hess and Torney found use of classroom symbols and rituals, for example, pledging allegiance, showing the flag or pictures of important events or men, singing patriotic songs. With the child's increasing interest in institutions rather than persons, more attention is given in successive years to specific political institutions. This curriculum content has special empirical and normative perspectives. Empirically, it ignores events and conditions that contradict the ideal descriptions of the political system. The normative content emphasizes compliance with rules and authority while skimping citizens' rights to participate in their government (other than by voting), which leads to a de-emphasis on parties, interest groups, and partisan behavior.[18]

At the secondary level, although more information is provided the student, it bears little relationship to the world portrayed by social scientists. As a spokesman for a group which has closely studied this educational phase has concluded,

> Today's high school student studies about government in much the same way that his parents studied government. Current high school

civic and government courses continue to be based upon legalistic descriptions and ethical prescriptions. The social foundations of political behavior and the cultural forces that shape political roles and decisions are neglected. The relationships between certain kinds of political behavior and socioeconomic status, ethnic identity, or primary and secondary group memberships are ignored. Little or nothing is said about basic concepts of current political science such as political culture, political socialization, status, role, reference groups, and function. . . . The political world presented . . . bears little resemblance to the world of the politician.[19]

The major elements of distinguishing the perceptions of politician and teacher is the absence of controversy in the teacher's world. The clamor over issues about which contemporary Americans sharply divide rarely enters the classroom; even those issues which divided our ancestors may still be handled gingerly. Characteristically, American history courses leave little time for the current scene; sometimes it is not even reached, as the course fuzzes away somewhere between World Wars I and II.

The blandness of the curriculum may be attributable to two major kinds of fault — lack of teacher competence to handle controversy and pressures upon teachers, textbook publishers, and school boards by interest groups. These possibilities engage us in the following sections, where we will note the pressure of "curriculum evangelism" to assure a neutral if not favorable treatment.[20]

Textbook Content

Textbooks are obviously another major instrument for political socialization. They played a powerful role in the decades after the Civil War in citizenship training in history and patriotism, when, in Wiggin's phrase, the textbook was "Teacher to America." Indeed, the perspective of the Southern white saturated the national perspective of Reconstruction because of the dominance of some Southern historians whose ideas dominated secondary textbooks. But even in more recent decades, the historical function of citizenship training still dominates those books.[21]

Again, the findings are much like those for the total curriculum — textbooks are characteristically as bland as the curriculum they serve. Noncontroversial, offering few conceptual and analytical tools for understanding political reality, jingoistic and narrowly moralistic (only the rare book mentions any mistake the United States has ever made in domestic policy and none in foreign affairs), naive in descriptions of the political process, overly optimistic about the system's ability to handle future problems — the criticisms of such books are repetitive and insistent. Instructional methods are not much more useful. At a chapter's end appear questions for review that stress formal facts. The naturalist fallacy pervades such instruction, that is, by assembling enough empirical facts, one can make value judgments.[22]

One illustration of such textbook blandness is the treatment of minorities. Despite the past and present highly minoritarian basis of American social life, until very recently what students might learn about this social fact in their school books was scant and stereotyped. Jews, Negroes, and other immigrants, as well as Indians, were often not presented at all, or only as picturesque "human interest" facets of history. They were never shown having an impact on American history. The "melting pot" thesis of such books is the implicit reason for not presenting such historical evidence; somehow, the immigrant stepped off the boat and into a giant social fondue. Often explicit was this view of the harmony in which all groups were said to have lived, except for the regrettable aberration of the Civil War. Negroes disappeared from history textbooks after that war, except for an occasional patronizing reference to George Washington Carver — but rarely to Frederick Douglass and never to William Du Bois. Indians were presented as quaint natives who sometimes caused "trouble" that was quickly put down. America was "discovered" by an Italian or a Swede but never by Indians. It is hard to parody such a narrow view of the pluralistic basis of American history; the actual presentations do so on their face.

Yet, at the end of the second third of this century, as a result of political and educational protest, minorities began receiving more realistic treatment of their roles in history. A comparison of textbooks from 1949 to 1960 found some improvement for Jews, but still little for Negroes and immigrants of other races. By the late 1960's, however, a fuller exposition of the Negro's role — including changing references to the "black" role — as well as removal of offensive characterizations, were widely evident in these books. Pressure from the urban centers by the increasingly politicized blacks was a major force in this change.[23] The rate of adoption of these textbooks, however, was still very slow by 1970.

The Role of the Teacher

Intervening between curriculum-textbook and the student, the teacher has been regarded as a potentially powerful instrument for political socialization since the days of Athens; and, as Socrates learned, societies have placed constraints upon such power. Examination of teacher-preparation requirements provides important clues to the direction of such constraints. Despite some acceptance of social science courses by midcentury, teacher training continues to emphasize preparation in history. Even the common "social science major" requires one-third to one-half coursework in history, with the rest spread among numerous other fields.[24]

The problem is that the outlook, training, and methodology of the historian is not that of the social scientist, the former having resisted the latter's behavioral revolution of the last quarter-century. As a consequence of this orientation, "the student comes to think of human activity in a descriptive, sequential, and narrative fashion rather than in an analytical and predictive way. History and historians do not address themselves to the problem of systematically developing theories of human conduct." [25] Moreover, such training inculcates a past — not a present — orientation in teachers that necessarily keeps them from directing their students' eyes to the social world around them. This facilitates the indoctrination of non-critical attitudes about the political and social world.

Further, as social science courses are increasingly added to the secondary school curriculum, the gap may grow between the actual competence of the teacher and the potential quality of the offering. Despite great student interest in government in the 1960's, for example, few teachers were or are qualified to offer the new thinking of political science as analytical tools. Many have had only the introductory course in college, which is often years behind them, and some have had none. In Kansas, "14.6 percent of the government teachers and 25.5 percent of the citizenship instructors had never had a college course in government." Better preparation will probably come, although not necessarily from teacher-training schools but rather from the upgrading of high school curricula by the professions and by recent United States Office of Education projects.[26]

Some qualities of civic teachers may be of considerable importance in their socialization function. Lack of controversy in textbooks was matched by teacher avoidance of controversy in Zeigler's Oregon study. The safer the topic, the less the reluctance to express views. Yet those who were younger, more liberal, and more politically active consistently expressed themselves more openly. This avoidance by most of the sample was partly a function of what one taught; those in social studies, English, and languages were more expressive and liberal than their colleagues in art and music. Issue avoidance in class did not carry outside the room, however, as most teachers agreed they would express themselves in their role as citizen. Yet, "even for the expressive teachers the closing of the classroom door means goodbye to the world of politics." [27] We shall later note some changes in this behavior, however.

Timidity — or lack of competence — in the face of controversy is not new. Thirty-five years ago Beale asked, "Are American teachers free?" and in his classic study found that they were not.[28] Countless other studies, dissecting the ties that bind the teacher to his community and profession, urge him not to get involved in controversy, an insistence backed by sanctions of disapproval or dismissal. Efforts to put constraints upon teachers, then, are not the monopoly of any group in this society but a recognition of their purported power as socializing agent. We have mentioned minority pressures that have recently moved textbook publishers to present a more full and honest treatment. Similarly, teachers have felt such pressures in terms of charges of racism and bias from these same groups, while right-wing elements charge subversion if teachers change. Unsafe, because controversial, issues appear consistently in accounts of these conflicts. Favorable — or even any — reference to the United Nations, the right to dissent, civil rights, current politics, evolution (only in 1970 did federal courts overturn the last of the laws forbidding teaching evolution), the role of blacks in our history, the Soviet Union, sex education, family life, class and status conflict — again and again the same items of curriculum appear as the nub of a local community conflict with an embattled teacher.[29]

One curious feature of the teacher-as-socializing-agent is the wide evidence that his adherence to values normally defined as democratic is not very strong. Teachers' responses to attitude scales on civil rights raise questions about their knowledge of and attachment to these values. This feature, if prevalent, fills in a picture of this socializing agent as not particularly well trained for his task, noncombative, sensitive to community pressure, and uncertain about if not antipathetic to at least part of the democratic credo he ostensibly is to transmit.[30]

Upon review, these instruments of political socialization appear to share common features. They are uncritical of the political system, unconcerned with contemporary social conflict, and undemanding of the student. Exposure to politics concentrates in the latter part of a student's years, although much of that focuses upon the past of the world and nation. The window opened to the student on his nation reveals a social monochrome, not a kaleidoscope, of peoples. They are seen characteristically interacting by accommodation but not by competition. The political system is a thing of institutions, and its presentation is formalistic; no live people man these positions of power. This system's values are offered as an unchallengeable heritage of the past, to be accepted as fact and not opinion, whose content is given and whose clarity is obvious.

In short, if diffuse support is created for a political system by exposing the young in a structured way to a uniform set of stimuli, then the instruments of American socialization surveyed in this section are just such stimuli. The allegiant-harmony model prevails, offering students "one nation, under God, indivisible, with liberty and justice for all." The instructional design, explicit or not, is to cause children to see their oneness and ignore their distinctiveness, and to treat similarly their allegiance and dissent, their cooperation and conflict. In our terms, then, all of this, if successful, looks much like diffuse support.

Yet it remains to be seen what the effect is upon the young. When we ask how effective such socialization has been, we raise a more significant query than asking what the instruments are like. The answer here leads us into a more dynamic study of the citizen at the intersection of State and School.

THE EFFECTS OF POLITICAL SOCIALIZATION

The recent flood of research on this question must necessarily be summarized here,[31] but several conclusions may be offered. First, institutions other than the School are socializing agents. Also involved are family and peer groups, as well as reality signals produced by distinctive events in the life of the child. Second, those School instruments described previously are repeatedly found to have *little* effect for white, middle-class Americans but substantially more for black Americans. Third, the psychology of the socialization process is very complex. And fourth, little is known systematically about enough of these psychological aspects to generalize firmly about the socialization process. This research review should not be taken as unnecessarily critical, given the relatively recent focus upon understanding this complex process. Indeed, enough is known to conclude that current School theory of curriculum and instruction is misplaced and ineffective.

The Agents of Socialization

The scholarly disregard (until quite recently) of the School as a political socializer is seen in the fact that Hyman's seminal volume in 1959 emphasized research on family influence but totally ignored that on the School.[32] The primacy of family influence on the political socialization of children has been challenged recently by Hess and Torney's study of over 12,000 elementary children and confirmed in other details by a smaller national sample in the work of Jennings and Niemi. The family emerges from these studies as important in creating early gross attitudes of support for country and government and for shaping the child's party identification.[33] But for other aspects of attitude, value, and cognition about the political world, other agents operate, such as the School, peers, and media of communication. Clearly a more complex theory is needed to explain why the child is not the mirror image of the parent. Its general dimensions may encompass something like Dennis' suggestion: "The views of the socialized are likely to follow the socializers who most often interact with him, present more explicit political content to him, and have higher salience, prestige, and capacity to influence him generally." And yet, as Dennis concludes,

> The comparative assessment of these forces and the extent to which they operate in concert or disharmony has only begun. There are still remarkably few published findings comparing different agency inputs with their ostensible socialization outputs, or relating both to the properties of learner and teacher as intervening variables.[34]

In that case, what do we know about the effect of the School as a social-izing agent? It must be kept in mind that the School's socializing stimuli probably are not the same everywhere in America. Hence, variation in cur-riculum, textbook, and teaching quality, as well as in the local community's demands upon such instruction, is probably associated with variations in what is transmitted. Thus, Litt showed three communities with different status bases had different instructional emphases and value indoctrination in their young.[35]

Yet repeated research finds that the impact of high school civics courses is minimal for white, middle-class, American youth, who after all constitute the large majority of the audience. The most recent of these studies, by Langton and Jennings, found little change in student knowledge or atti-tudes, ostensibly the behavioral objective of such courses. Blacks, on the other hand, particularly those of low- and middle-class origins, did show significant increases in political knowledge, toleration, efficacy, and the desire to participate in politics. For them at least, the course content was new information; for whites it was redundant. The implication is that other agents, such as peer groups and family, can socialize whites before such courses enter their lives. But in what manner and with what comparative effect we simply do not know at this time. It is certain, however, that such limited socialization effect is hardly evidence of the political system's striv-ing to create diffuse support. Further, such null findings question much of what is now done in civic instruction in high schools. So much effort with so little evident result suggests the need for either change in traditional in-struction at this stage or a shift in instruction to earlier years where effects are more likely.[36]

A Theoretical Framework for Research

We have to this point focused upon School-related aspects of political so-cialization. But far more is involved, for other social agencies may have some part in this. It is not unlikely that the individual himself plays a part through his unique interactions with society and events. But understanding of political socialization reaches even further to questions about its devel-opment, duration, and distribution, and its outcome for the political sys-tem. Yet little is known of such questions, for the fact that much needs to be done is admitted by all scholars. We can best suggest the dimensions of such research needs by reference to Dennis' analysis of the ten major prob-lem areas, hoping that our summary does justice to his fuller study.[37] These areas will be posed as general questions, with a few notes on find-ings.

1. *What is the effect of Political Socialization (PS) upon political life, particularly the persistence and the stability-change dynamics of the politi-cal system?* Note here the diffuse-support function of PS; but such support

might also be obtained by the political system's reliance on force, or by output and structural adjustments to environmental stress.

2. *What is transmitted by PS to the young that has persistence consequences?* In general terms, there is agreement that PS learning focuses upon three kinds of political orientations — affective, cognitive, and evaluational. The objects of these orientations are three: political authorities (those who make particular decisions and handle the daily routine of governance); the political regime (the basic "rules and structures through the use of which demands are converted into outputs"); and the political community (the members who feel they desire to be related together politically).[38] Others, answering this question in less sweeping terms, focus on participation and ideological learning or on attitudes toward authority.

3. *When and how does PS begin, develop, and end?* Here the focus is upon the individual's maturation, with a common assumption that what is learned as a child is what the adult later perceives and believes. No known study traces the same group — or cohort — from childhood onward; instead, studies characteristically examine different children at different stages of the life-cycle within the same research design.

4. *What, why, and how extensive are the similarities and differences in PS between generations?* Here the focus is upon shifts between those in different stages of the life-cycle of a nation; this is the previous question writ large on the history of the political system. Little work has been done here, but the question holds special interest for students of new nations and is obviously of interest today in American concerns about a "generation gap."

5. *What, why, and how extensive are the similarities and differences in PS across political systems?* There is great current interest by political scientists here, and a developing body of empirical data on cross-cultural political attitudes, although confirmed hypotheses are few as yet.

6. *What, why, and how extensive are the similarities and differences in PS among a political system's subgroups and what difference does this make for that system?* Reference here is to social divisions of status, religion, region, and ethnicity and their political consequences. This has been explored fully only for sex and social class.

7. *How does learning take place in PS?* We have earlier studies of socialization agencies in such learning, but other questions barely touched ask whether the PS learning model is incremental or abrupt, sequential or random, continuous or discontinuous — and what intervening variables affect these models. The research emphasis has been upon how society gives the learner his knowledge, but little attention has been given to what he picks up on his own, that is, whether the learner is a dependent or independent variable.

8. *Who teaches the lessons of PS?* There are many studies of school,

family, peers, but almost no studies of comparative effect and how that effect varies among States, social strata, life-cycle stages, and so on.

9. *How extensive among society's members is PS, whether it comes from the political system, social agencies, or events?* Only implicit in most research has been the possibility of viewing PS as an output of the system whose extent among citizens may vary widely, with important consequences for the input side.

10. *How are potential political leaders socialized, trained, and motivated?* This query, which links Plato's philosopher-king to contemporary public administration training, has had very little study.

In these ten queries we can see an expanded conceptualization of political socialization, whereas most definitions work with only a few aspects. We are obviously far from having satisfactory answers to any one of these, much less to how all ten interrelate. A suggestion of that relationship is shown in Figure 2.1. In this linear-flow model, we cannot be sure of the proper placement of each component. The content of a new member's learning, for example, may be mediated by the factors indicated as operating be-

Figure 2.1 The Flow of Influence in Political Socialization Within a Political System

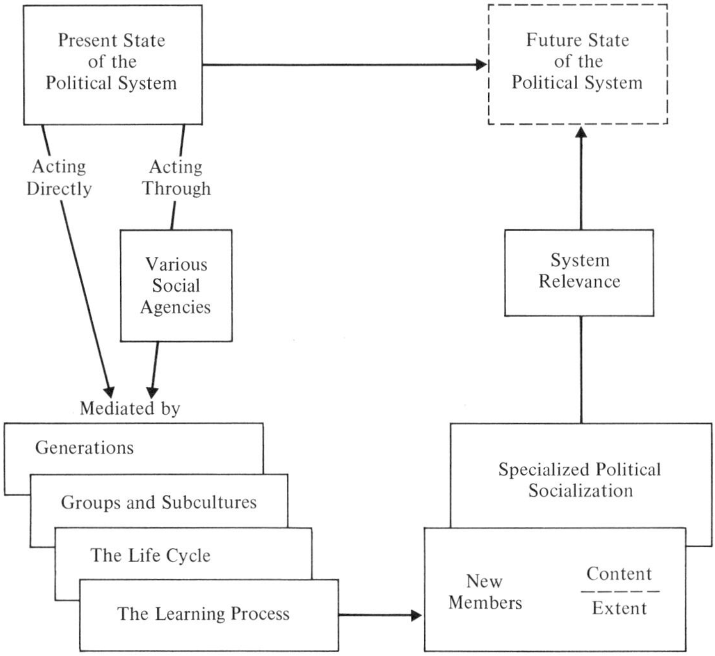

Source: Jack Dennis, "Major Problems of Political Socialization Research," *Midwest Journal of Political Science,* 12 (1968), 113.

tween himself and the political system. But new learning may abruptly short-circuit such intervening variables because of system failure or resistance to stress in which he is personally involved. For example, considerable evidence exists that adoption of affiliation with one major political party or the other is strongly influenced by familial training and is reinforced by group and subculture experiences. However, such transmission and retention are subject to a dramatic break when traumatic historical events intervene. Thus, the Great Depression brought in its wake altered affiliation patterns; before it, Negroes were overwhelmingly Republican, but by 1936 they had largely shifted to, and today a majority remain in, the Democratic party.[39]

Our ignorance of the exact linkage in this causal chain underlines the distance that research must go, but it also suggests some directions. There are exciting dimensions open to research, barely tapped by the recently renewed interest of social scientists. Thus, the once-common assumption of psychologists that little political learning occurs in childhood was the basis for curriculum theory requiring civics in secondary education only. But this assumption proved of doubtful validity when scholars searched for the first time for specifically political aspects of socialization during early life. It was found that as early as the second grade children conceived images of government and political leaders and held an extraordinary and unsuspected benign attitude toward both political objects; the School seemed more influential than the family in many of these respects. It is now believed that attitudes toward authority in the family may be transferred to political authorities, first via personalized attraction to idealized presidents and then to political institutions, accounting eventually for citizens' acceptance of the legitimacy of the political system. These findings differ critically from the state of knowledge ten years ago. They rest upon aggregate and not case-study data, provide a linkage to general learning theory, and suggest fruitful lines for further research. While this psychological conceptualization of socialization is not without its critics, at least the questions raised here have relevance for all other aspects of political studies.[40]

MODELS OF SOCIALIZATION
AND POLITICAL THEORIES

The socialization instruments of curriculum, textbook, and teacher need to be reviewed in light of Litt's three models of civic learning. His three learning possibilities were rational-activist (participation, compromise, rational discourse), integrative-consensual (harmony, allegiance, lack of conflict), and segmental-organizational (skills of intellectual analysis, manipulative in purpose). Findings on how School instruments for creating diffuse support have been employed should suggest which model prevails currently.

First, the direction of this research review is reinforcingly similar. School socialization emphasizes prescriptive learning but not analytical skills, selectively positive qualities of history and social life but not the problem areas, and harmony and unity of the political process but not its divisive and competitive qualities. In short, we see here many of the features of the integrative-consensual learning model with its allegiance to depersonified, abstract institutions of governance.

A second conclusion is not so evident. Most of the scholars summarized here are appalled at their findings, mainly because they judge from an alternative learning model that in some respects resembles Litt's segmental-organizational model. Note their criticisms that civic learning provides few political management skills, develops no techniques of analysis and inquiry to help the citizen understand political reality, and presents little knowledge of the pluralistic, organizational, group-conflict nature of the political world — and of who wins and who loses that conflict. They complain of textbooks and teachers pressured by representatives of that conflictual society into concealing the reality of the very world they represent.[41] For these critics, another view prevails of the appropriate civic learning model to link the political system and its citizens.

It is difficult to escape the further conclusion that just as people get the government they deserve, so the civic learning that prevails reflects dominant educational demands of the society. After all, the civic instruction portrayed here is functional for many people. The world of harmony and consensus is easier for the teacher to transmit than facts that emphasize complex and subtle conflict. School boards more easily deflect local pressures if civic content is at such a general, and hence acceptable, level that no group can take offense. Textbook publishers lose fewer sales if powerful group values are not questioned and the governing process is depicted as almost perfect. And, in terms of the larger political system, those socialized in this fashion are less likely to assert a right to participate more fully, to strive for more resources from government, and, if disappointed in that effort, to challenge the very legitimacy of the political authorities, if not of the regime itself.

In short, then, the important feature of the civic learning described here is not its incompatibility with other modes of civic learning. Instead, its very persistence indicates the functional role it plays and the satisfaction it provides for many elements of society. A learning model that emphasizes inquiry or that asks the student to look closely at the parade of reality is dysfunctional for all these elements. Socrates, it will be recalled, felt the brunt of the dysfunctional consequences for Athens of his urgings that "the unexamined life is not worth living."

There is one group unmentioned yet — the students. As we review the studies of socialization effects, two lessons of functionality in the American system emerge. School at the elementary level does seem to be shaping attitudes toward political authority more than believed possible, while at the secondary level the School is irrelevant, except for those receiving formal socialization for the first time. There are important implications for curriculum policy here. More might be done earlier and less later in a student's schooling if greater socialization effect is desired. There is a strong implication in these studies that secondary-school civics courses are probably a waste of time and resources if the students are white and middle class — as most Americans are. What might be done at an earlier age is only now being considered. There is an unused potential in these early years to transmit the formal knowledge and consensual appreciation of the political system — if that is one's civic learning model — as well as to experiment with analytical skills of the kind that social science has developed recently — if that is one's model.

A further conclusion is that the socialization content described here illuminates the theoretical perspectives of the opening section of this chapter. The tensions among plural, democratic values noted there are suppressed by a learning model that stresses acceptance of a consensual society, just as they are aggravated by one which stresses a conflictual society. Challenge to a consensual ideal by the reality outside the class is reduced by the School through several means. Especially important is a curriculum that avoids the contemporary political scene and postpones consideration of that scene to the last years of schooling.

Note the implications of this for systems analysis. The School's assertion that all is well and its avoidance of contradiction combine to provide an affirmatory socialization. As such, if effective in its transmission, it may well contribute more emotionally to diffuse support of the State than do other means. Further support may stem from a socialization that presents the political system as free from error in the past, as a set of impersonal institutions and not as contemporary men about whom passions rage, and as embodying vaguely a creed that ties all Americans together. This homogenized view contains elements of support for the political system's authorities, regime, and community.

Nor does it seem obvious that the student's increasing cynicism about government, which overbalances his earlier benign view, is directly attributable to the School's failure to provide diffuse support. After all, its efforts to transmit only positive signals are continuous and repeated, implying that other agents account for the growth of cynicism. Even that growth is suspect, both because it is not certain from the research that benign students actually turn into cynical students and because Americans possess a keen patriotism. They show a political-regime affect that is much higher than for citizens elsewhere viewing their own native land.[42] We suspect that the School's socialization disenchants the most aware students by offering civic instruction that is denied by reality thrusting in on their perceptions through the communication media. But again, there is insufficient evidence that this cognitive dissonance takes place often or that it does so for many.

Finally, we conclude that the inadequate knowledge we have of the socialization process and its effects makes difficult any full statement of the applicability of systems analysis, particularly to the relationship of School to diffuse support.[43] The extent of the queries raised earlier is enough to make this point for us. There are hints of validation, of course, but in sum these are insufficient. In chapters that follow we will deal directly with *specific* support of the political system stemming from satisfaction with system outputs. Yet for us, as for so many who study those psychological forces that bind people in community, the operational aspects are difficult to establish. What we see, instead, when we turn to the political conversion of demands into outputs, is not the simple, "clean" process presented by the Schools, but a divisive, sweaty struggle among conflicting groups. And yet, behind those forces, one senses a greater sense of unity — which nonetheless vanishes when brought close for inspection.

3 The Origins and Agents
of Demand Inputs

The political system is not subject to the input of support alone, for demands provide the more continuous, clamorous stuff of governance. We turn in this section, then, to the exchange across boundaries of wants that arise from unsatisfied values, which consequently generate stress in the social environment — some of which produce demands upon the political system. Essentially, then, such demands originate in the conflict between basic social values and are transmitted into the political system. The next chapter will carry us one step farther to examine the channels of access to the system's conversion process. Our present inquiry, however, will ask how stress arises through value conflicts and what agents transfer the resultant demands across the system's boundary.

VALUES AND THE ORIGIN OF CONFLICT

Individualism and Majoritarianism

The first, and perhaps still best, commentator on American political life noted a curious contradiction in its fundamental values. Alexis de Tocqueville pointed to the individualistic and the collectivist impulses whose clash provided a vital dynamism to the America he knew in the 1830's. Being a good aristocrat, he feared that the collectivist impulse would triumph with its adoration of the majoritarian principle. We believe that the stress swirling today in our society still stems from the confrontation between individual and group pressures to define life.

The fundamental value may well be individualism, with its roots in Greek and Christian beliefs. It is reflected in our economic processes, in our record of violence, and in the restlessness of spirit of the westward migration in the 1800's and the city migration of the 1900's. Sometimes rawly egotistic and selfish, but sometimes seeking freedom of mind and spirit, it forms the characteristic American *brio,* that vigor and strength more Roman than Greek — but always distinctive.

The political signs of this value may be seen in the bills of rights in national and state constitutions. These draw around the individual those lines which for government to cross constitutes tyranny. Such statements are also designed to guard any minority against an equally possible tyranny of popular majorities. Yet the problem is that majorities have special authority in a democracy, so the conflict of minority right and majority rule has been endemic.

The interaction of the two principles is influenced by the mediation of the political system. If all men are regarded as important, their wishes must be responded to by that system. But men's wishes are many and often conflicting, so, if it is to persist, government must regulate this conflict so that it remains within tolerable levels. The operating principle of such regulation is that a given policy will take the direction preferred by the majority. Of course, this is a simplification of a very complex body of theory, as "majority rule" is a concept whose ambiguity is exceeded only by its sister concept, "majority will." [1]

It is the case, nevertheless, that at a number of decision points in the political system, from school board to Congress, we find conflict resolved by a majority who vote on the relevant matter. That principle is justified philosophically because the majority's determination can best reflect the largest amount of individualism, even though other individuals in the minority will lose out. It also has the virtue, if accepted as a legitimate process, of being a conflict resolution device. Without it, at best there would be even more minority rule than now exists; at worst, without it no democratic society could be possible. Majority rule, then, has been the method of operationalizing the major cultural value of individualism.

If our history has evinced conflict between individualism and majority rule, our political practices and institutions have also reflected it. Thus, minority rights are protected by numerous devices, including the two-thirds requirement to pass school tax levies. Majority rule can be seen in the American concern to *elect* everyone in sight, including members of the 19,300 school boards (1970) — the only nation to do so. Many of the Constitutional principles are barriers against temporary majorities, e.g., separation of power, checks and balances, federalism, and civil rights. For example, school boards may issue policies, but they are subject to taxpayer suit, popular referendum, and even recall of officials. The national will may call for outlawing school segregation, but the power of Southern congressmen can long thwart that will. Or when passed, the law is faced by local minorities prepared to hold the line for another generation, if possible.

Such individualism operating in political channels might tear society apart if not checked. To a degree that is not fully clear, diffuse support for the political regime — the accepted, basic rules of governance — has contributed to the creation of a political community, the sense that Americans want to exist together. However, diffuse support is not absolute or thorough among Americans because of the splintering effect of individualism. Belief in a detailed set of political "rules of the game" is not widespread among all Americans; [2] individual as well as majoritarian impulses have continuously broken out into violence in our history; and a major civil war a century ago shattered the political community, leaving regional scars even today. [3]

Possibly this centrifugal pull of individualism has been checked by our tendency to live and socialize mostly with those who agree with us. In much of our past, American society was an archipelago of islands of conformity, each island oriented to different values and indifferent to or unaware of others. The Bible Belt schools could ignore evolution while urban Northern schools treated it fully; rural Protestant schools might require prayers while urban liberal enclaves ignored them. Such cultural isolationism broke down, however, when outside forces disrupted the civil serenity — the issue of slavery and Union a century ago, the movement from farm to the city seventy-five years ago, the impact of communication media in the last fifty years. These changes evoked new needs, stresses, and demands for the political system, and one of those demand sets arose over conflicting claims on the nature of schools.

Matched to the individualistic philosophy of Americans is a social scene of great heterogeneity. Social diversity runs in many strains through our history; even today, despite those who see only "mass Americans," scholars find the differentiating impact of ethnicity, regionalism, income, and sex upon a wide range of attitudes. [4] This variety is seen in our communities, which constitute a range of mixes of differing needs, resources, and preferences. Hamlets may not need, afford, or prefer an assistant superintendent for desegregation, large cities may be at the opposite pole, and intermediate cities distributed somewhere between. Or, what a community may prefer, it cannot afford, or what it needs it may not prefer, and so on in an unnumbered profusion of policy sets. [5] A cross-country tour passes through not merely jurisdictions but border stations of policy outcomes, seen in the change in road quality, street cleanliness, and schoolhouse styles — and what occurs within the schoolrooms.

This variety of group and region, policy set and community life, reflects that basic individualism in American life. Not for us a French school system where at a given hour every child of a given age in every school is learning the same thing. For Americans the very thought is unthinkable. Thus philosophic individualism reinforces social differentiation, and both are reflected in the kind of political system we have. The rate of exchanges between the environment and the political system is affected enormously by a value system which emphasizes that one *should* translate private preference and need into public policy. Such exchanges are also accelerated by an environment of great social diversity which necessarily generates more wants and demands than does a homogeneous environment.

Pragmatism and School Policy

An additional basic American value influences this series of boundaries exchanges — pragmatism.[6] While the political system began with all its subsystems relatively uninvolved in the lives of its citizens, that condition continued only as long as private action was competent to meet wants. When that failed, Americans showed no reluctance to turn to the political system and public policy. Such a resort was first restricted to local political authorities, but if this was inadequate, then to state authorities, and, in time, to federal authorities.

There are two special aspects of this political pragmatism: collective action in the name of individualism and a blitheness about ignoring "states rights" doctrine if necessary. First, in the name of individual goals our ancestors used collective action far more than we credit them. Alongside the individualism of Daniel Boone was the collective experience of Boonsboro, and the westward movement is symbolized not so much by the individualistic Kit Carson and the sod-hut farmer as by the group life of the wagon train and the Farmers Grange. Today, giant corporations still employ the symbols of individualism but the resources of collective power. The call for "community control" of schools in 1970 is but the latest in the collective impulse of Americans.

A second aspect of American pragmatism has been the lack of doctrine. Rejecting or not knowing the European traditions of an aristocratic social order and absolutist politics, Americans freed themselves to pursue highly disparate goals.[7] One result was an undoctrinaire approach to questions about the political and economic systems. If this meant at one time a minimum of government, so be it, and hence states rights was elevated as a principle of Americanism. But at another time, if wants could be met only by transferring them out of the social order as demands upon the political system, even if that meant federal law, so be that, too.[8]

We can see all this in the major expenditures of state governments today — welfare, roads, and education. Each policy is at different stages in this progression from private-individual-local to public-collective-national policy, but each had origins in private, local efforts. The poor, aged, and mentally ill were cared for primarily by the family in an earlier America; roads and schooling were provided as much by private as by public action in their beginnings; and all three were local in nature. By stages each received fuller participation by the local city or county authorities, then by the state, and today in varying degrees by the agencies of Washington. A policy inventory of even the smallest town today shows it to be hyperactive compared to its ancestor. Not even the shadow of much current policy is to be found in the records of these earlier towns.

What stands between the two eras is a host of environmental crises generating stresses which could be met only by individuals transferring their pressure from the private to the public realm. In seeking authoritative allocation of resources to reduce this stress, individuals let no doctrine stand in their way. One general cultural value — individualism — generated inputs into the political system which another value — majority rule — authorized as legitimate behavior. But in addition, pragmatism — undeterred by bonds of the past, stimulated by the challenge of a new society, and mobilizing collective, mutual interests — provided a crystallizing value. Combined with these other two, it made possible innumerable exchanges across that intangible boundary between the private and public systems.

We can illuminate this value complex in school policies. The desire for education has *not* been a major value from the founding of this republic, in the sense that everyone wanted it. Indeed, many reasons existed for opposing the establishment of early public schools, echoes of which are still heard today.[9] Yet along the way appear signs that many Americans *did* accept this value: the *national* commitment to use land sales to finance schools and colleges, e.g., the Northwest Ordinance of 1787 and the Morrill Land Acts of 1862 and 1890; the *states'* commitment to provide a free public education at least to the grammar school level, then to high school, and now to some college; local *communities'* efforts at private support to reinforce state efforts in the private academies and colleges of the nineteenth century; and the constant shaping of the curriculum to meet the special concerns of Americans, e.g., in farm, industrial, and military training classes.[10]

It must not be thought that all this was a function of governmental action alone; of much greater consequence over a much longer period has been the nationalizing force of professionalism. The growth of professional standards for administration, teaching, curriculum, testing, and other elements of education — all were a phenomenon of the last and not this century. Before this force emerged, the fabric of American schools was plaid, and a rather ragged plaid at that. Experience drawn from testing a jumble of ideas, transmitted through new journals and new training for the emergent profession, did far more than the political system to impose a striking uniformity on American instructional practices. Pragmatism shows everywhere in the early history of this profession, for what worked well in one site was soon transmitted elsewhere and grafted onto new schools.

In the face of this powerful nationalizing force, the belief in local control of schools never wavered, nor does it today when the existence of that control seems much in doubt. Yet those ardent for local control in earlier times were also busy adopting innovations that professional administrators and teachers had proclaimed as the best methods. In this fashion, American schools everywhere accepted a standard set of graduation requirements (thus the Carnegie unit concept), learning theories and their instructional practices, teacher and administrator-training standards, and so on. Thus it is that the enemy of local control has not been Washington but the professional within the bosom of the community. The impact of professionalism is so great in closing off local authority that we explore it in depth in a later chapter on curriculum policy and in our conclusion on the future of education policy making.[11]

But Washington has come to play a more significant role in our time, just as opponents of federal aid to education feared and its supporters hoped. Federal authority, which played a limited role in the nineteenth century, expanded enormously in the twentieth.[12] Only after World War II did its resources come significantly into play, climaxing in the Elementary and Secondary Education Act of 1965. This is a far trek when one considers that the Constitution makes no specific provision for Washington to have power in this area, leaving it by implication to the states.*

If the political system's relationship to education has varied over time, so has the citizen's. The belief that "education is a good thing" has had different meanings in the pluralist perspectives of our society. Early on, education was important for religious training. In colonial Massachusetts, in what Meyer has called "The Bible Commonwealth," the first schooling law was known as the "Old Deluder Satan Act"; a favorite early textbook was John Cotton's *Spiritual Milk for Babes Drawn Out of the Breasts of Both Testaments;* and the enormously popular *New England Primer* featured a biblical alphabet, *A* being "In Adam's fall/We sinned all." [13]

Subsequently, schooling came to be endorsed for various pragmatic goals: transmission of basic literacy, i.e., the three "R's"; provision of trained labor, i.e., vocational training for farmers and industrial workers; molding into one culture the diverse cultures of our immigrants, i.e., "Americanization"; and the absorption of "culture" in the popular sense, i.e., humanist and liberal education. Then, too, across time this education has been supported by many — but not all — for the boost it provides their children in the economic and status struggle, or for its usefulness as a custody agent when parents are at work.

The factors discussed in this section combine to suggest how general cultural values operate in the systems analysis that frames our inquiry.

---

* While Congress was originally granted in Article I, Section 8, the power "to promote the progress of science and useful arts," this aimed only to undergird copyright and patent powers.

When filtered through the pluralist prism of our society, general values achieve different definitions. The private pursuit of these individualistic interests sometimes produces cooperation and accommodation. Yet other groups come into conflict and find that private subsystems provide insufficient resources for satisfying their values. As a result, some groups are rewarded and others are not. The consequent stress can generate a drive to mobilize other resources on the side of those unrewarded. One such drive can take the form of transferring the struggle from the private into the political system. That system, in turn, seeking to maintain support for its political objectives, finds different ways of adjusting to such demands.

The desire for education during the nineteenth century illustrates these general propositions about values and the political system.[14] When that century opened, most education was private, expensive, and restricted to a few Americans with economic advantages — although there was some charity schooling. In short, private economic power was used to achieve educational benefits for a few. When the century ended, however, education was public, free, widespread, and systematic, at least through the grammar school. What happened in the interim was that one resource — the political — was used to achieve another — the educational.

Early in the century, barriers against suffrage fell under the battering of egalitarian values. By mid-century, anyone could vote who was white, male, and over twenty-one, a sharp shift from 1800, when suffrage was limited to the wealthy and propertied. This enfranchisement gave political power to many whose economic and educational resources were limited. The desire for education, therefore, was realized by exchanging political resources — votes — for school resources in a system of free, public education. In the process, schooling became more uniform under the pressure of private professionalism, a pressure that eventually shook off the politicians who had originally supported the exchange of education for votes.

Basically, then, the nineteenth-century stress arising over the lack of education for one's children — or over lack of funds to obtain it in the then-few private schools — caused this transformation. Stress-generated wants, unsatisfied in the private subsystems of society, were directed across the private-public boundary to the political system as inputs, which were converted into outputs of the American public school system. It is this process that we treat throughout this book.

We do not wish to exaggerate the standardization that this historical process has achieved, for within the interstices of American public education a considerable variety thrives. This is reflective of a diverse people with, as we shall see, diverse notions of what their children should learn, how teachers should act, what role the professionals should play, and indeed, what the purpose of education should be. Standardized units of American history requirements do not mean that children are getting the same facts, interpretations, or teaching skills in North and South or in a poor hamlet in North Dakota and an affluent suburb outside New York City. Credits for teacher training may be standardized, but this does not mean that the teacher is getting the same preparation in an unaccredited black college in Mississippi and the Teachers College of Columbia University. While everywhere the superintendent is the link between elected or appointed board and the school professionals, in some places he is elected, but elsewhere — and mostly — he is appointed; obviously these pivotal figures vary widely in their preparation, leadership abilities, and political roles.

The reason for such variety is that each school system reflects to some degree the prevailing values in that district. At this level are the guardians of community values — religious, economic, patriotic — for whom schools are important instruments for keeping the faith. We have seen earlier how the indoctrination function dominates schools when they teach about our government. Given insulation from outside forces, such guardians of orthodoxy can exist without challenge. But in this century challenges have abounded — the growth of national communication media, greater geographical mobility stemming from the economy or wars, professionalism, and so on. Control over schoolmen locally has been weakened by professionalism, as noted above, or by the militancy of teachers increasingly uncowed into believing they must accept the dominance of parochialism.

However, we are nevertheless far from the bland homogeneity of the French school system. Some schools still hold the theory of evolution suspect; others offer calculus or Asian history. The decentralizing impulse of pluralism clashes with the centralizing pull of nationalizing forces, such as professionalism and now federal laws. In this, education is not unique, but merely reflects the tensions of a federal system that also emerge in many other policy areas. But whatever the particular equipoise between these forces in the earlier eras, it has been drastically altered by these new nationalizing forces.

But we need to know more about specifics of this exchange and conversion process. Thus, what are the agents that transfer demand inputs into the political system from their position on its boundaries? "Transfer agents" is an abstraction for which we need some flesh and blood referents. For our purposes, we focus upon the roles of interest groups, electoral mechanisms, and local power structures. Each should be seen performing latent and manifest functions. Latently, each is involved in boundary transfer activities that have consequences for the ability of the political system — in this case the school — to persist as it seeks to cope with stress-generated demands. Manifestly, each speaks for or transmits the variety of American individualism involved in the swirl and clamor of local school politics. Both functions tell us much about how Americans give their educational values a political cast when they seek to transfer private preference into public policy.

INTEREST GROUPS AS TRANSFER AGENTS

Interest groups, intermediate between citizens and educational political authorities, are involved in the full spectrum of private demands upon the school as a political system. That is, they urge claims for justice, help, reward, or recognition. But they do more than just transmit political desires from citizens to officials. As transfer agents for the political system, interest groups often reformulate the demands so that they are somewhat different from citizens' desires. Moreover, interest groups do not confine their activities just to the input and conversion phases of the political system; they also provide feedback on implementation of school policy. Often they are mobilized by competing claims for the scarce budget resources of educational agencies. Despite such political activities, however, the tradition that overt politics and schools should be separate has shaped the particular nature of school interest groups.

Differences exist among these groups, e.g., in their temporary vs. permanent organization, special vs. broad interests, and large vs. limited resources — categories quite like those found in other kinds of interest groups. The National Education Association (NEA) illustrates the qualities of permanent organization, broad interests, and large resources, while taxpayer-revolt groups illustrate the temporary, narrow, and limited-resource type. But a major distinction we wish to employ for a closer examination of such groups centers upon the thoroughness of their interest in the many facets of education. Thus, we divide such groups into those for whom education is an end and those for whom it is a means to other ends. The first is filled with professional educators or those professionally oriented, the second with special interests wishing to use the school to serve other values, such as reducing taxes, protecting moral or patriotic values, and so on.

Professional Interest Groups

For many years the most numerous interest group — teachers — had only potential political power. Traditionally, school teachers have been reluctant to employ collective action to transmit demands to political authorities either within or outside of school systems. Further, the doctrine of the school administrator played down the usefulness of collective organizations of teachers, stressing instead the use of negotiations by individual professionals. This traditional doctrine also emphasized the "authority" of the superintendent and played down "democracy" and "participation" in their current popular senses.[15] Even the more recent conception of administration favours teacher participation only for its effects of morale building and consequent improved performance. Not surprisingly, until recently the views of teacher spokesmen differed only slightly from the administrators' tenets.

A review of the history of the NEA will help to illuminate the professional educators' norms of a unified profession that should not split into opposing interest groups competing for scarce educational resources or should not engage in public conflict over competing educational values. The NEA, as the leading national organization, concentrated its efforts at the national and state level. It gave only scant attention to local interest groups of teachers or collective pressure to change local school policy. Schoolmen of all types were inculcated with the "professional" need for a harmony of interests and the resulting agreement on educational goals for young children. Group activity, when reinforced by formal arrangements such as interest groups, would only lead to unnecessary and harmful conflict. With that perspective, the NEA as a national organization focused its concern until the past decade on standards and ethics, lobbying for general federal aid for buildings and salaries, conduct and dissemination of research, and technical assistance for state affiliates.[16]

The group's resources are not minor. It has over a million members, about 52 percent of our public school teachers. It has an extensive bureaucracy and hierarchy, although policy is usually made by the executive staff with the concurrence of a board of ninety-two directors and an executive committee of eleven.[17] Every state has its own teacher's association that is frequently a powerful interest group at the state level. There are over 8,500 dues-paying local school affiliates which filter their money through the state affiliates.

At the national level, the NEA is an umbrella for major segments of the profession. Within the national organization there are over seventy-five "Departments," "Divisions," "Commissions," and "Committees." Separate professional organizations reflect the big happy family of superintendents, principals, curriculum supervisors, and elementary teachers — all under one roof on 16th Street in Washington, D.C. Separate professional organizations within NEA exist even for audio-visual specialists, as well as for home-economics and speech teachers. The Council of Chief State School Officers is housed rent-free at NEA headquarters.

While NEA divisions serve these diverse organizations in such functions as research, public relations, and lobbying, its structure also reflects the norm of a profession which enables it to align its political resources and act upon public officials — without seeming "political." Thus, typically, teachers in Oregon NEA affiliates in the early 1960's wanted an organization "above politics," with emphasis on professional and educational activities for teachers. But while they felt politics should be avoided, it was approved if used for defending their current rights.[18]

Now, however, the NEA houses in one building groups with special orientation and values that increasingly compete with each other in the political system. More often now, teachers will not let the administrators' association be their spokesman for "good educational policy." Principals and counselors feel they are not represented by spokesmen for either teachers or administrators but are in an intermediary position. These divisions over priorities for money and values within the profession have spawned professional competitors who argue their cases before school boards and legislatures.

The most noticeable competition exists within the teaching profession itself. The American Federation of Teachers restricts its membership to teachers or to administrators with no direct authority over teachers. The AFT has state affiliates, a membership concentrated in large cities or their immediate environs, and a budget about 20 percent that of the NEA. While the two teacher groups can take common positions on some policy issues, e.g., increased state aid for teacher salaries, their differences on others are not concealed.

AFT executives contend that professional unity is a myth, because value conflicts are inevitable between teachers and their managers who administer the school.[19] AFT rhetoric is replete with *we* and *they,* terms reflective of a split between an aggressive labor union and its employer. The AFT's willingness to resort to a strike has proven attractive to big-city teachers but has shattered the professional ethic of low-profile interest-group activity. Observing that administrator groups such as the American Association of School Administrators have usually been a majority on the NEA governing boards, the AFT brands the NEA a "company union." AFT wants to write major school policies into union contracts. The organizing success of the AFT in the 1960's led to a more militant stance by the NEA in stressing collective sanctions, i.e., boycotts against accepting positions in local districts where working conditions are not suitable.

The division is not merely over goals but over organization of political efforts. If the AFT has succeeded more locally, the NEA has been more effective at the state level, where its affiliates, one of the largest organized groups in the states, spend much time dealing with state politicians.[20] The AFT, on the other hand, has few effective state federations, concentrating its efforts at the local level. Both groups have Washington offices, but until 1968 neither had been very successful in having its political demands approved by the president and Congress.[21] Frequently, the major administrative groups of superintendents and principals now make different demands on the political system and maintain their own offices at the state and federal levels. The National Association of School Boards has traditionally joined forces with the administrator-teacher groups at the state and federal levels — but not when these groups cannot agree.

These divisions among professional educators should not be overesti mated, for other forces work toward their unity. The tradition of a unified profession and the common training and experience of professional educators have led to an agreement on many fundamental values, a factor tending to restrict the range of interest-group activity. For example, most administrators have come up through the teaching ranks. Too, accrediting associations are staffed on a full or part-time basis by professional educators. Indeed, the faith which the public has in accreditation makes regional accrediting agencies a professional interest group of considerable importance, bringing irresistible pressure to conform to their standards of faculty, budget, facilities, and curriculum.

Professionally Oriented Interest Groups

Other groups, although not composed of professionals, are also interested in educational policy as an end in itself. Like educators, they provide schools with diffuse support, but also like educators, they differ on some school aspects and hence provide demand inputs. This may be their whole purpose or only one of secondary interest.

The National Congress of Parents and Teachers is not only the largest of these but the largest volunteer organization in the nation. The PTA is a loose confederation of 43,000 local units (with over 9 million members), concerned primarily with *specific* problems facing a *specific* school. Although most influential and active at the local or district level, its strength diminishes greatly at the state and federal levels, where its heterogeneous membership precludes agreement on controversial issues.[22] Although the membership now includes one-third males, there is little doubt that the organization is still dominated by women.[23] In states with historically segregated schools, there operates the National Congress of Colored Parents and Teachers.

Analysts of PTA accomplishments stress the generally dependent and close relationship it has to school administrators. Koerner expressed it this way:

> the American PTA is rarely anything more than a coffee and cookies organization based on vague good will and gullibility. It is chiefly useful to the administration for raising money for special projects and persuading parents who are interested enough to attend meetings that the local schools are in the front ranks of American education.[24]

The National President of the PTA stated in 1969, "The PTA in a school is just as good as the principal wants it to be — it's the kind of organization that he envisions that it ought to be." [25] This supportive function is validated in a survey of superintendents in Massachusetts which indicated that the PTA is seen as most influential when it supports school budget increases or new building programs.[26]

The PTA's role locally is amplified at the national and state levels, where it does not provide an independent source of demand inputs into school policy but rather proceeds as an instrument of schoolmen who use it to reinforce or implement *their* policy inputs. Indeed, the national PTA is a resolute member of the "Big Six" — a coalition of three professional groups and three lay groups in education: American Association of School Administrators, NEA, Council of Chief State School Officers, National School Boards Association, National Association of State School Boards, and National Congress of Parents and Teachers. At another level, a study of three states in the Midwest concluded that the PTA is viewed by legislators as a useful friend but not a very bothersome enemy. In Missouri, the PTA office is in the Missouri State Teachers Association Building in Columbia, and "its political efforts are similarly linked." [27] In effect, the values of the PTA leadership and the school professionals are similar and as a consequence the PTA does not sponsor many conflict-oriented demands.

The PTA states that its goals are

> To bring into closer relation the home and the school, that parents and teachers may cooperate intelligently in the training of the child.
> To develop between educators and the general public such united efforts as will secure for every child the highest advantages in physical, mental, social, and spiritual education.

The PTA is not, however, the only professionally oriented interest group. The Council for Basic Education is an organization that has emphasized values different from those of the PTA and hence has become known as a "critic of public education." The CBE believes that the schools have neglected the fundamental intellectual disciplines in their purported overemphasis upon social adjustment. Its intentions are to see to it

> that school administrators are encouraged and supported in resisting pressures to divert school time to activities of minor educational significance, to curricula overemphasizing social adjustment at the expense of intellectual discipline, and to programs that call upon the school to assume responsibilities properly belonging to the home, to religious bodies, and to other agencies.[28]

The CBE attempts to influence the school authorities primarily through publications, conferences, and other uses of the media to disseminate its viewpoint. It does not have local chapters but has provided material to local groups who are interested.

Professionally oriented interest groups can also be found among numerous organizations that embrace education as a secondary concern, e.g., the League of Women Voters and the American Association of University Women. These exist for general social improvements, a part of which touch on school programs and processes. Most of these groups attempt to influence the political conversion process for education only when the members are deeply and widely concerned about a particular aspect of school policy. This occurs only at intervals, however, such as the revision of the state constitution for education. Like the PTA, these are non–issue-specific groups that provide support for the ongoing system and inject little conflict into it. They also constitute a resource upon which decision makers may draw in times of crisis.[29]

Transcendental Groups

Several kinds of interest groups view the schools as a means to accomplish ends that transcend the schools, e.g., reducing their tax burden, eradicating communism, etc. Taxpayer organizations began around the turn of the century to mobilize the support of those who valued the elimination of "wasteful" public spending. Of particular interest is the finding that taxpayer organizations have been *supporters* as well as opponents of increased tax support — depending on the tax source. Forty-five percent of the superintendents in Massachusetts reported that taxpayers associations were the primary source of pressure against school tax increases and bond proposals.[30] On the other hand, Bailey and his colleagues found the Massachusetts Federation of Taxpayers Association an influential advocate of increased state aid, which would obviously require less reliance on local property taxes.

Distinct from those whose main interest is material are those whose concern is the moral instruction of schools; the overlap of the two, however, needs study. The educational function of moral indoctrination of our schools' colonial origins never really disappeared with the *New England Primer*. Indeed, the concern for the religious instruction function has not disappeared, either, as witness the continuing outcry against and disobedience of Supreme Court decisions against Bible reading and school prayers.[31] Less explicit moral concern is seen in the outcry against the current dress style of high school students, whose clothes are regarded by many, parent or not, as a symbolic challenge to the prevailing morality.

The main function of groups like these is to guard orthodox values. Their support of the schools is secondary to their concern for maintenance of community norms. The school is viewed as only one of a number of institutions whose moral sanctity must be protected against subversion or direct challenge. Constituting what LaPiere has called "societies for the prevention of change," they maintain a protective surveillance over teachers' drinking and dating in small rural towns, students' music, dancing, and clothing in suburbia, and teachers' and administrators' "Americanism" everywhere. Few such groups have more than a local organizational basis, although their frequent church associations might imply otherwise. Their tactics lean heavily on direct contact with suspected deviants who are challenged to prove their moral worth. These tactics can escalate into board confrontations, or, in small towns, into whispering campaigns. In smaller communities, more homogeneous and hence with fewer independent bases for defense of those challenged, schoolmen have little recourse. They walk a very narrow line, not only in their individual morality but also in what they transmit to students.[32]

One such group with a national organization is the John Birch Society. The views on schools espoused by the society reflect the special values of its founder: "We know something of what is taking place in the field of public education in an attempt to convert the whole system into an indoctrination and thought-control agency of a Socialist Big Brother Government." [33] The society urges its members to "take over the PTA," get society material into school libraries, and pressure local boards for history texts that reflect "American, patriotic history." [34] Like the NAACP and its concern for integration, right-wing groups are ideological, acting to inject conflict into the system and to make conflict salient for decision makers.

Crisis Interest Groups

Despite the large variety of interest groups in public education, not all interests or values are reflected in organized groups. Moreover, interest groups in playing their role of transfer agents may choose not to convey certain demands to school officials. Recall that subsystem stress over value concerns will produce organized activities seeking to satisfy these claims directed toward the political system of American schools. However, this stress may also activate persons who share the same attitudes and values but for whom no existing interest group reflects their special values.

In a typical illustration of this phenomenon in a Northeastern suburb, two new organized interest groups were created in one year but dissolved after the school-board election.[35] A "Taxpayers Association" was formed to defeat three board members and cut back school expenditures. The superintendent countered with an interest group called "Save Our Schools" in order to reelect the incumbent board members and pass the budget. Both groups played important roles in conveying the special values — and articulating the demands of citizens in a political system where local interest groups had not traditionally been important. Integration crises across the country frequently spawned "Mothers to Preserve Neighborhood Schools" as a counterweight to civil rights groups advocating integration. These neighborhood school groups have also disbanded after the integration crisis passes.[36]

Testing Agencies and Foundations

Several groups that do not fit the usual conception of an interest group influence the outputs of the political system of American schools. One such, for instance, arises because, although this country does not have a system of national exams, we have several national testing agencies. The most important is the Educational Testing Service in Princeton, N.J. Most American schools do not have a choice in providing their best students with courses in most of the subjects covered by College Board Achievement Exams. Because high schools want their students to score high on these exams, they do not have absolute flexibility to teach what they want. These external constraints reflect value judgments on what should and should not be taught, albeit urged in the interest of "professionalism." This is one of those forces of professionalism that we earlier argued may be a more powerful external constraint on local school policy than local demands or federal laws.

Further, while private philanthropic foundations are not thought of as interest groups, they have exercised a major influence on such school issues as curriculum reform, teacher training, testing, finance, facility design, educational television, and so on. The foundations have used their grants to generate stress over value concerns. When the Ford Foundation finances the development of a battery of instruments to assess national progress in education, it is helping to create a political issue that will pit those who oppose national testing against supporters of increased accountability by professional educators. A decision on whether to permit national assessment had to be made by conversion processes at all levels, e.g., local school boards, state departments of education, and the United States Congress. Consequently, the questions and approach in the approved assessment represented many compromises.[37]

In short, a foundation does not behave like a conventional interest group by seeking access to a legislature and then advocating its case for public money or public support. However, by using grants to start experiments and demonstration projects (often reflecting special value orientation), foundations may make value conflicts more visible. This in turn may create a new demand that provides an existing (or new) interest group with an issue. These interest groups may substantially modify the content of the demand as it is transmitted to the school board or state legislator, but these foundations need the interest group in order to reach the political authorities through collective pressure. We need much more research on the political impact of foundations in school policy. The Ford Foundation–funded community-control experiments in New York may be only the tip of the iceberg.[38]

Protest as a Political Tactic of Interest Groups

Protest has grown in frequency and intensity as a means of seeking the support of potential allies and as a channel to communicate with school authorities. Among other things, the use of protest indicates that standard interest-group tactics have been ineffective in presenting demands. Lipsky has defined protest activity as

> a mode of political action oriented toward objection to one or more policies or conditions, characterized by showmanship or display of an unconventional nature, and undertaken to obtain rewards from political or economic systems while working within the systems. The "problem of the powerless" in protest activity is to activate "third parties" to enter the implicit or explicit bargaining arena in ways favorable to protesters. This is one of the few ways in which they can "create" bargaining resources.[39]

This definition draws on earlier research suggesting that protest activity could be conceived of as a bargaining exercise in which the basic problem was that protesters, lacking political resources to exchange, used protest to create them.[40] Protesters realize that twenty people picketing the school board office is not likely to influence the board to make new policies. Rather, the protesters' strategy uses public display as a communication device to appeal to a wider public to which the school board is sensitive. The goal then is to have "reference publics" or target groups respond to the protest so as to add their political resources to the protesters'. In the early 1960's, for example, civil rights groups used pickets and sit-ins in order to attract support of liberal, white, third parties. Such groups as Democratic Party reform clubs then joined with the protesters in presenting demands to the school board.

This conception of protest should be distinguished from labor union strikes and boycotts, where the protest groups already possess sufficient resources with which to bargain. Instead, protesters who lack political resources must rely on the public media for communicating their demands. Often the content and amount of media coverage will determine whether third parties will join the protesters and pressure the school board. A student boycott of classes may generate news coverage but alienate liberal allies who have a different value orientation to begin with. On the other hand, police brutality may be featured in college student newspapers and galvanize support from student groups who were previously unconcerned. In high school the mobilizing issue may be restrictions on student dress.

The participants in protest organizations often limit the flexibility of the protest leadership. Negro school protest in the Deep South has been inhibited by the expectation and reality of retribution, such as job losses or housing evictions.[41] On the other hand, when young children and their parents made an expensive bus trip from Mississippi to the Office of Economic Opportunity headquarters in Washington to protest Headstart cutbacks, the courage and expense created respect and attention among third parties and the mass media.

This example suggests another facet of protest, its status and dramatic basis. Protest became particularly useful for many low-income school parents who lacked money to maintain the expert staff and public information service required by effective interest groups. Protest-oriented groups do not try to provide "objective" data but rather rely on dramatizing issues. These issues will then often become demands that are considered by school authorities. The parent and student boycotts of schools in many communities clearly display these characteristics.[42]

Political protest has been used more often in our history than most people viewing recent events realize; nor is it new in school history, although it is on the increase.[43] Whenever it appears, however, it is a graphic indicator of large-scale stress in some subsystem and of the failure of existing interest groups and conversion personnel to deal with that stress effectively through normal processes. Protest also highlights the conflict between the values of individualism and majority rule. Protesters resort to this tactic in some cases because of their unwillingness to accept further the legitimacy of the decisions made by bureaucracies that are supposedly responsible to majority rule. Yet their very claim to a more equitable distribution of school resources is most often made in terms of majority rule. Thus, the "people's" or the "community's" wishes not being heard is the frequent claim justifying protest. The minority of "bureaucrats" must be compelled to stop the obstruction of the community's will — all of this a clear appeal to the basic American value of majoritarianism. Little work has been done to define the conditions under which protest succeeds and fails,[44] partly because social scientists have not, until the late 1960's, begun to study the non-consensual forces in our society.

CONCLUSION

This chapter has introduced major components of the conversion process by examining only the input side. We have suggested some of the basic values in the social environment that influence the conversion process and have indicated how interest groups act as transfer agents for these values. The energizing force that impels the input phenomenon is environmental stress arising out of unsatisfied values. This phenomenon generates felt needs whose satisfaction is sought by turning to the political system. When such a force is set into motion, it crosses the boundary between private and public systems in distinctive ways. The presentation of demands by interest groups is not a distinctive education-policy process, as interest articulation is widespread among nations for different policies.

Such a conceptualization of values, transfer agents, and school authorities calls for empirical analysis employing more than just the case study usual in such research. Illustrative of the far more useful approach — because it yields wider generalizations — is found in Jenning and Zeigler's recent survey of over eighty school boards, which measures the interest groups discussed above by the intensity of their activities.[45] By *intensity* is meant the extent to which interest groups come to the attention of school boards; it is an assessment of the quantity of interaction rather than of influence or success. This survey concludes that (1) education interest-group activity is substantially more intense in metropolitan than in rural school districts; (2) as public confidence in board policy declines, it is articulated by increased interest-group activity; and (3) surprisingly, right-wing interest groups have a more episodic involvement with the social board, whereas the intensity of left-wing groups is greater, more continuous, and has impact on more issues.

We now move closer to the political system and its reaction to stress by a study of elections and local community power structures. These are the target of inputs from interest groups articulating social values, and hence partake of a partial or preliminary allocative function. The process of electing members to local school boards is a formal, visible, and legitimized point of access for stress-generated wants. The operations of a community power structure in treating school policy is informal, often covert, and not legitimized. But both are alike in processing demands and setting the conditions by which authoritative allocations are made in the conversion aspects of the school's political system.

4 Access Channels to School Policy Making

THE ARROYOS OF SCHOOL BOARD ELECTIONS

Modes of Citizen Political Control

While demands originate outside the political system, some become political when they "are voiced as proposals for decision and action on the part of the authorities." [1] Some enter the political system; others do not, partly because of the kind of value interest seeking legitimation (Mafia interests, for example, are excluded) and partly because of the available resources each interest can aggregate (thus the exclusion of the very poor). Public preferences, which have some weight in the outputs of a democratic system, have concerned schoolmen long before the recent interest in the politics of education. Given the condition, rare among nations, that our citizens vote upon school governors and programs, it is not surprising that these officials have long sought to detect and defend themselves against such control. We have mentioned this in reference to the "depoliticization" of education around the turn of this century; but even after this change had flowered, citizen participation was still a potential political control. Reformers could depoliticize by substituting nonpartisan for partisan elections and election at large for election by ward — but citizens still possessed the means for controlling those given authority over school matters.

In the past, educators have concealed concern for this participation under the rubric of "community relations." Such literature in educational journals has been much preoccupied with methods of selling professional views to the public. But little of this rested upon empirically researched propositions; often it was, and still is, anecdotal in form, a nice little story about how a bond issue was maneuvered to success in Hoggsville, Ark. But in the decade after World War II, validation of some propositions was

61

appearing, as in Hamlin's report on increasing citizen participation in school decisions.[2]

That participation has traditionally taken two primary forms — election of officials and referendum on issues. The referendum we hold to the next chapter, because it partakes more directly of conversion than does the election of officials. The election mode operates independently of political parties, a separation we have earlier noted, the attitudes underlying which need not be recalled here. The question is the degree to which political parties serve as linkages between citizen desires about educational policy and subsequent governmental response. This model of democracy posits political parties soliciting votes with the promise of securing desired policies, with elections serving as mutual exchange markets that link citizen to party to government. Contrary to popular impression, political parties at the *national* level have sought to serve as a linkage between citizens and school policy. Brown demonstrated that for almost a century of national party platforms, education has been among "the predominant forces in operation during election years." But it is important to note that in a nation believing in direct citizen control of officials at all levels, there is little evidence that *local* parties provide linkage of citizen to local schools.[3]

Yet schools have not escaped citizen control by avoiding the clutches of political parties, for there is popular control both direct and indirect. Directly, there is the widespread practice of electing school boards at the local level and boards and superintendents at the state level.[4] Indirectly, control exists in the election of state legislators, executives, and judges, among whose broad responsibilities lies authority over many aspects of public education.

Local Board Elections

While 85 percent of local school boards in this country are elective, the politics of these elections is a great unknown.[5] We are aware that these officials, five to seven on a board, seek their three- or four-year terms almost always on a nonpartisan ballot. We know that the board appoints a superintendent, usually professionally trained, who operates under its general policy guides and who may be removed by it. The exception to this pattern is the appointment method found most often in our biggest cities. But for the usual community, the theory of democratic control places the board member as a pivot between community demands and school operations. Thus the election of these board members is ostensibly a major channel for inputs to the political system of the schools.

Whether that is the case in reality, however, we simply do not know because of the inadequate analysis of these vital linkages. Not until quite recently have we seen any testing of the linear relationship between voter preferences reflected in elections and board decisions. Thus, Walden studied 117 school districts in southern California to determine whether incumbents' defeats and superintendents' turnovers were related. If popular will were effective, the incumbents' defeats should have been followed by superintendent turnovers; he found just such a linear relationship.[6] Yet much more needs to be known about the process of board-member nomination and election, their response to group pressures, and the effect of their need to return periodically to the public for electoral confirmation. In short, do these representatives have a mandate to guide them, and, if they do, what is its course?

Students of the politics of education do share some general impressions about this citizen–board-member interaction, although such knowledge raises more questions than it answers. It is clear, however, that citizen turnout is very low for such contests. Is this because of the nonpartisan myth of school politics or because elections are held in off years and at primary dates when turnout is low for all contests? If states and cities do vary in degree of citizen participation, what accounts for it? Does the mere requirement of nonpartisanship preclude political parties playing a direct role — for they do operate in Detroit — or do voters' party identifications shape their choices — as they do in some city council races? Could low turnout and the spacing of elections, as well as their timing out of phase with general elections, benefit some groups but not others? That is, might not board elections represent more often the weight of Republicans — more often voters than Democrats — and consequently more often the viewpoint of groups attracted to the GOP? [7]

Another clear finding is that campaigning in school contests is very limited, candidate visibility very low, and the contest rarely based on specific policies. Is this attributable again to the nonpartisan myth, which requires political participants to act as if they were not engaging in political acts? Or to the lack of highly visible issues on which candidates might stimulate popular interest? What are the kinds of conditions under which election contests become visible and the public highly participant? Further, although most boards are filled by elections, a minority in significant American cities are appointed. What difference does this make in representative roles? Is there any difference in policy orientation under the two methods, and can such differences be traced directly to the methods? Crain has shown, albeit with a limited sample, that boards immune from elections were somewhat more able to move toward school desegregation.[8]

The directions we need to take are again well illustrated by Jennings and Zeigler's study of boards in eighty-eight school districts referred to in the last chapter. They wished to account for the variation in board responsiveness — that is, its manner of "acting on the basis of expressed preferences by constituents." They found elected boards more responsive to individual interests and appointed boards to group interests, i.e., the appointed boards operate under as many — but different — constraints as the elected board. Whether members are elected at large or by districts seems to affect their group responsiveness very little. Nor was the existing competition for office a cause for greater responsiveness by members. In fact, the competitiveness of such elections was quite low. About a quarter of the members had no opposition; almost half of the districts had no incumbent defeated over the previous several elections; and many members had been first appointed to office or solicited by board members to serve — all symptoms of a closed rather than open structure. The delights of such noncompetition, however, seemed slight, for on one-half the boards no more than one-quarter of the incumbents were committed to serving another term.

Far more important in shaping the pattern of board responsiveness than these electoral conditions are other community factors. Thus, Jennings and Zeigler found that metropolitanism and urbanism were more important indicators of board responsiveness. There was some effect associated with the electoral factor, however, which refused to disappear in the wake of sociological factors. The authors conclude that

> electoral characteristics of the school district do leave an imprint on the responsiveness of school boards . . . because [they] provide differential settings within which the strong elements of socio-political complexity (and mass support) operate. It seems probable, therefore, that tinkering with the legal framework and fostering more competition for office would — sooner or later — affect the response linkage between constituents and school boards.[9]

In previous paragraphs we have illustrated major research directions still unexplored and recent ones pursued in queries about these 121,000 board members, the most numerous of all American elected officials. Observers report massive citizen disinterest in these contests, but whether this arises from their preference for such low-profile activity or because of indifference to it cannot be judged from aggregate data about low voting turnout. Yet from time to time, this channel for input swells like an arroyo after a flash flood. The occasion tends to be highly singular, focused on one event — conflict over a busing proposal is currently the event. What may be said systematically about the conditions provoking such volatile voting is very tentative, particularly as to its causes, objects, and outcomes.[10] So it is that the enormous pool of school elections remains largely untapped for what it can tell us about the larger picture of Americans' participation in their political system. While we know much about participation in presidential elections,[11] we know far too little about how and why we chose those responsible for the education of our children.

State and National Elections

Partisan elections to higher state offices also have consequences for the nonpartisan local schools because of the state resources allocated to schools. Increasingly, the budget fight in the legislature over school appropriations — in particular, the amount of the state subvention for local support — becomes in every state an annual drama for all those intimately connected with the educational system. The governors and legislators who make such decisions, therefore, have a direct bearing upon school quality. Nor does the appropriation battle exhaust the state role in local schools. Given the many aspects of that state role — in teacher preparation and certification, curriculum, textbooks, attendance, and pupil safety — "local control" may be more imaginary than real. Further, what the legislature says about the taxing authority of local units is vital, not only to the operation of the schools but to the pocketbooks of most citizens as well.

However, the role which citizens perform in providing inputs to these state officials through the election channels is unknown. We need to know more about:

1. citizen perception of the relationship of legislature and governor to educational policies
2. given some awareness of this relationship, the degree of salience that education policy has compared to others by which citizens may judge state authorities
3. the degree to which partisan identification, so vital in understanding presidential voting, affects citizens in their voting for governor and legislators, so that their educational concerns become suppressed if not invisible
4. the degree to which state parties regard school policy as important or not as a voter mobilization device and the strategies for stressing or ignoring certain kinds of school policies
5. the role of state educational interest groups in seeking to mobilize popular support for their stands through election channels
6. the conditions under which the state electoral channel becomes flooded with demands and the results this has for education policy making *

There is one further channel for popular participation: elections of congressmen and the president. If the range of issues facing political authorities is extensive at the state level, the reach becomes enormous nationally. This should mean that the saliency of school issues for most voters becomes reduced at higher governmental levels. That is, concern over school taxes or what they are teaching Johnny becomes reduced in comparison with the issues of war and peace or the national economy. However, citizens more closely follow national than local affairs — and state affairs least — that is, when they do pay any attention to public affairs.[12] Yet we have little information on popular use of resources designed to affect

---

* Some of these queries will appear for discussion in later chapters.

national authorities on school policy. Citizens may have *opinions* on Washington's policies, as we shall see, but the gap between popular opinion and action on many issues is enormous. Citizen input in the forms of demands — or even attitudes — on federal policy may be so diffuse as to be nonexistent.

Some input is provided, however, through party channels in the form of partisan issue stands. Rather consistently, those identifying with the Democratic Party have in the past been stronger supporters of federal aid to education than Republican identifiers. The professional politicians of either party were even more widely separated on these issues than average party members.[13] As federal funds became increasingly available in the late 1960's to local school budgets already straining under an overloaded property tax, this partisan difference apparently began to disappear.

But the diffuseness of citizen attitudes about federal school policy can sharply crystallize under some circumstances. Thus, there was very strong support for the "GI Bill" after World War II; to oppose this was to oppose the soldiers' efforts in that war. National attitudes in the late 1960's, on the other hand, coalesced intensely in opposition to school busing during the desegregation controversy, as we shall see later. The point, here, however, is that citizen attitudinal input into national decision arenas deals little with educational policy, and there is little evidence that it flavors the decisions of voters in federal elections. Yet it may well be that under some circumstances — such as a perceived threat to a value more dear than most — opinions can crystallize to have electoral importance.

Summary

In summary, then, although elections serve in the United States as a potential channel for citizen inputs to school outputs in a fashion rare among the nations of the world, they seem to be very little used. This channel can affect board members' responsiveness to group or individual demands, particularly when it is hit by local environmental stress. Flashes of such storms in the mountains over issues of patriotism, curriculum, and morality can race through the normal channels in a flash flood, swamping an incautious school board. But such storms are only occasional, albeit dramatic, episodes; in the normal course of events the channel runs in a feeble trickle.

In another sense, board elections are barometers, normally reflecting little pressure from the environment but subject to enormous change because of hidden disturbances. Indeed, a systematic examination of the disastrous weather changes that produce "rancorous conflict" would be immensely valuable.[14] Such analysis would have several uses, practically in describing the conditions under which professional administration of the schools excites public concerns, and theoretically in developing an understanding of the linkages between private wants and public outputs under stress conditions. These practical and theoretical concerns generate interesting questions. Practically, how much can the superintendent support external professional demands for quality when community standards reject or resist them? Does the frequency of superintendent turnover — chronic in the profession and especially so in larger cities — inhibit or enhance this schoolman's efforts at financing, curriculum and staff improvement, or desegregation? What different community-relations strategies operate when board or superintendent are appointed rather than elected — and does either system enhance policy change? What coalitions by these schoolmen with other local or state political authorities are employed for mutual benefit?

The theoretical questions must confront the available evidence of American schools' receiving a minimum of significant input through the direct channel of elections. From this, one must not conclude that the wants of citizens are ignored by the political authorities of School or State. It suggests rather that elections — whether viewed as channels or barometers — are little used for exchanging demands across the boundary between the environment and the school's political system. That they may serve this purpose mainly as a threat to elected officials, causing them to act in anticipation of future defeat, is not supportable in light of the Jennings and Zeigler study; most board members, they found, did not plan to remain in office. Yet the possibility always remains that an issue which deeply agitates a community or the nation may suddenly turn to the exchange mechanism of elections, throwing out the old and bringing in the new, much as for other public policies. After all the rhetoric of local control of schools, this flash-flood phenomenon may not amount to much; but schoolmen cannot ignore it.

COMMUNITY POWER STRUCTURE AND SCHOOL POLICY

Another exchange mechanism is less visible and formal than elections — community groups with special influence upon school policy. What inputs enter the political system for conversion, and how the conversion process itself operates, may be shaped by those who are not formally in the school system — but who nevertheless control it. One can conceive of nations dominated by a particular subsystem — the military, clergy, wealthy, aristocracy — which in turn dominates the political system. Indeed, much of the literature of political science from Athens to the present concerns itself with whether such subsystems do or should dominate,

In the last several decades, one aspect of the study of private and public power has focused upon how power is organized in communities to make public decisions. Under the rubric of "community power studies," much research and polemical literature has appeared, often pitting sociologists against political scientists, debating whether local power is hierarchical ("elitist") or segmented ("pluralist"). This literature is partly theoretical, methodological, and normative, although the distinctions among these modes of knowledge have not always been clear. We do not propose to detail this "search for community power," but we will summarize its contours as a preface for noting its relationship to schools.[15]

Four Queries in Power Studies

We suggest that this complex intellectual debate centers around four questions. What is meant by "power"? How is its presence and arrangement discovered in the community? What accounts for differences in such power arrangements as exist among American communities? What differences for community life stem from these different power arrangements? Each of these deserves book-length treatment for adequate exposition, but we shall be brief.[16]

Despite enormous fascination with power, social scientists have little agreement on its meaning, except that it involves the capacity to cause or inhibit change in men's behavior. But this modest consensus falls far short of being a theoretical statement that can help explain and predict the outcome of social conflict. As March's survey of the term's meanings concluded, "On the whole, however, power is a disappointing concept. It gives us surprisingly little purchase in reasonable models of complex systems of social choice." [17] Much of the conflict in the whole field may well stem from this ambiguity at the heart of the inquiry.

With different interpretations of the nature of power, its measurement methods have been equally various. Most research has dealt with the problem of how to detect community power, and, once the methods were justified, what was found. It may be too strong to say that much of this was trivial, compared to the larger scholarly questions in this list; maybe, too, the problem of method had to be tested in research before we could arrive at the present situation. But for a decade after the publication of Hunter's *Community Power Structure* in 1953, the pages of the journals of sociology and political science were the forum for a strong, even bitter, clash over methods — positional, reputational, decisional, combinational. Part of this may have reflected a bias stemming from disciplinary training for such research, but this seems unlikely in light of Clark's analysis.[18] At any rate, by the mid-1960's it was clear that no one method was sufficient, for judicious combinations were needed to trace the dimensions of community decision making.

The third query, what accounts for differences among community power arrangements, required first the building of a pool of comparable data.

That task has been slow in achievement. One approach was to compare a small number of communities within the same methodological framework; thus, Agger *et al.* in the mid-1960's developed a theoretical and conceptual framework for the study of four communities. Another approach was to compare what was known about existing case studies, in order to test hypotheses about different power arrangements arising under different conditions. But the limited-sample approach was not a sample, so generalizations were limited; at best they were a modest advance over the host of case studies. On the other hand, analysis of pooled case studies faced the problem of the varying methodologies and research questions that motivated each study. By the end of the 1960's, the third approach was getting underway, that of working with a large number of communities to which were applied unified theory, concept, and hypothesis. The announcement of a "permanent community sample" of fifty-one American towns with resident community analysts opened a new possibility; here was a more established data base from which to raise research questions about policy outcomes and decisional arrangements.[19]

A final query is one which has been often implicit in all this research: what difference does it make for the community whether power arrangements are "elitist," "pluralist," "amorphous," etc.? Far too often, of course, each analyst dealt with but a single town in answering that question, hardly the basis for meaningful generalization. Nevertheless, the first major works on community power, the Lynds' *Middletown* and *Middletown in Transition,* were critical of the quality of life they found in a community dominated by one family. Many later writers never quite abandoned this normative approach. Much research has had an implicit criticism of the arrangements found (particularly the "elitist") for what they meant to democratic values and the way people lived. For these writers, even the somewhat less narrow power arrangements found in "pluralist" studies were criticized for seeming to justify a *status quo* that defeated the democratic promise.[20] The emergence of new federal programs and their resources for those who were formerly resourceless attracted scholars concerned whether this development might rearrange power at the local level.[21] In this development, the "mobilization of bias," which locally works to the advantage of the few who set the local agenda and mobilize the maximum resources to achieve their ends, could be overcome and power returned to the people. The overtones of Populism and Progressivism are recognizable in such programs and in the scholars they attract to study them.

School Policy in the Power Literature

Even this highly condensed description of a complex problem in social research may seem inordinately long and vague to one new to the subject. For him, the question of greater importance is: what is the significance of this research for schools? A fair question, but one that can only be sketched here before turning to analysts of that query. The general response, however, is that its utility here is like that of any knowledge of the community. A fuller picture of the interrelationship between school and community enables teachers and administrators better to carry out their professional tasks. A little less generally, though, one could note the queries of a leading school administration textbook: "For example, does the administrator become subservient to the power structure when elements of it are known to him? Or is he then in the position to become manipulator? Or in a better position to provide constructive leadership?" [22]

We can illustrate some of what is implied here. If the community is dominated in public and private decisions by one small group that shares the same values about community life, i.e., is "elite," schoolmen who wish to pursue educational programs that are new must know what the group is whose support they must enlist. Educational innovation that proceeds with no notion of what community values are, of who the guardians of this orthodoxy are, and of what resources they have is an empty exercise. If, however, the community has a number of groups, each important in shaping policy in one domain, or has shifting coalitions which form temporary majorities on each issue area, another strategy will prevail. Here, one has a better chance of finding alternative bases of support in the community for innovation — or for protection of accepted practices newly questioned. In sum, then, if it is true that the school is part of the community, power research provides information about that relationship and suggests strategies for working with it.

Oddly, this scholarly debate has not dealt much with the schools. Illustrative of this neglect are the four major works that mark the major developments of the controversy — by the Lynds, Hunter, Dahl, and Agger et al.[23] Further, a review of the hundreds of research studies in this field would yield support for this finding; not even the recent aggregate, comparative studies show interest in this policy area.[24] A recent exception is Alford's study of the political cultures of four Wisconsin cities.[25] Among these four, different degrees of bureaucratization (i.e., professionalism) and citizen participation are at work. But in none is there evidence of any elitist control — other than the educational interest group of administrators and PTA's. In this work, schools are clearly seen as a proper policy concern for the analyst because of the size of the resources they expend and the occasional flash flood of citizen concern about school actions.

The relevance of such study for schools has been drawn primarily by educational administration scholars, a handful of whom have provided a bridge from these other disciplines to their own. Not much of even educational scholars' work is available, however, and little of it is comparative. In late 1967 a listing of community power studies provided merely 10 out of 310 citations that were clearly related to educational policy; two of these had the same author, and four were unpublished dissertations.[26] This literature went through the stages noted earlier of cases and then comparative study. The theoretical perspective in these earlier studies was limited, most found "elitist" arrangements, and all urged such study upon superintendents so they could better fulfill their jobs.[27] The comparative phase was ushered in by the little-noted 1956 study by Webb of three small towns in Wyoming, one delightfully named "Wideroad." [28] Utilizing reputational techniques of Hunter (whose work he curiously ignores), matched with opinion surveys from samples in each town, Webb unearthed community control in the hands of a few men who were unknown in the main both to the average citizen and to the school administrators. The work has a limited theoretical basis, yet in its comparative aspects is a considerable advance.

Some years followed in which case studies still prevailed in the limited research on schools and power structures. A study of two towns by Foskett showed that economic elite dominance did not exhaust all the possibilities, but the work was primarily descriptive.[29] But then in 1963–64, there flowed a freshet of publications whose quality was a quantum jump above those preceding. These emphasized the comparative method, their theory and concepts were well developed, and the consequent hypotheses and empirical grounding brought the study to another level entirely. Most still cited the utilitarian value of such study, this incessant and unnecessary pleading of scholars to their audience of professional administrators that learning is a good thing. Yet to be faced was the question of what difference for school outputs did a specific form of local power make? Such a research orientation guided the Syracuse volumes of the early 1960's.

Chief among these for our purposes is Bloomberg and his associates' analysis of four New York suburbs. This "study of values, influence and tax effort," while theoretically oriented, also sought to help those who want to learn how to raise school taxes. Whereas the power arrangements in these suburbs were quite similar, they "displayed major differences in their levels of relative expenditure and tax effort." Hence, little consequence for school policy would flow from administrators and teachers establishing friendship lines into the business and civic clubs. The critical variable seemed to be the distinctive community attitudes about school programs and needs, although specification of that relationship is quite complex.[30]

But where these authors found power arrangements irrelevant to financial differences, Kimbrough a year later found that they controlled many school matters in four Southern counties. This volume is a strong plea by an educational scholar to administrators on the difference that such knowledge makes for job performance.[31] The two books contrast sharply in their findings, illustrating Bloomberg's suggestion that the lack of any policy differentiation traceable to power arrangements might well change in communities with different power potentials. The Kimbrough work has been widely cited in education literature on the intervention effect of covert groups upon the entry and determination of inputs before the school board.[32] One way such groups may have effect is upon the superintendent's tenure; McCarty has suggested that much of the variation in their tenures is explained by just such variations in local power arrangements.[33]

The theoretical climax in the study of school and power arrangements was reached in 1964. A collection of essays edited by Cahill and Hencley contain a wealth of research strategies, questions, typologies, hypotheses, and interactional analyses. While the opening section discusses the politicalness of education and its implications for studies in power, the major contributions come in the central section. As the editors correctly note:

> For all their distinctiveness, the chapters in this section convey a promising impression of convergence on central themes. It is as though each were focused on a single quartz crystal, but each on a slightly different face, through a slightly different lens, and from a slightly different vantage point. Collectively, they represent a set of mutually reinforcing guidelines for the future development of research in community politics and education.[34]

The theoretical and practical utilities of such comparative study are seen in Crain's recent examination of school desegregation in nine major cities.[35] The sample is small, of course, but the data are worked with great care to illuminate the relationship between desegregation and community power. The complex conclusions work against the purported power of the "civic elite" in the desegregation process. However, this elite does seem to set the "political style" of each city, it indirectly influences appointments to school boards, and it demonstrates a North-South distinction on the extent of elitism. In another of those ironies that our conflicting basic values occasionally thrust at us, desegregation proceeds more evenly if the board is more independent of the general public.

A major study of the kind needed appeared in 1968 in the work of Johns and Kimbrough.[36] This incorporated a comparative research design with financial effort as the dependent variable and other factors — such as the kind of power structure in existence — as the independent variables. The focus was on fiscal policy for seventeen years after World War II in 122 school districts over 20,000 population in the states of Illinois, Kentucky, Georgia, and Florida. In-depth power studies were made in twenty-four of these districts, six in each state (three having high and three low financial school efforts), while surveys of the attitudes of schoolmen and citizens were employed. There emerges a four-fold typology of community power structures, described in Table 4.1; these collapse into two "closed"

Table 4.1 Criteria for Power Structure Continuum in Johns-Kimbrough Four-State Study

Monopolistic elite	Multigroup noncompetitive	Competitive elite	Segmented pluralism
Singular structure	Considerable overlapping of structural groups	Limited overlapping of groups	Segmented structure
80–100% overlap on projects	70–80% overlap on issues	50–70% overlap on issues	50% or less overlap on issues
Issues contained	Minor issue competition	Competitive on issues	Segmented or specialized competition on issues
One dominant group over period of more than one election	Incomplete separation of two or more groups; consensus at times	Two or more well-defined power groups over time	Many competing groups separated due to different interests
Communication line upward and downward within group	Communication between groups allows consensus on major issues	Communication is with satellites; little with competing groups	Communication through political office-holders; little otherwise
Voting participation is low; 40–50% or less of registered voters	Voting participation approximates 55% over time	Voting participation approximates 60% over time	Voting participation approximates 65% or higher over time
Membership in groups is general	Much overlap in membership between two or more competing groups	Overlap in membership between groups	Little overlap in group membership
Few, if any, regime conflicts	Little regime conflict	Regime conflicts between two or more groups	Regime conflicts involving many groups

Source: Roe L. Johns and Ralph B. Kimbrough, The Relationship of Socio-economic Factors, Educational Leadership Patterns, and Elements of Community Power Structure to Local School Fiscal Policy (Washington, D.C.: Bureau of Research, Office of Education, HEW, 1968).

or noncompetitive and two "open" or competitive systems, measured by the degree to which power is diffused. This work had hypothesized that the closed system would be associated with lesser financial effort, and such was the case. Of the nine competitive structures studied, seven were high- and two low-effort programs, while of the fifteen noncompetitive, five were high and ten were low. Table 4.2 displays the twenty-four communities (with fictitious names) and their variety of power structures related to population and financial effort.

The lengthy work is studded with interesting findings, but in light of our concern with the degree to which power structures provide open and closed channels to the political system of the schools, one set is particularly meaningful. If a system is closed and noncompetitive, we should expect to find citizens less participative, but more participative if the system extends them more opportunity to be so. This was the case, whether participation was measured by proportions of voter registration, voting, or

Table 4.2   Classification of Power Structures in Johns-Kimbrough Four-State Study

District[a]	Financial effort	Population	Type of structure	State
McKinley	H	228,106	Segmented pluralism	Florida
Everest	H	76,895	Competitive elite	Florida
Logan	H	54,539	Competitive elite	Florida
Whitney	L	455,411	Monopolistic	Florida
Ranier	L	67,131	Multigroup noncompetitive	Florida
Shasta	L	36,208	Multigroup noncompetitive	Florida
Andrews	H	234,757	Competitive elite	Georgia
Ford	H	46,365	Multigroup noncompetitive	Georgia
Scott	H	23,632	Monopolistic	Georgia
Anderson	L	39,154	Segmented pluralism	Georgia
Benne	L	30,652	Monopolistic	Georgia
Carter	L	20,596	Competitive elite	Georgia
Oak	H	209,138	Segmented pluralism	Kentucky
Pine	H	69,096	Competitive elite	Kentucky
Cedar	H	42,471	Monopolistic	Kentucky
Hub	L	58,148	Multigroup noncompetitive	Kentucky
Farm	L	37,439	Multigroup noncompetitive	Kentucky
Scenic	L	22,050	Monopolistic	Kentucky
Allwin	H	78,000	Monopolistic	Illinois
Brookston	H	49,450	Multigroup noncompetitive	Illinois
Camelot	H	26,630	Competitive elite	Illinois
Marleboro	L	83,270	Multigroup noncompetitive	Illinois
Tareyton	L	51,860	Multigroup noncompetitive	Illinois
Winston	L	36,271	Multigroup noncompetitive	Illinois

Source: Roe L. Johns and Ralph B. Kimbrough, *The Relationship of Socio-Economic Factors, Educational Leadership Patterns, and Elements of Community Power Structure to Local School Fiscal Policy* (Washington, D.C.: Bureau of Research, Office of Education, HEW, 1968).
[a]The names of the districts shown are fictitious

organizational membership and activity. Citizens tended to misperceive drastically the power condition in their community, in the direction of seeing more competition than actually existed. But if they perceived more or noncompetitive and two "open" or competitive systems, measured by competition, they felt more efficacious. The typology of power structure showed little relationship to the civic, economic, and educational beliefs of community influentials, teachers, and registered voters.

This design is a prototype of future work in this area. Its findings, interestingly enough, suggest that the best explanation for why a district had a given pattern of financial effort or expenditure was whether it had employed that pattern in the past.[37] Only a fraction of these districts moved from one financial category to another during this seventeen-year period. Much of this was related to the amount of available resources, of course. The independent effect, therefore, of such community forces as the power structure, superintendent's role or influence, and citizens' values was grossly limited. Nor did the closed-open dichotomy explain all variation in effort or citizen behavior; some closed structures exhibited high financial effort and not low, and the reverse was true for open structures. However, the wealth of findings exhibited in this massive study stands in stark contrast to the limited case studies of the past, even though the authors caution against generalizing too far from their work.

From such works, the concept of community power study and of its relevance to school decisions has made its way slowly into the social foundations texts and the training of educational administrators.[38] That professionals should relate to their communities is not a new idea, of course. But now the emphasis shifted to the uses to be made of the knowledge that a few influentials may shape community outputs by controlling the access of demands to the school system. Similarly, this training adopted more explicitly the pressure-group concept of policy making. Whether these forces were valuable or not for the administrator's tasks was not clear, for some writers rejected lay pressures, while others insisted they were a necessary and inescapable part of the job.[39] No matter how slowly this facet of school politics was working itself into the cognition of administrators, scholars were well ahead of them, as the Johns-Kimbrough study demonstrates.[40]

While these scholarly concerns were much like those of others in the field, they may be somewhat belated. For the findings of most studies are time bound in a society that is changing enormously. Gilbert's reanalysis of power structures in 166 communities, using time as the independent variable, shows that political processes are changing, tending to become more pluralistic: "power . . . is less and less in the hands of a privileged few and is increasingly dependent upon the broker, be he elected official or not, who can bring together (to the extent he can bring together) the various elements in the community." [41] Walton has also emphasized the possibility that the intervention of major forces from outside into local communities may well be rearranging power all over the nation.[42] Too, we have earlier mentioned the recent nationalizing force of federal school laws following upon the older nationalizing forces of professionalism. We suggest that such intrusion into the school scene may well diminish not merely the weight of any local elite in decision making; it may also narrow the options for decision by *any* power form.

DEMOCRACY AND SCHOOL POLICY

In these two chapters we have sought to trace the relative incidence in the use of various channels of access for demands seeking entry into the schools. One finding seems rather consistent: relatively few citizens use whatever channels are available to register their educational needs. Popular participation is episodic, providing more a spasm than a steady flow of demands. When finally aroused it does not focus upon broad policies but upon specific aspects. Of late, this involvement has taken the form of increasingly failing to pass local school levies, from almost two-thirds passing in the mid-1960's to only one-third by 1970. Against that increasing flood of dissatisfaction with public schools by an apathetic public there are occasional waves aroused by a sex education course, a too-liberal textbook, student dress regulations, and other item-specific causes.

Thus, interest groups may be the most frequent form of participation, but few citizens belong to them; the difficulties of PTA's in getting members enrolled and turned out are well known. Even groups seeking wider popular authority over local schools through "community control" programs have had great difficulty in getting "the community" to participate. As for board elections, they are rarely enticing enough to pull out more than a small minority; they are dominated by the success of incumbents; and competition is negligible. The potential does exist for sweeping out of office the "school rascals" and replacing them with members with different ideas, as we noted earlier. Elections can operate in this fashion — but usually do not. Community power structures in some form probably exist in every community, but we can say very little about the frequency of different kinds. The Johns-Kimbrough study's look at twenty-four districts' power systems is to be measured against the 19,300 districts in the nation. Their finding of closed systems' being more frequent must be related again to another finding. The greater the frequency of closed power systems, the less effective is public participation in school decisions.

Yet to say that relatively few of our citizens participate is not to say also that this frees the school authorities to do whatever they wish. The power of one parent with a complaint raised against a perceived injustice is enough to agitate administrators, and can, if not met, escalate into a flash flood from the community. To a degree that is not really known, school authorities are guided by the "law of anticipated reaction," shaping their actions in response to what they believe the board or public will permit. While the day-to-day life of official or teacher in the school system is filled with simply administering past directives from the public and his profession, the potential exists for new waves of citizen inputs. At any given moment, then, the school system is caught between the forces of popular participation and bureaucratization, as Alford has noted. Over time, the latter prevails, but also through time the influence of the former may be felt as pressure to relieve unsatisfied old demands or just-realized new demands. This does not mean that school authorities live in a constant, quivering sensitivity to community and group demands — far from it, if one accepts the continuous criticism of school bureaucracy. Nor does it mean that the authorities are so inertia-driven that they cannot be changed in their course — the history of educational reform belies that charge.

Under some conditions, then, demands do enter the political system of the school and make their way through to policy outputs. The conditions under which this is true at the local and state levels are the subjects of the next three chapters.

5 The Local Conversion Process: Boards and Subsystems

Through channels and agents described earlier, environmental demands move into the political system of the schools. Some are rejected, others are converted into issues, and some become outputs. This conversion process involves interaction with state and national political authorities, but it primarily occurs among forces within the local schools — school board, superintendent, bureaucracy, teachers, voters, and so on. While forces outside the school provide some inputs, others inside the system also affect conversion. The latter contribute what Easton terms *withinputs,* "the effect that events and conditions both within and without a system may have upon its persistence [whose study] sensitizes us to the value of looking within the system as well as the environment to find the major influences that may lead to stress." [1] It is this set of interactions at the local level that concerns us in the next two chapters; thereafter we move the focus to the state capitol.

The term *withinputs* may be new, but the concept is in part a familiar one. For long, political scientists have revealed its effects upon public policies in their focus on structural arrangements within American government, e.g., separation of power, federalism, a two-party system, and so on. The first major empirical work by an American political scientist — Woodrow Wilson's *Congressional Government* of 1885 — focused squarely upon the force of such a withinput in national lawmaking. Many of the subsequent Progressive Movement's reforms (e.g., nonpartisan elections from citywide districts) were directed at altering political processes that had created corruptive withinputs in support of special interest outputs. The recent behavioral revolution in political science broadened its focus to examine how withinputs are both response to and cause of stress as well as stress reduction. [2] Thus scholarly interest in the internal dynamics of policy

78

making is not new; what is new is the broadening intellectual perspective that relates internal to external factors in that process. Easton's additional concern, the manner in which withinput analysis tells us something about system persistence, moves us into an even more general conceptualization of policy making.

This chapter explores the formal, professional subsystems of the school system — board, superintendent, and so on — in which is performed most conversion activity on a day-to-day basis. As with so many men in any organizations, the thrust of their work is to bureaucratize activity in order to rationalize objectives and economize resources; a latent consequence of such effort is to maximize system persistence. A second major force here — voter influence — provides episodic inputs to the school system, best conceptualized as a set of anticipated constraints upon the school author-ities — a relationship whose elements are not altogether clear. In these chapters, then, we move from the environment directly into the interior of the political system of American schools. In many respects, however, the view is not unlike that observed within any other organ of governance at city hall, state capitol, or Washington.

SCHOOL BOARDS

It is the school board and professional educators who authoritatively allo-cate values in formulating and administering public policy for education. But the board, whether meeting or blocking a demand for black studies, is not static or its members value-free. Schoolmen modify, regulate, innovate, or refuse political demands in response to professional or other value preferences. On the one hand, they are not unrestrained in this conversion function; subsystem elements conflict within the system, higher system lev-els constrain, and voters may always disrupt. In short, board members and administrators are not "passive transmitters of things taken into the system, digesting them in some sluggish way, and sending them along as outputs." [3] Rather, school boards to some degree reflect a very personal element in the interplay of school politics. Policy output, then, depends in part upon the feelings and values, failures and successes, of human beings. Consequently, it is important to know something of what school board members are like.

Although the most recent survey of the social characteristics of board members was taken in 1958–59, those findings had changed very little from a 1927 survey. More than three-fifths of the board members were either business owners, officials, and managers or they rendered profes-sional technical services. Farmers ranked third, accounting for 12.4 per-cent, and then housewives for 7.2 percent. The main change between 1927 and 1958–59 was the decline in the number of farmers, reflecting the farm closures and rural-school consolidations. The proportion of women remained remarkably stable at around 10 percent. The income of board members was well above average for the nation, reflecting the fact that board members were drawn primarily from advantaged economic positions.[4]

Demographic qualities are not as interesting as psychological ones. Why do board members serve? McCarty investigated the motives of fifty-two board members from seven communities in Illinois and Wisconsin.[5] By their own statements, 54 percent expressed "self-oriented" motivations for seeking office; they were interested in achieving personal goals or in representing interest groups reflecting special values. Another 46 percent had "community-oriented" motives; they were interested in advancing the objectives of the school system so as to benefit the community generally. The method of selection was an important factor in the type of individual who served. For nominating candidates, some districts use a nonpartisan caucus open to all registered voters. Because caucus nomination usually leads to election, the nominee need not campaign. McCarty found that this caucus system produced more of the community-oriented candidates. That is, this open election process permitted the selection of candidates with a "wider range of motives."

Another study in Wisconsin found a vital relationship between social class and expectations for the board of education. For example, upper-class citizens (as measured by family income and education) expected the board to be decidedly more liberal than did lower-class voters with respect to expenditures and to academic freedom for teachers and pupils.[6] A conflict existed because these Wisconsin board members were primarily middle and upper class, but their expectations on key educational issues were not congruent with those of lower-class citizens, who comprised a large majority of the voters. This finding highlights the increased likelihood of value conflicts when the citizenry in a school district is socially and racially heterogeneous. On the other hand, upper-class, suburban school districts can be expected to experience less conflict, and Minar has shown this to be the case.[7]

Such research suggests that, given the great diversity of school districts in size and status, a large range of conflict patterns exists among school boards. Generalizations that will apply equally to New York City, Scarsdale, Waterloo, and the rural South will thus be difficult to find. However, a recent survey of local school pressures found that districts within a metropolitan area experienced much more conflict and interest-group activity than did those outside it.[8]

Whatever the variety of board members and their values, there are serious questions about the board's effectiveness in dealing with conflict. Obviously, boards are not always rubber stamps for school administrators. But their influence is restricted by a lack of time and independent staff, other than a legal counsel. Board members usually hold very demanding full-time jobs on their own and can meet at night only once or, at times, twice a week. They are rarely presented with performance criteria or objective output data upon which to question the professional judgments of the superintendent and his staff.[9] Budgets are not related to academic programs (such as reading or science), and curriculum proposals rarely analyze student attainment data.

Moreover, as we indicated in an earlier chapter, elections seldom provide board members with a specific mandate or policy platform. Since most boards are elected at large, they usually do not feel they represent the views of a specific city ward or neighborhood. Indeed, the prevalent norm for years was that the board should not differentiate the educational program for a section of the city, a specific economic class, or a racial minority. The city is viewed as a unity for purposes of the school program.[10]

This question of the board's function within the school system may better be understood historically. When public schools began, no administrators intervened between teachers and board, as the board itself was an executive body. Each member undertook responsibility for a special school function, much like the contemporary commission form of local government. Chapter 1 outlined the chaos resulting from this structure, whereby the board formed a special subcommittee for each new problem. The growing details of that job which accompanied the growth of enrollments, plus the growing expertise of the new crops of professionals, transformed the board into a legislative body. Now its major function was to set broad policy guidelines and sit as watchdogs over their administration. But even that function has been transformed in this century with the growth of control over local schools by state and national laws and the growth in power of professional administrators and teacher unions. Now the board has become mediator or adjudicator among contending school factions, limited sharply by a set of constraints that can only be touched on here.

In Figure 5.1, Guthrie has captured symbolically the walls of constraint surrounding the big-city board on matters of fiscal and budgetary policy. These walls narrow its autonomy as much as that "divinity which doth hedge a king." However, the autonomy may be wider for non-budgetary matters; the 1950's dispute over "why Johnny can't read" saw boards imposing new directions in reading curriculum over professionals' protests. Too, the autonomy may be fuller in small towns. But the available evidence suggests that the constraints of Figure 5.1 typify much of what big-city boards attempt to do. Thus 80 percent of the budget is usually frozen in personnel salaries, which cannot be lowered by the board.

School boards, then, more often mediate major policy conflicts, leaving important policy issues to the professional staff or to higher levels if there is no evidence of community concern — and even in mediating they may do little. In the process, they legitimate the proposals of the professional

Figure 5.1   Constraints on Big-City School Boards' Control over Budget Policy

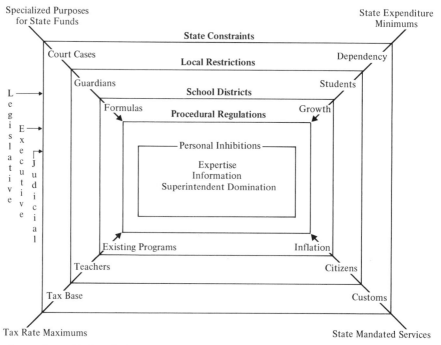

Source: Suggested by James W. Guthrie, University of California, Berkeley.

staff, making only marginal changes, rather than representing citizens.[11] One study of board members found that they spent over 80 percent of their time on managerial details.[12] In big-city integration crises, however, where the professionals have usually handed the issue back to the board with no specific proposal or compromise among the conflicting groups, boards have been the major political decision makers.[13] The professional educator has often regarded integration as a social issue that is more appropriate for the board to settle. It is obviously also an issue where the professional's expertise has little influence on resolving value conflicts.

It is not difficult to present an alarming picture of the policy constraints on the school board. It is increasingly hemmed in by state and federal statutes, confronted by teachers organizations threatening strikes and sanctions, and threatened by community demands that an inadequate financial base or teacher/administrator tenure provisions will not permit it to satisfy. As one observer remarked,

> It must be plain from all that has gone before that in three major aspects, all vital to public education [integration, teacher militancy, and

finances], the American school board has reached a point where what was mere inadequacy has come close to total helplessness, where decline and fall are no longer easily distinguished.[14]

Perhaps this is too harsh a judgment, for it raises serious questions about the persistence of our present form of school government. It is also one cause of the conflicting demands for community-controlled school boards by inner-city blacks and for metropolitan school boards by some whites.

The Nature of Community Demands

Some of the problems of school boards stem from the types of demands received from the community. Citizen perception of schools was more negative than positive, especially on big schools, during the 1950's.[15] Other studies show, however, that citizens know very little about the substance of education or major policy issues.[16] Most often the public is concerned only with minor details or emotional issues, such as dress codes, discipline, and sex education. It is to these demands, then, that the school board will be most often reacting. This has led to board sessions where the budget, a building plan, and major curriculum changes are considered only superficially or postponed, where a dispute over a dress code or teacher retention leads to a serious loss of confidence in the superintendent. In short, if the school board is frequently bogged down in details or emotional issues unrelated to broad policy, this is in large part caused by the lack of communication with, and the style of demands of, the community.

The evidence shows that it is not merely the average citizen who has little knowledge of his schools or is interested only in marginal details. Community leaders are in much the same position. In the early 1960's, Martin, in surveying a large sample of suburban citizens, mayors, presidents of local Leagues of Women Voters, and officials of local Chambers of Commerce, concluded that they too indicated no

> particular interest in curriculum, textbooks, subversive activities, personalities, athletics, race relations. . . . This suggests that these areas provide a reservoir for what we have called episodic issues — issues which emerge under unusual or special conditions and shortly subside. Thus, it is not textbooks which cause concern, but a particular textbook under a special set of circumstances.[17]

Gallup's 1969 survey indicates that Martin's findings are still accurate. These "episodic issues" continue to account for the types of demands that school boards are forced to focus on, and for the consequent frustration and turnover of superintendents.[18]

This is not to deny the weight of community pressure in innovation in educational programs that would not have come from the school bureaucracy. Indeed, one study has concluded that "the most direct and clear-cut cause and effect relationship with innovation appears to be public participation." [19] While there were only six cities in this study, the conclusion does suggest the potential power resting in a community if it transmits demands for substantive change to an understaffed and often overwhelmed school board.

Popular participation is thus a factor in explaining the board's role in policy making. Minar's study of superintendent–school board political interaction in the suburbs of Cook County, Illinois, revealed this relationship in clear terms.[20] Generally speaking, school districts with high levels of voter participation also exhibited high levels of dissent. Dissent was measured by the proportions of votes cast for losers in board elections and proportions of "no" votes in referenda. High-dissent districts tended to have low social status, while other social characteristics, such as urbanism, mobility, and size of district, bore no significant relationship to this behavior. On the other hand, districts with low levels of community dissent and of participation in school policy making were characterized by high family income, prestigious occupation, and more schooling. Low-dissent districts also tended to use the town caucus to nominate board members.

A follow-up study of four districts produced some evidence that in low-conflict, high-status districts, the superintendent had a great deal of latitude from the school board for independent action. Here, the board was inclined to approve the superintendent's actions and to be concerned chiefly with broad policy issues. Boards in high-conflict, low-status districts permitted less independent action by the superintendent and focused on details of what the superintendents described as "administrative matters." While Minar is careful to point out that the study can be considered only suggestive because of sample size and other qualifications, he does support the linkage between community socio-economic characteristics, political stress, and schoolmen's political relationships. Jennings and Zeigler also found this linkage in a significant correlation between high interest-group activity among districts within metropolitan areas. Nonmetropolitan districts, with less complex environments, had much lower interest-group intensity.[21]

Such research suggests a direct correlation between a community's social base and its style of school politics. Where there is higher social status, dissent is minimized, interest-group activity and board-election conflict are reduced, and the board restricts its attention to general policy while the superintendent is given a free hand in administration. Where social status is lower, however, political activity is much higher in elections, referenda, and interest-group involvement. Here, dissent moves more easily and more often into the school and affects the board, which becomes preoccupied with the details of administration, and upon the superintendent, whose autonomy is thereby lessened. More often than not, however, citizen inputs to school policy making is quite minimal.

SCHOOL PROFESSIONALS

If the community is active only occasionally and if the board has serious limitations on its political efficacy, school professionals retain a greater influence on policy issues. While the board is the ultimate local authority in school politics, professional educators have their resources, too. They define alternatives, produce research, provide specific policy recommendations, and recommend the formal agenda. In these and many other ways, professionals generate subsystem pressures and information that shape the board's deliberations and policy decisions. In Easton's framework, the school superintendent and his staff provide "withinputs" to the school board and all levels of the school bureaucracy. Moreover, many specific policy issues may never reach the school board if the superintendent and his staff are acting under broad discretion from the school board. Consequently, both board and superintendent act as authorities seeking to maximize support from the community through the use of appropriate outputs in the form of budget, curriculum, teacher selection, and so on.

While the professional staff has been found to be a major source both of change and obstruction in school policy making, they do operate under certain constraints. Thus, they must anticipate reactions of board members to their actions, for they are cognizant of the basic power of the board to fire them.[22] Too, they learn that the ultimate power of the electorate, if provoked, can remove them by changing the board composition. In recent years, this hiring-firing (or resignation) cycle for superintendents appears to be getting shorter. Boards have jealously guarded their prerogative to hire the superintendent, although a screening committee of outside educators provides nominees. Further, it is likely that the superintendent would act in accordance with the school board's wishes on many issues even *without* the threat of removal from office. The board hired the superintendent, and it is natural to assume that board members would hire a man whose values were similar to their own. In effect, the board's impact on specific decisions may be more indirect than direct, but they are real nevertheless.

If the board hires, however, most superintendent resignations are caused by defeat of board incumbents and their replacement by those who do not share the values of the superintendent. Thus, in California in the 1960's the defeat of one or two incumbent board members preceded conflict on the board and was foreshadowed by a series of nonunanimous school board votes.[23] The substantive conflict in the school subsystem then centered on the leader of the board insurgents opposing the superintendent, while the latter tried to work with the long-term school board members to preserve the *status quo*. Frequently in such a context, more incumbent board members were defeated and involuntary turnover of the superintendent followed. A new superintendent from outside the district was then chosen by the reconstituted board.

Defeat of incumbent board members in the suburbs has often followed a new population influx from professionals and technicians. Their views on education often conflict with the older population that is oriented to agriculture and related enterprises.[24] This conflict in values is channeled through the board election to defeat incumbent board members and ultimately to change superintendents. Similarly, the growth of minority populations in core cities may set off stress and value conflicts that will most likely lead to defeat of upper class, white, incumbent board members and the same cycle of involuntary superintendency turnover.

Earlier we noted that in school affairs, a community's social mode influences its political mode, but now we suggest that when the first is changing, the latter should also. Demographic changes that bring in new groups with new school demands trigger an altered social mode. The California and other studies suggest that there then ensues a readjustment in characteristic patterns of school politics, leading eventually to a new board and superintendent. More importantly, there emerges a new mode of political interaction among citizens and schoolmen as well as a new set of educational values implemented in school policy.

School Subsystems: The Bureaucracy

Despite these potential constraints, school subsystems most influence what happens in the school. During his tenure in a school district, the superintendent or his staff maintains predominant influence over such internal issues as personnel, i.e., tenure, hiring, promotions, and assignment. His views on facilities and remodeling are usually decisive except where the location of a school causes substantial community concern and opposition.[25] Another area where the board customarily bows to professional expertise (as we shall see in Chapter 10) is curriculum development, where the educator's training and other factors have not granted a large role to lay views.

In short, although the prior discussion indicates that a superintendent may have a limited tenure, his role extends beyond merely implementing the board's wishes or general policy decisions. As Martin has concluded, "he is as much a policy maker as he is a manager in the narrow sense; for he enjoys an expertise, a professional reputation, and a community position which combine to give him an almost irresistible voice in school affairs." [26]

The influence of this "irresistible voice" has changed since Martin wrote a decade ago. A former big-city superintendent described a commonly held view of the current political role of the superintendency:

The most important single thing that is happening today is the shift in the power structure. What we used to conceive of as the role of a board of education and the superintendent is greatly truncated. The federal funds generally add new programs to the schools, not aid old programs; it adds burdens which it doesn't fully finance. But at the bottom is the organization of teachers which is at least three years ahead in its demands of any available resources. The ceiling moves down as the floor moves up; and the administration gets squeezed in the middle along with the school board.

It used to be that a school superintendent, if he was at all successful, would have the feeling that he had the ability to mount a program and carry it through successfully. I think at the present time very few superintendents would be able to say honestly that they have this feeling. They are at the beck and call of every pressure that is brought to them. They have lost initiative. They don't control their own time. One of the problems today is that the teachers are so well trained; they know as much or more in their own specialization than any administrator does. The community is better organized and more outspoken. Mid-administration is very much floundering. They don't know whether they are teachers or administrators.

There has been a change in the role of the superintendent from one who plans and carries through to one who works with groups of people in joint planning and ultimate realization of something the group can agree on.[27]

The increasing complexity of school policy making tends to provide considerable influence to those who control detailed information and analyses of policy alternatives.[28] The control of information highlights the role of the school bureaucracy vis-à-vis the superintendent. At this point, our research has not progressed far enough empirically to differentiate in a large number of school districts the influence of the superintendent from his own staff. But we do know much about this pattern in the big city schools. There, the central office staff has accumulated a vast amount of decision-making authority in such areas as curriculum, personnel assignment, and facilities that restricts the role of outlying district administrators and building principals. As we shall shortly see, this condition has helped lead to a widespread demand for decentralization and/or community control. Under present conditions, however, the principal is too involved with day-to-day management of his school to participate effectively in broad policy making. District superintendents are primarily concerned with assuring that policies set down by central headquarters are followed by the schools in their districts.[29]

The top officials at the central office are traditionally chosen from within the system by the superintendent or his committee. In some districts, the board must ratify his recommendations. But a new superintendent cannot always bring in a new team of top administrators. Few incumbents are removed or fired from the district; [30] indeed, San Francisco administrators actually have job tenure. Given the turnover discussed earlier, the superintendent may find himself unable to implement policies through his administrative officers. For example, Rogers concluded that in the school desegregation program in New York the policies of the board and superintendent were emasculated by contradictory or evasive directives and actions from some line administrative officers.[31] Indeed, the central office made official policy statements, but the operation of the school system was highly decentralized with various bureaucrats ignoring the central desegregation policy and going off in conflicting directions.

Again, we run into the problem of generalizing from one case study in a large city to other dissimilar districts. At this point we need much more information on the political role and effectiveness of the various middle-management and central-office administrators. Evidence indicates, however, that some large-city bureaucracies are able to "pocket veto" policy changes established by their superintendents and school boards. To what extent is the condition elsewhere as characteristic as Rogers summarizes it in a statement about the bureaucratic politics in New York City?

> Indeed, this is a system that is strangled in red tape; mired in inertia . . . insulated from its clients and from outside institutions; and fragmented into power blocs (teachers, principals, district superintendents, divisions, bureaus, staff units at headquarters and districts, a Board of Examiners) that veto new ideas and prevent the efficient use of resources by failure to coordinate. It is, in addition, leaderless; it has no adequate auditing, monitoring, or information system to evaluate programs and see if policies are carried out; it faces continued subversion of headquarters directives for change by field officials; it protects mediocrity through outdated civil service standards; it is highly inbred, allowing protectionist power blocs inside to develop and solidify their baronies and vested interests against client demands for change; it is then accountable to nobody but itself; and it victimizes almost anybody who comes in contact with it, including its superintendents and lay boards, who are emasculated with regularity by the professional staff, and whose efforts are absorbed by the cumbersome workings of the system.[32]

COMMUNITY CONTROL AND DECENTRALIZATION

The situation Rogers describes led in the late 1960's to proposals for major institutional change through decentralization and community control.[33] The most drastic change, community control, would create several local educational agencies out of one central system and thereby empower several new community-based school boards of lay members. Particularly favored by

minority groups who lack the resources to influence the central administrators, this new concept envisions a board able to remove personnel
employed by the old centralized board and with complete discretion to
reallocate budget priorities. Little support exists for this among school
professionals.

Decentralization, on the other hand, is supported by teachers, principals,
and administrators in the individual schools who find the present system
cumbersome. They complain that they cannot get supplies and personnel
from the central office and are prevented by overall regulations from making curricula and teaching reforms. The assumption of this group is that
better education will result if more locally based, professional educators
have more discretion. Their goal is decentralization within the present administration and under the single central school board. In effect, field
administrators would gain power from central administrators. Under community control, however, lay board members and citizens (particularly
from minority areas) would ostensibly gain more influence than when —
as at present — they confront all the professionals as well as city-wide
voting constituencies.

The politics of decentralization and community control revolves around
several value conflicts.[34] Perhaps the most important, that between democratic control and professional autonomy, is latent in the American school
system. Advocates of community control assert that their model would
make professional educators more accountable and responsible to parents.
Supporters of professional autonomy, on the other hand, contend that
although it is proper that laymen should set broad limits on policy, educators, like doctors and lawyers, cannot perform their tasks well under
close lay supervision.

This controversy is also related to differing views on substantive and
procedural values in policy formation. Advocates of community control
value highly the side effects of certain procedures for setting educational
policy. As Lyke points out:

> In particular, extensive citizen participation is valuable [because] only
> by regular, meaningful participation can individuals become aware of
> what is happening in the community and develop the skills and under-
> standing necessary to make a rational contribution. Moreover, it is
> agreed that participation enables an individual to develop his personal
> values so he can act as his own agent, not unwittingly as someone
> else's. This theory is currently appealing to black theorists, who feel
> that only through participation in black communities can black people
> begin to shed the values and perspectives inculcated in them by white
> society.[35]

Opponents of community control believe that any particular procedure for
making decisions is not nearly as important as a decision's impact on

educational attainment. Lay "interference" in "professional" judgments will purportedly weaken the quality of those judgments.

Finally, there is the inherent conflict in values between community development and societal integration. Community control of the schools is viewed as an important step toward that community revitalization, participation, and pride deemed necessary to overcome the numerous problems — housing, jobs, health — of oppressive slums. Advocates of centralization, on the other hand, warn that community control will only exacerbate and harden the barriers to racial and class integration and that without integration in an economic and educational sense, community development is unlikely. Clearly, if community control is complete, then the task of school desegregation becomes impossible. For some, both black and white, that represents no serious criticism, for they reject desegregation. For others of both races, however, this is of serious concern.

These conflicting values have been articulated by interest groups for school boards in most major cities.[36] In New York, Detroit, and Los Angeles, the pressure has come principally from minority groups who want community control. In Chicago and Washington, D.C., decentralization has been developed by the school system itself, but minority groups are also pressing for community control. In these two cities, decentralization is viewed as an experiment to be confined at this point to one or two neighborhoods. As the debate rages across the nation, it is important to keep in mind that decentralization and community control are fundamentally political issues over who shall have the right to authoritatively allocate values.

Community control, unlike decentralization, will necessarily involve new state legislation to create new school districts. This means that state legislators will have to decide the issue on the basis of the value conflicts sketched above, with school professionals on one side and minority groups on the other. But the stance of the school professionals has varied widely among the cities. The Detroit administrators and teachers union were neutral on a decentralization bill containing elements of community control that passed the Michigan legislature. On the other hand, the Los Angeles professional staff lobbied vigorously against any state legislation mandating community control or decentralization. The initial results across several cities indicate that state legislators are more responsive and sympathetic to school employees than to community groups.

The specific issues that have caused the most conflict in large cities concern district boundaries and personnel procedures.[37] If the community is now to control — who constitutes the "community" and where does it live? District lines under community control determine not only the access to educational opportunity but also the political character of the neighborhood. Even though "community" lines could be drawn on the basis of economic or class measures, race has been the overriding consideration. A related issue is how large a "community" should be if it is to enhance professional accountability to parents. Each of the ten decentralized New York City districts is larger than the whole district of Rochester, N.Y., hardly conducive to the closer relation of parents to schools.

Once the boundaries are defined, the goal of community control for many has been the right locally to hire, fire, and promote school personnel. As LaNoue points out, "Community control can be simply a demand for a share of the pie of school positions which are now relatively well paid in most cities." However, the plan's support can be a judgment about the cultural gap between middle-class teachers and ghetto students. Much of the debate about community control in New York City was motivated by a fear that white teachers were bent on the cultural "genocide" of black youngsters. In response, teachers' unions have declared their willingness to strike if their tenure and other rights are not carefully safeguarded. However, the increased attractiveness of the voucher plan and performance contracts with private firms could cause associations of school employees to view decentralization as a more palatable form of "accountability."

Community control is only one form of community participation, and while discussion grows, no one knows how widespread and prevalent it is. A large survey in 1965 indicated that another form of community participation was not widespread when Jennings explored the incidence, direction, and outcome of parental complaints.[38] The incidence of grievances varied widely among his ninety-seven sample schools, although only a few experienced much unhappiness. Only 13 percent of the 1992 parents complained over curriculum and only 27 percent over other matters such as methods of instruction, services, personnel, etc. These parents are not necessarily those most isolated from political life and hence most alienated. Indeed, much of the objection (particularly by fundamentalists) was about curriculum — matters of morals, ethics, and religion — with politics running second to this grouping.

But the method of redress attempted by the aggrieved parent is what is important to us; did he take group action, which means political action, in order to correct the complaint? Over a majority did nothing whatever about it — 62 percent on curriculum matters and 52 percent on other concerns. Of those who did seek redress, only about 10 percent took "corporate action with the school." This represented only about one in 25 of all parents with a grievance. Parents who took corporate action on any matter were remarkably few — 0.5 percent on curriculum and 1 percent on other matters.

Some schools showed more grievances, of course, but the overall impressions are that a large majority have no complaints about specific matters and an even larger majority have never taken political action to correct complaints. Of course, while few in number, the aggrieved can create extreme factionalism, and this incidence is a measure of environmental stress. But for most constituents of the school system, little community participation exists in the form of organized protest as an input on local school matters.

THE SCHOOLS AND GENERAL GOVERNMENT

Compared to bureaucratic politics, more is known about the interaction of school officials in "external issues" that require negotiations with political authorities and actors *not* primarily concerned with the internal administration of public schools. Tax increases, integration, and community control are examples of such external issues. The influence of school administrators is substantial in these external issues, even though their tactics are less overt than during decisions on administrative promotion or curriculum. The superintendent often defines the issues, proposes alternatives, provides technical ammunition for his supporters, and in the end implements or evades the decisions arrived at. But the school board, mayor, city or town council, and many interest groups may also be involved. A decision on the overall amount of a tax increase and school budget is a frequent example of these external negotiations.

Chapter 1 showed how the reform politics at the turn of this century was designed to limit the number of these external issues. These reforms advocated the divorce and isolation of school policy making from the influence of local government, political parties, and the mayor. This was a reaction against a spoils system that selected teachers and ward-based school board members who were more receptive to the needs of city political leaders than to those of the students. For example, "Big Bill" Thompson, running for mayor of Chicago in 1927, concentrated much of his campaign on the issue of school control; he called the superintendent a lackey of King George and the British and promised to fire him.[39] Educators have sought protection from such big-city politics, which led to what they regarded as educationally irrelevant attacks. One tactic to provide this protection was to proclaim the unity of professional educators and the inclusion of teachers and administrators in the same organization. Local politicians could not attempt to gain votes and influence by appealing to one education group against another. For many years this fundamental unity of purpose among educators prevailed, and the mayor was not a crucial participant in teacher salary negotiations. The traditional doctrine was that each teacher should negotiate with the superintendent.[40]

In some cities, however, general government officials were involved in negotiations with the board and superintendent over the overall amount of the budget increase based on the mayor's and city council's concern for tax rate increases. But several studies have shown that city officials did not attempt to change the program judgments or priorities of education officials. Moreover, the role of the mayor and other city officials on program judgments does not appear to differ depending on whether the school district is fiscally dependent or independent of general government. Under fiscal independence, the board of education has its own taxing authority and does not need to submit its budget for review to local government officials. Indeed, one study of six large cities found that mayors have historically been happy to insulate themselves from such responsibility on school issues.[41] This attitude stems in part from the force of the "no politics" doctrine for schools, partly from the political costs of becoming involved in school conflicts where large blocs of voters will be alienated, and from the mayor's fear that he could not produce effective change in the schools anyway.

Recently in many districts, however, mayors have played a mediating or decisive role in teacher salary negotiations. In New York City, for instance, teacher salary demands are not settled by the superintendent or board. Serious negotiations begin when the mayor, who must review the overall school budget, enters the picture. At this point, the divorce of school politics from general government ends. The school budget becomes a very visible political decision for the mayor and city council, who must answer to the voters for tax increases in fiscally dependent districts. This trend, now extending to many cities other than New York, signals the end of unity for professional educators and the consequent involvement of city or town officials in exploiting or settling disputes between the teachers and the administrators and boards.[42] Even in fiscally independent cities, mayors have attempted to mediate when teacher strikes are probable.

In such situations, stress generated within the school subsystem between teachers and administrators breaks through the boundaries that have tended to separate school politics from the political system for general local government functions. Stress in subsystems external to the school can create political demands for school authorities, as Chapter 10 will show for curriculum reform. Similarly, internal stress that cannot be authoritatively settled by school authorities creates political demands that reach out toward local government officials, particularly the mayor. This is reflected in recent trends in teacher militancy which indicate that the New York City situation will reach many smaller and medium-sized districts.

EMERGING STUDENT ROLE IN POLICY MAKING

Our discussion of subsystem elements contributing to school withinputs and conversion would not be complete without reference to a recent phenomenon — the emerging political influence of students.[43] A New York

City group called Schools Defense Network, in a pamphlet entitled *Schools Belong to Students,* reflects this new viewpoint of student power.

> Students are the people who suffer the most from the way schools are run. Students must be heard and heeded if education in the schools is to become "relevant." . . .
>
> Because of the way the school system and the Board of Education have acted in the past, you cannot expect your rights to be given to you. They will have to be won.

The pamphlet advocates several political tactics for "winning your rights" in such diverse areas as dress, publications, records and grades, curriculum change, discipline, and police in school. One tactic is for the students to organize as an internal pressure group within the school system: "If you have been working in a student group, start with the group in making your call for help. The best method the school system has to destroy a student group is to divide and conquer."

Yet another student tactic is to seek an "advocate" outside the school officialdom who can present demands on behalf of students.[44] In effect, these interest groups are potential allies of students in generating stress that will result in political demands upon the school authorities. If students cannot exert influence within the school system, they may go outside and use protests or interest group allies. The existence of the organizations cited above reveals the inadequacy of large city PTA's in reflecting the special values of reform groups or in using aggressive political lobbying.

The emerging trend of high-school activists using collective protest contrasts markedly with the docile role of powerless adolescents described in studies only a few years ago. The picture then was one of student government so coopted by its faculty sponsors that it had little influence over significant issues or changes in important policies. Student unrest in the recent past enabled educators to deal with individual students who cut classes, fought, and failed to do their homework. The new era in high school student-administration relations involves students aggregating their power and transmitting their demands outside of such traditional school channels as the student council. The search for new channels clearly marks the inadequacy of the old for representing new values, particularly those challenging "professional" standards. The characterization of these organs as "sand-boxes" by disgruntled students may be cynical but true.

In a preliminary study of this new student role, Nystrand found little evidence in five cities that protest leaders were "recalcitrant trouble makers of long standing." [45] Rather, they were often leaders in athletics, debate, student government, or other traditional status activities in high school. The demands of the students upon school authorities were similar. In four of the five cities, dress and grooming were an issue. In all cities, students wanted more attention to minority culture. Nystrand distinguished three types of student demands: (1) those growing out of specific situations for which students advocated immediate and specific redress, e.g., firing a particular teacher; (2) demands relating to student dignity and self-worth, e.g., employing minority group teachers; and (3) improving educational programs as school people have traditionally defined them, e.g., smaller class sizes or more counselors.

There were underlying causes in each city that created the stress. Among these were student awareness of increasing criticism of the schools for their failure to serve minority students effectively. Also important was an awareness of an "action ethic" generated by contemporary society; students have observed the success of collective action by teachers and community organizations. It is noteworthy that the students' strategy was to use collective protest (demonstrations, boycotts, etc.) as opposed to dropping out or utilizing impotent student governments as a basis for withinputs inside the formal governing apparatus. In most instances, negotiations went progressively to the central administration and then the board of education.

PARTICIPATION VS. BUREAUCRATIZATION

This brief review of inputs, both from within and outside the school's conversion system, suggests that most policy is affected by a few actors, particularly those inside. This emphasis upon professionals as policy makers reflects an interesting tension in our schools that arises from conflicting values. On the one hand, Americans talk much about democratic controls on education, and the school's closeness to community opinion is much stressed in the literature of educational administration. On the other hand, "We want the best for our children" is an also-stressed popular value, one which requires surrender to the expertise of professional educators. Thus there exists this tension in education — and in most other public policies — between popular control and professional autonomy, which in most cases results in the latter triumphing.[46]

But one form of popular input remains as a potential control device, election of school boards and referenda on school issues. We must examine these more fully before understanding whether the general public or the professional dominates the conversion process of American schools.

6 Referendum in the Conversion Process

By the last of the nineteenth century, many Americans had become disgusted with their representative government. The republic had begun with high hopes for the legislature as the primary decisional forum. But the excesses of those bodies had within seventy-five years brought restraints on their operations and an expansion of executives to balance off the corrupt assemblies. But as the century moved toward its close, neither office received much praise. Political parties were everywhere seen as corrupt links between the two, the judiciary was equally tainted, and the beneficiaries of this degradation, in an era of rampant capitalism, were not only politicians but businessmen. Two political movements struck out against this union of private and public theft, Populism and Progressivism. Although their membership and some objectives differed, on some things they agreed. More democracy must be a part of the operations of the institutions of democracy, and more control should be provided for common men over the corrupters of the political and economic weal.

Under this banner, a number of innovations entered the political system under the title of "direct democracy" — initiative, referendum, and recall. It is hard to realize today how radical these once were regarded, for in our time, as Goldman has wryly noted, they have "become quaint; one thought of them, as one remembered Teddy Roosevelt's teeth, in a haze of mezzotint sentimentality." Their promise of democratic control has not been met by reality, for little evidence exists that they rearranged interest-group power in state politics. These devices stand today as a testament to the power of the Jacksonian and Jeffersonian dream of the importance of all men in the political affairs of life.

But not all men consider them important enough to use. Aside from the occasional, controversial issue that precipitates a large turnout, most referenda pull out far less than a majority. Yet the hollowness of the earlier promise is not complete, for one reality that policy makers have to keep in mind is that these devices *can* be turned on if their actions become too offensive. Earlier advocates spoke of their power as "a shotgun behind the door"; today, political scientists speak of their potential for creating "anticipated reactions" in officials who then ostensibly curb their excesses in anticipation of what the public will accept.[1]

Referenda continue to be more significant for education than for other areas of public policy. For our purposes the referendum is important in two perspectives. It is the necessary device for securing financial support of schools in most states. Also it may be conceptualized as a conversion process at the local level that bypasses the school board and authoritatively allocates values. We must keep in mind that, unlike board elections, referenda are direct policy-making processes. Passage or defeat definitely allocates school system resources, in general for operating levies and in specific for bond issues. The act of voting for or against — or not voting at all — relates the individual citizen to his schools in an intimate fashion unknown for other major policy structures.

That relationship may take several forms, however. Sweeping support of what schoolmen offer citizens reflects close correspondence between the preferences of the two. Ostensibly that condition arises when schoolmen carefully anticipate the limits of the public's demands, beyond which its support will drop off. Alternatively, however, the relationship may be one of closely divided but still a majority referenda support, reflective of community cleavage over public preferences. Here the schoolmen have less room in which to anticipate the public's acceptable limits. A third possible relationship exists when schoolmen are defeated on the referenda they urge; here their anticipatory wisdom was poor. Adjustments will vary depending upon the size of the defeat; a narrow loss is worth another referenda effort while a large defeat requires considerable rearrangement of the school policies which the referenda funds were to support.

Thus the collective act of the school referenda tells us much about environment, demand inputs, and the political system of American schools. In this section we explore what consequences this may have for school political authorities, and what citizens are doing when they engage in or refrain from tax referenda.

STRUCTURES, COGNITIONS, AND OUTPUTS

The striking fact about such queries is that research using aggregate tax referenda data is limited. Such data could be drawn from the elections themselves or from surveys of voters and nonvoters. This research gap is particularly surprising in light of the enormous number of school districts

and referenda available for study. In the 1960's, school districts were the
most numerous governmental unit in America, even though consolidation
was sharply reducing them, as we see in Table 6.1. Better than one-third of
all units were school districts in 1962; but by 1968 the 20,406 districts
remaining constituted more like one-quarter.[2] The number of school bond
and tax referenda was equally large — 1432 bond elections alone in 1961–
62, peaking to 2071 in 1963–64, and declining to 1341 by 1968–69.[3] Yet
we can point to only about a half-dozen aggregate studies employing these
data.

Structural Factors and Referenda Success

Undoubtedly the most massive study was that by Carter and Sutthoff
using data from 1054 districts over the period 1948–1959.[4] About 900
of these had held at least one bond or tax election in this time. Regardless
of district size, there was much similarity in structural provisions for them.
In most, the board alone initiated bond proposals and adopted the school
budget, without recourse to approval of voters or governmental authorities.
Most of these referenda were successful, but important variation in the degree of success could be traced to structural factors.

The measure of "strong" district success in the Carter-Sutthoff study
was winning 90 percent of the elections. In Table 6.2 we summarize their
calculations about what structural, political factors relate to such success.
Many of the differences in Table 6.2 are quite minor, however, and the
kind of election — bond or tax — obviously makes a difference in a factor's importance. Looking only at bond elections, we find in many large
cities that success is strongly related to boards (1) that are appointed,
(2) whose majority requires a longer time to change, (3) that need never

Table 6.1   Number of Units of Government
in the United States in 1952 and 1962

Governments	1952	1962	Percent change	Percent of total
Federal	1	1		a
States	48	50	4.2	a
Counties	3,052	3,043	-0.3	3.3
Municipalities	16,807	17,997	7.1	19.7
Townships and towns	17,202	17,144	-0.3	18.8
School districts	67,355	34,678	-48.5	38.0
Special districts	12,340	18,323	48.5	20.1

Source: Adapted from Charles R. Adrian and Charles Press, *Governing Urban America*,
3d ed. (New York: McGraw-Hill, 1969), 268.
[a]Less than 0.1 percent.

Table 6.2   Board Characteristics and Financial Election Success by Size of School District[a]

	Bonds			Taxes		
Characteristic	*Large district*	*Medium district*	*Small district*	*Large district*	*Medium district*	*Small district*
Method of selection						
Appointment	X	X	O	(1)	(1)	(1)
Elected	O	O	X	O	O	O
Term of office						
2–4 years	=	O	=	=	O	=
5–9 years	=	X	=	=	X	=
Time to change board majority						
1–2 years	O	=	=	=	O	=
3–9 years	X	=	=	=	X	=
Nominating method						
Petition	O	=	=	O	O	O
Self announcement	O	=	=	X	O	O
Other[b]	X	=	=	O	X	X
Kind of election						
Separate	O	O	X	=	=	X
Combined	X	X	O	=	=	O
Method of adopting school budget						
Election	O	O	=	(1)	=	X
School board	O	X	=	(1)	=	O
Number of miscellaneous elections						
1–5	O	O	=	=	=	X
None	X	X	=	=	=	O

Source: Adapted from tables in Richard F. Carter and John Sutthoff, *Communities and Their Schools* (Stanford: Institute for Communication Research, 1960), ch. 4.

[a]Key: X: most successful under this characteristic; O: most successful under other characteristic; =: less than 10 percentage points difference; (1): too few cases in one cell to include here. Note that chi-square measures are not as strong as they should be for some of these tables.

[b]Includes caucus, primary election, annual meeting, and official nomination.

go to the electorate for miscellaneous bond votes, (4) that enter office by partisan ("other") methods, and (5) whose election is held along with that for other offices. In bond elections the medium-size districts share with large districts three of these criteria of success, but they differ in having distinctively long terms and needing only board approval of the budget. Small districts are distinctive in few factors, but on two they differ from other districts; they are more often elected than appointed, and they do not share the ballot with contests for other levels of government. The basic inference from these data, the authors concluded, was that "larger district boards of control have a greater potential for effective control of fiscal policies." [5]

If referenda outputs are affected by structural characteristics of the political system, another effect may be seen in the degree of citizen participation, specifically, in the turnout. Carter and Sutthoff's strongest finding — with unsuspected ironies for believers both in the Jacksonian heritage of participatory democracy and the Jeffersonian heritage of the value of education — was that the fewer the voters who turned out (0–30 percent), the greater the chance the measure would pass. Turnout in the middle range (31–60 percent) was associated with more failures than successes; highest turnout (over 60 percent) found equal outcomes.[6] High-turnout elections were found most in small districts in the South Atlantic and East South Central regions; it was not said whether the inference is correct that the failures were also largest here. Further, turnout was highest for tax issues in large districts and for bond issues in the small ones. In general, the more money involved and the more it is drawn from local sources the larger the turnout. Little change in these patterns was found over the years studied.

Cognitions and Referenda Support

The negative relationship between referendum turnout and success is matched in its strength by the finding that turnout was generally low even when fever-pitch emotions may have been aroused — inferred in the syndrome of high-turnout–high-failure elections. To understand this phenomenon it is important to realize that cognitive and normative frameworks vary among voters both in content and completeness. Carter has shown in another study, utilizing extensive opinion surveys of laymen and professionals during the late 1950's, that the "normative view of education as a valuable institution, fully endorsed by the voters we interviewed, is missing in specific opinions and behaviors." [7] Furthermore, voters' informational maps about what their schools are doing are incomplete, just as their normative maps about what schools should do are often missing.

While these findings are uninspiring to those seeking to maximize democratic participation in policy making, they are simple. The citizen thinks schools are good in general, but he criticizes them in particular areas. He wants schools to teach loyalty and the fundamentals of literacy — the three R's — while eschewing local history, industrial arts, and "culture" — the fine arts. In what he thinks important to teach, he believes the schools do well, but "on tasks and services connected to the pupil's ability to stand on his own, economically and emotionally, performance is not nearly so much in line with the perceived importance." [8] His values about the function of schools, when they exist, form the significant variables for understanding whether he will vote for school financial measures. That is, his voting support is dependent upon a complex of school-related perceptions — what he thinks of school costs, teachers, the community, and the educational product.

The results are different models of voters, each a different mix of these independent variables.[9] The voter most favorable to school financial referenda was a young person with school children, a recent resident, and most likely a skilled union worker, clerk, or salesman. The most unfavorable was also young, but without children, or a long-time resident, and a professional or technician. There are other modes of participation than voting, of course, as anyone knows who has gazed curiously upon the work of the PTA. The active, interested participant is the young parent, well educated himself, usually a professional or technician. The interested but nonactive type is also a well-educated, young person, but most often male with no school children; he is a joiner of nonschool groups, which siphon his community participation energies. The nonparticipant is another kind of American — older, with little education, childless. A final type — active but not interested — is most often a young woman of little education whose children are in school.

To complicate this variety even further, these types also have different values that they wish the school to realize in their children and that cause them to evaluate the school's performance differently. This, too, is not unfamiliar to schoolmen who deal with these parents every day. The administrator's job is made even more difficult by the fact that the harshest critics are those without children in the school, often older and long-time residents, for whom everything in society is in decline since they turned forty.

Beyond the social characteristics of those who provide input to the schools through referenda lies a quality in the participants that is even more significant. This is a sense of efficacy — the belief, which varies among men, that what one seeks to do to change the environment can be effective.[10] This psychological energizer has been found in other aspects of social life as a critical variable, e.g., in voting in presidential elections, membership in a political party, and success in school.[11] Carter found with great consistency in four cities that about one-third feel that they have little to say about schools; another one-half see the vote as their only influence. Overall, over 40 percent think school policy too complicated to understand, even if they wanted to do something.

The efficacious voter shares many characteristics with the active, interested supporter of schools in general. He is younger and more educated. He most feels the pressures to be involved in school policies, pressures arising from within himself and from his child; the pressure flow most often is from school to wife to husband. This activity is considered part of the wife's role, although both share financial activities.[12] However, the family's role is variable, a function of the couple's background, values, and child status. Each spouse plays a distinctive role in influencing the other.[13]

STATUS AND ETHNIC SUPPORT

Carter's pioneering effort — still the broadest-based evidence for propositions on the subject — was followed by few others. Later research used either aggregate data on status characteristics of school districts or opinion survey data of voters in school districts; few sought to pair these disparate data sources.[14] The subsequent work did open up, however, understanding of additional variables operating in the citizen-school linkage. On the aggregate side, the support of educational finances among higher-status citizens was verified. Wilson and Banfield provided impressive evidence that higher-income sections of American cities were stronger supporters of a whole range of welfare and civic-betterment referenda.[15] Among these, support for increasing school taxes or constructing schools was consistently larger than the city average.

But, as Wilson and Banfield demonstrated, within each income level, ethnic identity separates high and low supporters of school issues equally effectively. The scholarly revisionism of the 1960's found that ethnic assimilation had not taken place — in Glazer and Moynihan's words, "The point about the melting pot is that it did not happen." [16] Holding the income level of voting precincts constant, Banfield and Wilson found that while low-income renter precincts were more likely to vote yes on most issues than were middle-income home-owners, within any one income group considerable variation in support was associated with ethnicity. Table 6.3 selects the only school referendum the authors included to demonstrate this typical relationship.

The saliency of ethnicity for voting in referenda may arise from the absence of partisanship or political party, which provide cues to voters on appropriate voting behavior. In the absence of such cues, ethnicity may be more emphasized — with an increased social cleavage as a result — as one study of municipal elections in New Jersey revealed. So it could be with

Table 6.3   Variations in Support of a Chicago School Tax Issue by Income and Ethnic Characteristics

	Low income renters			Middle income homeowners		
	Black	*Irish*	*Polish*	*Black*	*Irish*	*Polish*
Support percent	97.8	79.4	81.8	88.9	64.2	58.3

Source: James Q. Wilson and Edward C. Banfield, "Public Regardingness as a Value Premise in Voting Behavior," *American Political Science Review*, 58 (1964), 883.

referenda — particularly as they apply to schooling, where ethnic judgments seem to differ about the purpose of education.[17]

While more needs to be done with the quality and force of ethnic demands upon the school system as they are reflected in referenda, one relationship does emerge in all studies of ethnicity and public policy. That is the high support of the black and the highest-income, white precincts for many measures, including school finances.[18] That pairing may have been disarranged by the Northern school-desegregation conflict in the 1960's. Certainly there is no reason for the black endorsement of school referenda to falter, except as a threat against dilatory school boards.

The blacks' main problem has been their relatively limited participation in such elections. Compared to urban whites, blacks support tax referenda much more, but they turn out to vote less, and even when turned out they tend to vote less on school referenda. Supportive data for these conclusions, drawn from recent Detroit elections, are shown in Table 6.4. Although the two contests differ in turnout (again, higher turnout is associated with lesser tax support) and in favorable vote, race provides a common thread. A larger black population means a slightly smaller turnout but a much larger support — and a vastly larger failure to vote on the issue even with ballot in hand. Almost one-half in 1968 failed to mark their ballot on taxes in school districts with the largest black population. Joined with the characteristically low voter registration in this group, blank voting further reduces the supportive effect of black inputs.

Masotti's Cleveland study of this voting further showed that normally high black support can be withheld. The data in Table 6.5 include a 1964 election preceded by considerable black opposition to a school board slow to desegregate. In that election, as black leaders had threatened, black precincts produced a drastic falloff in support. However, by 1966, black support had returned to its high levels after improvements from the

Table 6.4 Race and Referenda Behavior in Detroit School Districts, November, 1966, and 1968[a]

Black percentage of total population	Turnout		Support		Blank votes	
	1968	1966	1968	1966	1968	1966
Below 25	80.5%	65.3%	26.5%	43.8%	13.0%	13.8%
25–75	79.3	60.6	32.3	55.8	35.4	31.5
Over 75	77.6	59.9	58.0	74.3	47.8	41.8
Total	78.8	61.9	37.5	54.0	32.3	26.6

Source: From data provided by Research Department, Detroit Public Schools, with the permission of Norman Drachler.
[a]Percentages are calculated as median votes in twenty-one high school constellations on millage referenda.

Table 6.5   White and Nonwhite Support for School Referenda in Cleveland, 1960-66

	Wards			
Date and levy	*White*	*Nonwhite*	*Mixed*	*City total*
May, 1960				
Operating	38.0	73.6	58.1	47.9
Building	33.2	73.5	55.1	44.3
November, 1960				
Operating	68.7	86.3	78.7	73.3
Building	67.4	88.0	79.7	72.8
November, 1962				
Operating	61.7	84.9	75.1	67.5
Building	64.7	89.4	79.9	71.3
May, 1964				
Operating	67.4	34.0	48.1	53.9
November, 1966				
Levy increase	64.6	84.8	72.4	70.2
Bond issue	61.0	81.1	67.9	66.0

Source: Louis Masotti, "Patterns of White and Nonwhite School Referenda Participation and Support: Cleveland, 1960-64," in Marilyn Gittell (ed.), *Educating an Urban Population* (Beverly Hills, Calif.: Sage, 1967), 253, 255.

black viewpoint. Again, though, low registration weakened this group's power.

TAX SIZE, TURNOUT,
AND REFERENDA SUCCESS

To this point we have examined elements ostensibly independent of the referendum that may affect its successful passage. Yet it could be argued that success is a function of some quality in the referendum itself, such as the size of the tax bite or the size of the voter turnout. Tax size is central to the referendum proposition. Turnout, however, may be affected by mediating factors, such as the community climate of opinion created by prior matters, as well as by the size of the tax that affects the current opinion structure. The tax-size factor to our knowledge has not been investigated.

We conceive of that tax as an output, designed by political authorities as an adjustment to needs arising from the school environment and to demands arising from the social environment. Yet not all outputs are well conceived; authorities make mistakes about the absence or presence of needs and demands, about the willingness of the community to support them, and in general about the compatibility of the output to stress-generated inputs. One area for error is misjudgment of the public's tax tolerance. A board's decision on the tax it believes will be approved involves its estimate of the tolerance of its constituency. At one end of the board's options is a tax of such size that all know it will fail, but it is still sought because needs are judged to be so great; at the other end is the option of reducing taxes. Between these, other options exist — seek only the existing tax, seek a slightly larger tax, etc.

The obvious hypotheses are that the higher the tax increase sought, the more regularly will it be defeated (higher taxes hurt more than lower taxes) and the corollary that the decisions to reduce or maintain taxes at the same level are more likely of acceptance than increases (the former minimize stress). Is it true, then, that the more one plucks the golden goose the louder the squawk will be? Table 6.6 provides data for the proposition which we draw from three recent years of California tax elections. The data are bound by time and place, of course, but they suggest how the query can be pursued.

If the options are to lower, maintain, or increase school taxes, it is certainly clear from these data that seeking the same tax rate is most successful, even more than seeking a reduction. It seems as if change of any kind is more opposed than the *status quo*. Moreover, increases have only about half the chance of succeeding as the other options, and the larger the increase sought the lesser the chance of passage — but with some interesting exceptions.

We do not wish to make too much out of limited data in a single — and

*Table 6.6   Tax Increase Size and Success
in California, School Districts, 1966–70*

Tax size	1966–67		1967–68		1969–70	
	N	Won	N	Won	N	Won
Lower	2	50%	4	100%	3	67%
Same	26	96	25	96	28	100
Increase						
1–20 ¢	17	47	17	53	8	12
21–40	60	42	28	68	48	54
41–60	64	48	21	57	59	41
61–80	21	33	14	64	42	31
Over 81	19	21	13	46	73	34
Subtotal	181	42	93	59	230	40
Total	209	48	122	68	261	47

Source: Calculated from data provided in California Department of Education, "Tax Rate Increase Elections," annual reports (Sacramento: Bureau of School Apportionment and Reports).

singular — state, but Californians had a quite high tolerance of how much increase they would endure. In 1966–67, when about half of all measures passed, increases in the wide range of 1¢ to 60¢ had about the same chance of passing; thereafter stiff resistance set in. In the more supportive year of 1967–68, when two of every three referenda passed, chances of success actually *increased* as the tax size increased, and the range of support was broader, 1¢ to 80¢. Not the least important finding here is that study must not focus upon single years; we have seen, in both Tables 6.4 and 6.5, great variation from one year to the next. In sum, for California and these years the range of options on tax size was matched grossly with a range of likely outcomes, although for the option to increase taxes these publics seemed highly elastic in their responses to demands of their schoolmen.

This is not the only matter in which elasticity exists. The rate of turnout affects the success of such measures, as Carter reported for the period 1948–58. As we see in Table 6.7, the negative relationship between turn-out and success continued to exist over a decade later, at least in California. This variation exists not merely in one state in one year, but across years, although not all districts are voting in all three years. But in all three years, the proportion of success for each turnout rate declines smartly, except for the districts with greatest turnout. Further analysis would probably re-veal these last as the districts where, as Carter noted, high affluence and participation join to provide upper-middle-class attitudes more supportive of schools than those found in the middle class.

Yet we must not perceive most of these as hotly contested affairs. The truth is that most state bond referenda have secured a sizable majority of votes in the last two decades for which data exist, as we shall show in the next chapter. Such elections even in the twelve states requiring an extraor-dinary majority for passage were very successful; except for 1968–69, well over one-half of the referenda won every year, and two-thirds won over all the years. For eight years in the twelve states with high majority requirements, there were ninety-three sets of elections. In only thirteen sets did a state fail to pass over one-half of its referenda for that year, and in

Table 6.7 District Turnout and
Tax Referenda Success, California, 1966–70

Percent turnout	1966–67		1967–68		1969–70	
	N	*Win*	*N*	*Win*	*N*	*Win*
0–19.9	26	62%	8	87%	13	69%
20–39.9	71	58	53	70	91	42
40–59.9	67	45	30	73	113	50
60–79.9	26	38	25	52	41	46
80 and over	9	44	6	67	1	100

Source: See Table 6.6.

four of these a vote of over 50 percent — but still less than the extraordinary majority — was secured.[19] In the decade for 1948–59, Carter and Sutthoff found in 1054 local school districts an even higher support both in bond and tax elections — 85 percent.[20]

We stop to emphasize these data because of their importance for understanding the school's conversion process. When, seeking financial resources, schoolmen find support high or consistent, then this referendum is not a substitute for or a bypass of the school's political authorities. Instead, it then becomes a process for the public to ratify policy. If so, it has value not only for the authorities but also for the citizens, who obtain a sense of participating in their destiny as the democratic credo provides. For policy makers, it is a legitimating instrument for their own decisions.

Two considerations preclude our designating this use of the referendum as mere obeisance to the prevailing myth, a ritual like the Greeks pouring wine on the ground before eating. First, to a degree that needs fuller substantiation than the literature provides, these authorities may restrain or shape what they do in recognition of limits that they know their public will not permit crossing. The "law of anticipated reactions" has been a higher ground of retreat for those who, disillusioned to find little democratic input to policy making, still wanted to perceive democratic controls upon political authority. We raise it here, not as a normative defense but as a hypothesis. It may explain conditions under which the referendum is not merely a ratification but an agreement among citizens that the authorities have correctly perceived what they want.

After all, the literature of educational administration is filled with advice to leaders to establish "community relations" with elaborate "lines of communication" into and "citizen participation" in schools. This suggests that the successful administrator comes to know what his constituency wants and guides himself by their expectations.[21] But the question is: how often and for how many political authorities in our schools is this the case? Certainly it is one model of interaction between policy makers and the environment, but its incidence is unknown as the subject has been studied very little. If this model is real, the referendum is then something more than a gesture.

Another consideration that makes this hypothesis possible is that referenda are sometimes lost. In a later chapter we will show that in some states like West Virginia this occurred regularly, and in all states with increasing frequency as the 1960's ended. That reality must cause schoolmen to trim their policies to these adverse winds. In these cases, and again the research is limited, the referendum is not a mere ritual but a stentorian command. How it is understood may well vary, though, as some schoolmen may choose to ignore it and cast it up again for another vote. Or programs may be slashed severely — schools may even be closed — to fit the available monies, as schoolmen hope that reaction against such cuts will mobilize voter support the next time. Yet other authorities may deem the setback as final, and reshape services and staff to accord to the demand perceived here. Implicit in these different strategies are alternative models of role behavior. Board members and administrators adopt these out of their personalities and values, i.e., from orientations drawn less from the community than from officials' life-styles.[22]

Whether the referendum is effective because of officials' expectations or election threats, a special insight may be had into this device's operations in closely contested elections. Marginal contests reflect high cleavage, that stressful environment which, in Easton's concepts, the political system works to avoid or adjust to. One measure of the scope of stress is the frequency of closely contested elections, those where the final results are in the 45–55 percent range. The distribution of the proportion voting for school taxes, among districts or among states, is also a rough gauge of that condition.

We explore this condition in Table 6.8, where the California cleavage is displayed for recent years. This shows that only about one-quarter of these tax elections (where only a simple majority is needed for passage) were marked by cleavage, regardless of whether it is a year in which many or few referenda won. Most elections were in the range of very high support (41 percent of the referenda received over 54 percent of the vote) or of very low support (33 percent received under 45 percent of the vote). Almost 3 in 4 of these elections, then, were in these extreme ranges identified with low community cleavage. Of course, the patterns for other states or this state in other times are not inferable from these data; we merely suggest the utility of the marginal contest as a stress indicator.

LOCAL CONVERSION, STRESS, AND THEORY

This reference to high stress returns us to the considerations that began this section. We had conceptualized the referendum in alternative models of

Table 6.8 Distribution of Yes Vote
in California School Tax Referenda, 1966–70

Percentage of yes votes	1966–67		1967–68		1969–70	
	N	%	N	%	N	%
Below 34	35	17	8	7	30	11
35–44	41	20	22	18	62	24
45–54	59	28	29	24	86	33
55–64	34	16	29	24	41	16
65 and over	40	19	34	28	42	16

Source: See Table 6.6.

school politics. Was it a local conversion mechanism for citizens directly to control the conversion processes within the school system? Or, on the other hand, was it a device for schoolmen to reach directly into the environment for support of their decisions? We have noted the enmeshment of this device with community conflict in analyzing voter turnout and referenda results. If the reduction or elimination of environmental stress is a driving force for most political authorities, they should use referenda only when certain that it will reduce and not increase the stress upon them. In short, if this conceptualization is correct, most referenda should succeed because schoolmen would call for them only when and in the form that could guarantee victory. As we have seen, that is exactly what does occur, judging by the record of the last several decades.

Because schools cannot escape the matrix of local conflict, schoolmen learn how to work with it so as to reduce its impact. What Minar has termed schoolmen's "conflict-management skills" then come into play in reducing stress. These skills operate more often in high-status communities that characteristically have low dissent and give superintendents much discretion.[23] Also involved in stress reduction are the adequacy of judgments about public tolerance of school decisions. Much conflict can be reduced also if citizens agree that the subject matter is "professional" and not "political."

As we have see here and before, whether because of skilled conflict management, wise anticipation of reactions, or convincing definitions of public policy, school authorities have successfully kept disruptive public inputs to their system at a minimum. Escalating conflict threatens schoolmen's control and the system's persistence. Consequently, low-key community relations prevail, the decisional forum withdraws somewhere into the crevices of the professionals' world, supporters both inside and outside the system are maintained and reinforced, and so on. This picture of limited citizen control over schools is broken, despite the schoolmen's rhetoric, only occasionally by episodic events. But even these do not often go directly to major policy, focusing as they do on peripheral and quite specific issues.

In this description one sees much of both systems analysis and democratic theory in operation. As Minar concluded from his study of many suburban districts, "There is reason to believe that the reduction of public conflict is something of an ideal toward which school systems tend." [24] In this, if true, we see signs of system persistence, of coping with threatened stress by shaping the required referenda inputs and of forestalling eruptive demands. All this is done in an effort to anticipate community demands. The result is an output reflective of both public and professional needs and wants.

In this too we see the conflict of majoritarian and minoritarian values raised in an earlier chapter. The rhetoric of majority rule is strong in our school districts, but the reality is minority decision making, which is regularly confirmed by referenda in all but a few communities. Much of this condition arises from the predominant influence of the school professionals, who move the system toward goals which they — and not often the community — define. Board members' ties to the community are tenuous and ambiguous, while their control over the bureaucracy is limited and general. At best, they are adjudicators at the margins of school policy. When groups not satisfied with this minority control seek changes through the prescribed channels, they often find the professionals' control unassailable. It is these conditions of system maintenance that students, ethnic members, parents, and teachers are currently attacking.[25]

Yet some change by schoolmen is likely in the face of this challenge; dissenters are presently finding some "give" in the structure. But it is highly unlikely that professional control will be altered in the end. One suspects that the result will be concessions affecting few people on a few issues. But the real, continuing authority to allocate school resources at the local level will remain where it has been since Americans entered into a covenant with professional schoolmen that educational policy was not like other policies. Already there are signs of teacher unions shaping themselves to the system by rejecting claims for more jobs arising from ethnic minorities. The causes for system maintenance are many, of course, but not least among them is the fact that it is schoolmen who oversee the administration of policy — even if they do not always shape its origins — and hence can influence the kind of outcome desired.

Such is the nature of a conversion process at the local level that we shall see again as we turn to state and national levels. For the tension between majority and minority infuses all elements of the American political system.

7 The State Conversion Process

Although popular folklore conceives of schools as locally controlled, the state has taken a hand in them for many decades. Indeed, by 1970 as we have seen, it is highly questionable how much local control is a reality. But the components of that political authority termed the *state* need further specification. For such authority is partly formal, a matter of state constitutional requirements and state officers, and partly informal, a matter of pressure groups and current values. Given the variety of American federalism discussed earlier and its accompanying individualism, there should be differences in these political authorities and hence in these conversion processes. It may be that such diverse political cultures can operate to fend off the nationalizing trends noted earlier. In that case, the values of a diverse localism, deposited from our past, still give some reality to the notion of local control.

GROWTH OF THE STATE ROLE IN LOCAL SCHOOLS [1]

Most state constitutions make local education a legal responsibility of the state. The United States Constitution is silent with regard to education; consequently, education is a reserved power of the states. These three levels of educational government interact on policies, but only state statutes stipulate in detail how schools are to be governed. In effect, although much control is delegated to district boards, the states vary considerably in the independence of those boards from the state.

The contemporary arrangement differs sharply from that existing at the nation's opening, for there was no state school administration then. Early school laws of the American colonies stemmed from the state legislature

111

and other organs of general government making education policy directly. Schools were small, with unspecialized curricula, and the state role was to "protect and encourage" schools rather than financially support them. Thus there were no state boards of education or chief state school officers. By 1820, however, thirteen of the twenty states had developed constitutional provisions for education. The position of chief state school officer (CSSO) had emerged in some states in 1836, and by 1870 most states provided for them; state boards of education appeared about the same time. A number of the early CSSO's played a crucial role in leading public opinion to support public education.

From these early beginnings, state involvement in local schools has expanded both in programs and personnel. Over time, several important decisions have come to be made at the state level. Most states *define the program scope,* such as kindergarten, vocational education, or junior college.[2] The legislature usually delegates to the state board of education the prerogative to *set minimum standards* for curriculum, pupil promotion and graduation, and even instructional materials. Some state boards *adopt a standard course of study* or detailed guidelines for subject areas such as civics or math. Southern states in particular *adopt textbooks* that are distributed to all public schools. State regulations and statutes are even more detailed with respect to requirements for *certification of teachers.* Most states stipulate the length of the training program, define some specifics on its content, and accredit training institutions.

The most visible state political issue has been financial support for education. Some states set tax limits for local districts and require certain local budget breakdowns. A state property equalization board can be a crucial factor in providing for adjustments in local property assessment practices.[3] In all of these areas, however, policies among states vary enormously. Table 7.1, showing the state proportion of total school expenditures, reflects this diversity, with a range from 8.5 percent in New Hampshire to 87.0 percent in Hawaii.

Generally speaking, the state role has focused on establishing minimum standards in education while encouraging local districts to exceed them. This role stems from one aspect of American egalitarianism, the belief that the general welfare requires a floor for educational opportunity.[4] State employees must inspect local districts to ensure that this floor is provided through certain courses, minimum school attendance or minimum tax levies. To encourage local initiative, most states provide tax leeway for local districts that want to exceed state minimums, e.g., matching incentive payments for districts whose tax rate exceeds the state minimum.

This state role arises from another consideration, the pull of localism. The evolution of state influence on and financial support for local schools has been replete with philosophical and practical political struggles between

Table 7.1   Governmental Contributions to School Revenue, 1969–70

	Public elementary and secondary school revenue receipts, 1969–70					
	Per pupil in ADA		*Percent by source*			
			State			
State	*Amount*	*Rank*	*Percent*	*Rank*	*Local*	*Federal*
United States	$ 907	–	40.8	–	52.5	6.7
North Atlantic						
Connecticut	1068	6	33.1	35	63.2	3.7
Delaware	1026	8	70.6	3	21.8	7.6
Maine	792	29	44.9	22	49.8	5.4
Maryland	1055	7	35.2	29	58.4	6.4
Massachusetts	960	15	20.0	47	74.0	6.0
New Hampshire	785	30	8.5	50	87.2	4.2
New Jersey	1113	3	28.5	41	67.2	4.3
New York	1430	1	45.4	20	51.1	3.5
Pennsylvania	1020	10	46.9	17	47.3	5.8
Rhode Island	919	16	34.5	32	57.5	8.1
Vermont	759	33	28.6	40	68.1	3.3
Great Lakes and Plains						
Illinois	1109	4	34.4	34	60.5	5.0
Indiana	896	19	34.9	31	61.0	4.1
Iowa	892	21	30.1	38	65.9	4.0
Kansas	965	13	27.1	43	65.5	7.4
Michigan	859	24	45.1	21	51.0	3.9
Minnesota	962	14	43.4	24	51.2	5.4
Missouri	817	28	34.5	32	59.2	6.3
Nebraska	672	42	20.0	47	73.6	6.4
North Dakota	744	35	27.2	42	65.8	7.1
Ohio	783	31	31.6	36	63.7	4.7
South Dakota	678	41	13.6	49	75.1	11.3
Wisconsin	992	12	29.4	39	67.4	3.2
Southeast						
Alabama	524	50	63.0	4	22.5	14.5
Arkansas	592	48	45.5	19	37.5	17.1
Florida	821	26	56.5	10	34.4	9.1
Georgia	625	46	58.7	8	30.7	10.6
Kentucky	693	39	52.6	11	33.6	13.8
Louisiana	701	38	58.3	9	30.9	10.8
Mississippi	582	49	51.6	12	26.4	22.0
North Carolina	726	37	70.9	2	18.2	10.8
South Carolina	657	43	61.6	6	25.1	13.3
Tennessee	620	47	49.3	14	40.4	10.4
Virginia	821	26	36.6	28	54.3	9.1
West Virginia	737	36	48.2	15	39.4	12.4
West and Southwest						
Alaska	1199	2	43.7	23	30.6	25.7
Arizona	893	20	47.5	16	43.7	8.7
California	1023	9	35.0	30	59.8	5.2
Colorado	837	25	25.3	45	68.3	6.4
Hawaii	1019	11	87.0	1	3.9	9 1
Idaho	691	40	43.2	25	49.1	7.7
Montana	897	18	30.9	37	63.2	5.8
Nevada	898	17	39.2	27	54.8	6.0
New Mexico	771	32	62.7	5	23.3	14.0
Oklahoma	626	45	40.8	26	49.2	10.0
Oregon	1078	5	20.6	46	73.5	5.8
Texas	636	44	46.9	17	42.0	11.2
Utah	757	34	51.4	13	43.0	5.5
Washington	879	23	58.8	7	35.3	5.9
Wyoming	887	22	25.4	44	52.3	22.3

Source: National Education Association, *Estimates of School Statistics, 1969–70* and *Rankings of the States, 1970* (Washington, D.C.: NEA), research reports 1969-R15 and 1970-R1.

state and local jurisdictions. The constitutional power of state government has been in constant tension with a widely held value that the soundest educational policy is determined locally. "Local control" has become a powerful and pervasive political shibboleth, in many states restricting the financial and leadership support of state agencies. A study of the Northeast concluded that "the most pervasive and persistent of depressants on state school subsidies is rural localism." [5] We shall return to this issue subsequently but move now to a fuller review of state school political authorities.

THE AUTHORITATIVE STATE POLITICAL SYSTEM

Governors and Legislators

One area of historic controversy has been whether educational policy should be in the effective control of the governor, a separate board or boards, the legislature, a commissioner, or a combination of these. Almost every state has had its peculiar battles about this question. However, the legacy of "no politics in education" has helped to shape the outcome of this question, often ending in restricting the influence of elected officials such as the governor and legislature.

For instance, when in 1784 the New York State Board of Regents was established to formulate educational policies for the state, the governor was very powerful. Key politicians, however, had a central role in appointing and managing the board, often composed of legislators and big city mayors. After only three years, however, a new act reduced the control of these leaders, and the regents became a fourth branch of government — independent of governor, legislature, and even court. Bailey and his associates concluded:

> What is true of the New York State Board of Regents is true to a lesser degree of the other state boards of education in the Northeast. Although in the other seven states, appointment to the boards is made by the governor (often with legislative consent) rather than by the legislature alone, the effective independence of the boards from direct political pressure and from the political rhythms of gubernatorial and legislative elections is a long standing tradition.[6]

Any proposals to reduce this political independence in New England has brought resistance from professional schoolmen, because it would "inevitably plunge educational leadership and the schools into a maelstrom of partisan politics to the detriment of all concerned." [7]

The governors and the legislatures, however, maintain control of state financial-aid legislation. Issues of educational finance inevitably involve judgments on educational programs and priorities, so the constitutional separation of education from general state government can never extend to many important educational issues. Indeed, in most if not all states, public education is the largest single state budget item, and politicians, of course, know that the electorate responds to tax increases. Money is obviously a basic resource, and the amounts available for education are so large as to attract considerable political attention. As close analysts of governmental costs have noted:

> More public funds are expended for education [1964] than for any other domestic service of government, and this has been true consistently throughout this century and probably for a considerable time before that. In fact, until World War II, the peacetime costs of education substantially exceeded those for national defense.[8]

The weight of such monies gives much power to those who dispose it, and in the states these are the governor and legislature. Any governor is a hard man to fight when he wants to hold the line on state finance. Appropriation committees in the legislature are also watchdogs for the state treasury, ranking at the top of all committees in seniority, prestige, and power. In any given year, however, tight budget constraints are rarely aimed at education alone but extend across all state government functions.[9]

Enormous differences exist among states in the scope of gubernatorial and legislative concern with and expertise in education. Thus, in California, the legislature, which has a large, full-time staff for its education committee, between 1961 and 1967 passed bills in such areas as licensing of teachers, school redistricting, the measurement of student achievement, and teaching of reading and foreign languages. Elsewhere, state legislators are part-timers, paid less than $5,000, and with no staff that has expertise in education policy. In some of these states, education legislation is confined to desegregration and routine financial aid. But in Texas, where education finance revision is the major state issue, 40 percent of the members of the House are serving their first term, obviously inexperienced in this issue's complexity. Such variations should not conceal some similarities among the states, however. Everywhere financial problems dominate legislators' perception of education, and everywhere the gap between demands and resources is hard to close.[10]

The evidence we now have suggests that state legislators find education not to be an issue that provides much political leverage or attracts many votes. For example, a study of three midwest states concluded, "Relatively few public school proposals entertained in the legislative halls of the three states studied result from general public pressures or from wave-like 'public' protests."[11] Legislators and governors may feel they should respond to and support regularly the professional education lobby, but they have not been forced by widespread citizen demands to develop a continuing insight into educational issues or to mount a consistent educational crusade. As we noted earlier, education interest groups have attempted to mute competition between their professional organizations and other competing interests for state dollars, thereby reducing the conflict level and the pressures over school funding.

The role of the governor in education has been restricted by the lack of expert staff in his office with a viewpoint independent from the state department of education. In some states the CSSO is a member of the governor's cabinet; in others he is a separately elected official. Some governors have no education specialist at all, and others operate with only a one- or two-man personal staff.[12] Experience in several states indicates a leadership role in education by one governor which is then not continued by his successor. In effect, some governors have wanted to establish their statewide reputation through leadership in public education, but their effectiveness (or lack of it) has caused the successor of either party to attempt leadership in another field in order to build a separate record and political image.

State Boards of Education

The state board is primarily a legitimating agency for broad policies; it leaves administration to the state superintendent and state department. Again, we find tremendous differences among states. Some boards are elected, some appointed by the governor, and some are constituted *ex officio*. Their size ranges from three members to over twenty; some meet weekly and others quarterly. Again, the variety seen here reflects the mosaic of American federalism with its underlying individualistic notions of how to govern.

But regardless of how they are selected, Sroufe has shown that state board members comprise a singularly homogeneous population of professionals earning high incomes.[13] Forty-five percent have served on local boards, and three-fourths have lived in no more than two states. There appear to be two streams of activity that might lead someone of high education and status to become a state board member. One path is increasingly responsible experience at the local level, then moving on to some state study groups or special commissions, and finally elevation to the state board. The less common route is to gain eminence within a non-educational sector and then be "tapped" for the board. Sroufe found that at the time of selection, state board members do not seem to have highly specific educational goals or to be concerned about certain educational issues. Indeed, over half the appointed board members reported that they first considered the work of the board only when the governor asked them to accept.[14] The influence of political party elements in securing appointment is considerable, despite the nonpartisan myth surrounding much of education. Table

7.2 reveals this when it presents the views of state school board members about the persons considered most influential in nominating candidates to the state board.

As for the alternative selection method, elections, these can be accurately described as non-events; about half of the elected respondents to a recent survey did not campaign at all. The typical candidate issues just one press release, so that public awareness and interest are minimal. The winner receives no pay, little publicity, and, not unsurprisingly, the position is rarely a political stepping stone. In short, elected members do not differ from appointed members, because, unlike most other statewide political contests, this election process is of low intensity.

This leads to Sroufe's speculation that the "reason board members are so much alike is that no one expects the board to be very influential in the formulation or implementation of state educational policy." [15] In fact, we know very little about the policy role of the state board, although it is clear that the electorate finds it exceedingly difficult to make substantive choices for membership to an unknown board. Popular disinterest is shown in the gap in total votes between this and other state offices in most elections. This would suggest that public demands for change in educational policies are probably transmitted more to elected political leaders and the state department of education rather than to the less-visible state board.

Functionally, the state board acts both as an implementing arm of the legislature and as a legislature in its own right. Indeed, its work covers the three traditional governing functions of legislating, administering, and adjudicating. Much of this arises because the discretion provided by the legislature is often quite wide. [16] For example, the legislature may set general requirements for administrative credentials but permit the state board

Table 7.2   The Influentials in Nominating Candidates to the State Board of Education

Influentials	Percentage of respondents assigning first rank
Political party member, outside the legislature	30
Members of the legislature	19
Current board members	16
Chief state school officer	12
State education association	11
Governor's aids and advisors	3
Other school groups	2
Other (variety of noncombinable categories)	7

Source: Gerald E. Sroufe, "Recruitment Processes and Composition of State Boards of Education," paper presented at 1969 meeting of the American Educational Research Association.

to specify courses, experiences, and other requirements. Other customary functions of the state board are to act as court of appeals in disputes, define racial imbalance, create statewide testing, direct preparation of statewide syllabuses or courses, and oversee consolidation. Despite such authority, Koerner has concluded that the state board's potentially vast influence is used in only the most general way. "Either it allows the state department of education to make policies . . . or it yields a great deal of its power to local school authorities. Southern state boards are apt to be more domineering than northern, but all are permissive." [17]

The board's problem is that localism makes enforcement of its policies very difficult. Local districts can find ways to circumvent the state because the board usually has no clear enforcement strategies. Further, state boards have little time or inclination to check carefully on local compliance but must rely for staff work on the state superintendent and his staff. Recommendations, analyses, and outlining of alternatives are the responsibility of the state department civil servants and the CSSO. State boards rarely have their own independent staffs but rather view the entire state department as a resource to draw upon.[18]

State Departments of Education

A reading of state constitutions and statutes would lead one to believe that the legislature and state board of education are the sole sources for the authoritative allocation of values. The state department of education (SDE) is usually described as the executive or implementing arm of the policy-making state board. Traditionally, the SDE has close ties with the professional statewide associations of teachers, administrators, curriculum specialists, etc., who provide demands and supports for its decisions and recommendations to the board. In fact, as we have seen, the SDE actually has broad areas of policy making delegated to it by the state board, which then exercises minimal administrative oversight. Moreover, the state board relies on the SDE to prepare its agenda and provide recommendations.

In effect, then, this state agency is the locus of a considerable amount of authoritative allocation of values, whether in formulating specific regulations, allocating federal funds to local districts, or executing the more detailed decisions of the state board. The administration and interpretation of the general and flexible mandates of the state board have a differential impact. Consequently, because the values and actions of the SDE enhance the benefits of some groups and individuals rather than others, we need to explore its impact and orientation.[19]

How much influence the CSSO has depends on several factors — primarily the strength and activism of the legislature, governor, and state board.[20] Some state superintendents have dominated weak boards. Others have been limited severely by a strong legislature. Most superintendents find themselves somewhat constrained by the board and the legislature but

have been able to exert a substantial, independent influence over state policy. Consequently, the CSSO and the staff of the SDE, through detailed
regulations, actually write the final version of policies passed by the legislature and state board. The SDE's are less constrained by the state board
and the legislature in the allocation of federal money funneled through the
state. As we shall see, this federal money has given SDE's a greatly enhanced role in determining the content of local education programs and
the priorities of intrastate financial allocation.[21]

The CSSO is almost always a member in good standing of the professional education fraternity. The pay and prestige of the office are low —
lower than most big city superintendencies. His low pay depresses the
salary range for his administrative officers and hinders recruitment of able
and aggressive people. Despite these limits, SDE personnel have high
responsibility and authority as the executive arm of the state board. Consequently, they are involved in such activities as teacher credentialing,
technical assistance in subject areas, operation of agencies for handicapped
children, and distribution of large amounts of state and federal aid.
Conant's comment in 1964 about the political orientation of SDE's appears
still true today.

> The major weakness of all state departments of education I have en-
> countered, with perhaps one or two exceptions, is that they are too
> much a part of the educational establishment. That is, I found many
> of these agencies . . . to be no more than "willing tools" of the inter-
> ests and clientele, particularly the education association (that is, the
> state NEA affiliate). In more than one state I heard highly placed edu-
> cation and political officials claim that state departments of education
> "follow a party line" or reflect the public school mentality. . . . A
> grave shortcoming of our educational leadership at the state level, in
> my opinion, is often its unwillingness or incapacity to respond to forces
> outside the establishment. These agencies seldom solicit the opinions
> of educational experts or critics who are not associated with public
> schools or professional education, and in those rare instances when
> they do ask the advice of "outside experts," I suspect it is largely for
> symbolic purposes. Too often, educational leadership at the state level
> — official and unofficial — has been open to the charge that it was
> unwilling to examine public school needs critically.[22]

In fact, because there have been no comprehensive studies of the
political role of the SDE's and CCSO's or of their impact on local educational agencies,[23] it is not possible to verify Conant's observation. But the
evidence is more than suggestive that he was correct. We know that in the
past many CSSO's derived the bulk of their political support from key
local superintendents, and probably owed their appointment or nomination
for election to them as well as to leading professors of educational administration. Bowles's evidence suggests that the CSSO emerges not as a top

influential but as a unity candidate who supports rather than initiates policy.[24] As teacher and administrator groups have begun to compete, however, this monolithic structure has been breaking up. We simply do not know how CSSO's are chosen or nominated now. It appears that fewer governors and politicians are willing to listen to the advice of the professional education organizations, but their influence in selection of the CSSO is an open question.

Undoubtedly, the main movement for SDE's is toward more control and influence over local districts. For many years this state agency responded to its constituency of professional education interest groups and of malapportioned state legislatures, both favoring rural areas. The increasing role of state and federal aid, however, is bringing more attention to the cities and hence to an increased SDE role throughout the state.

The federal influence on the growth and reorientation of the SDE has been dramatic since 1965. Title V of the Elementary and Secondary Education Act of 1965 provided support for increasing the state professional staff, usually doubling it, as we see in Table 7.3. Three-fourths of the present staffs of all states have been in their jobs less than three years.[25] While Title V could be used flexibly for non-federal program services, other titles included a federal allocation for state administrative functions. The result in one large state department was that 16 of its 26 departments were devoting all or part of their attention to federally related programs, and 64 of the 135 professional personnel were involved in federal projects.[26]

In short, the new national legislation has made SDE's even more dependent upon federal funds. These officials lament the expanding federal role in their affairs but in most cases cannot get money from the state legislature

*Table 7.3   Impact on State Educational Staff Size
from Federal Funds, 1962 and 1968*

	Professional positions	
State	*1962*	*1968*
Alabama	43	140
Minnesota	100	154
New Jersey	69	197
New York	277	557
Rhode Island	35	61
South Dakota	19	58
Texas	173	300
Utah	38	77
Vermont	29	73

Source: Advisory Council on State Departments of Education, *The State of State Departments of Education* (Washington, D.C.: Government Printing Office, 1969), 15–32.

and governor to expand their staffs. One long-time observer of SDE summarized the current situation this way.

> Most . . . , instead of interacting with federal agencies and even with local school districts as equals in a major enterprise, appear to be simply responding to forces about them. [SDE's] engage chiefly in regulatory activities as required by their respective state legislatures. Responses to the federal legislation have been of the same general nature; when functions are imposed by Title I and Title II of the ESEA and the Vocational Act, they are more or less willingly assumed. More and more the agendas of most [SDE's] are being set by the federal government.[27]

One counterthrust has been the formation of the Education Commission of the States to improve their coordinated action and studies.[28] The commission, presently representing forty-two states, administers the National Assessment of Education program. The initial hope was that a group of states could exert more influence in federal relations by presenting united views on policy issues. But although the compact has become more of a forum for discussing common problems, it has failed to develop a mandate to lobby in Washington in order to transmit specific demands to federal leaders.

Reviewing the impact of these recent changes, it is appropriate to ask whether SDE's have now become merely extensions of the federal government. We note in response that the value orientation of representatives of different levels of the federal system are frequently not the same.[29] This is especially important because administration of federal grants by the states requires program judgments by state officers. For example, what types of vocational or compensatory programs should have preference? Which local districts are most in need of funds? By contrast, the bulk of the state-provided aid is distributed automatically through a legislative formula based on such factors as average daily attendance, assessed value per pupil, and local tax effort. The SDE's function is merely to compute the formula and send money to local districts, unlike its role in federal funds where it has more flexibility. Although new program discretions are given with federal funds, Table 7.3 suggests also the growth in SDE resources provided by Washington. This interaction is important enough, however, that in a later chapter we will focus on the politics of intergovernmental relations and consider in detail the implications for federalism of the issues discussed above.

STATE SUBSYSTEMS

The conversion systems that allocate educational resources at the state level do not operate independently of their environment. Much like their local counterparts, these political authorities are the object of demands for particular allocations of state resources that give priority to certain values. These demands are transferred from society to the political system by education interest groups and by citizen participation in elections and referenda. We turn, then, to considering how such demands are mobilized, aggregated, and articulated.

Interest Groups

Since board members have few strong views on specific policies and SDE's have traditionally responded to rather than exercised leadership, the impact of interest groups has been substantial. They have not only been the principal advocates for increased state aid, but have provided support for preserving what they deem to be professional considerations in such regulatory areas as curriculum and certification.

The most important single interest group has been the state teachers association — the National Education Association affiliate. Although it has grown rapidly in big cities, the American Federation of Teachers has not concentrated its lobbying or organizational efforts at the state level. As in other areas of state politics, the state NEA affiliates differ considerably in the amount of political pressure they can exert. The Texas State Teachers Association, for example, is strong enough to commit state legislators to its salary proposals during the campaigns or primary elections; it has been notably successful in overriding the Texas governor's budget recommendations. On the other hand, the California Teachers Association has been unable to commit a majority of the state legislature to its school finance proposals.

The importance of teacher groups for generating demands in the political system was substantiated by a study of three large-membership state affiliates in the Midwest.

> The groups and individuals who articulate the policy proposals, the innovators, so to speak, are those who have a direct and tangible stake in the outcome of the decisions. . . . [I]n each of the states we surveyed the major group was the state affiliate of the National Education Association. . . . These groups have a relatively high degree of organization, a principal spokesman, a wealth of information about school needs, and generally favorable access to at least some points in the formal decision-making structure.[30]

All three of these groups presented information about school needs by stressing the "objectivity" and expertness of their educational analyses. They avoided identifying, allying, or competing with groups not directly concerned with education. In short, the image was of professionals "above politics," expert and objective. Anything beyond persuasion through testimony was regarded as "desperate" or "critical"; avoiding these labels

hopefully separated the teachers from charges that their views were politically inspired. At such "critical" times, however, the capitol could be
flooded with telegrams and letters from school professionals supporting the
NEA views.[31]

This does not mean, however, that the demands of teachers associations
are always, or in some states frequently, converted into policy outputs. In
large part the result has depended on the cohesion and competition of the
various education lobbies, as we shall shortly see. In some states, moreover,
the NEA affiliate lacks aggressive leadership, is hobbled by poor relations
with the governor's office (where the budget is formulated), and competes
with a large, city-based AFT. Further, the power of teachers is not always
credible. Some politicians suspect that much of the membership belongs to
NEA only because belonging to it is a professional norm, and that the
leadership cannot mobilize the teachers to vote against politicians who do
not follow the teachers' advice.[32]

Teachers are not the only statewide education interest groups. There
often exists an affiliate for school administrators that has divorced itself
from the NEA teacher affiliate. For instance, the Michigan Association of
School Administrators (MASA) represents 96 percent of the city superintendents and assistant superintendents. It retains a formal affiliation with
NEA, but its viewpoint is usually somewhat different.[33] The administrators
association's influence lies in the nature of its membership — school superintendents are highly respected members of their communities with an
image as local experts on education. Consequently, they enjoy easier access to state legislators than do teachers. In Michigan, the NEA is regarded
by the legislature more as a teacher-welfare bargaining agent. MASA
officials use the tactic of making sure that the contact with legislatures is
locally initiated, related only to the specific local tax situation, and is not a
statewide lobbying effort. Again, the objective is to have the membership
be seen as educators, not politicians. This orientation leads, however, to a
lack of political sophistication and interest by the members, as substantiated by the executive secretary's belief that his biggest problem was "getting our boys interested." [34]

Another politically active organization in some states is the affiliate of
the National School Boards Association. The national office is hindered
in its political activities by the conflicting interests of 19,300 heterogeneous local school boards. Probably 90 percent of the local school board
members in any state, however, belong to the state affiliate. As more of the
governing authority has shifted to the state, board members have organized
in order to gain access to the new points of decision. State school board
associations, unlike their professional education counterparts, do not maintain large staffs or generate policy proposals. Rather, they act as watchdogs
over public school legislation introduced by others and then provide support or opposition. School board associations view themselves as not being

on the public payroll and consequently as acting in the best interests of education. Since school boards represent both the schools and the taxpayers, the associations contend they should represent schools at the state capitol instead of public school employees. In some states, such as Michigan, this orientation has led to rivalry between the two types of interest groups. For example, as teacher groups stress salary increases in state budgets, school board associations may hold out for a broader focus.[35]

Another potential lay interest group is the state affiliate of the National Congress of Parents and Teachers. The PTA's size alone is a source of some strength because it includes hundreds of thousands of voters in large states. However, not having a natural degree of cohesion, it is a reluctant entrant, especially in partisan situations. The mass of PTA members are rarely stimulated to such militant action as letter writing and phone calls, but the association does use face-to-face contact between its leadership and the state legislators. In short, politicians find the PTA a useful friend but not a bothersome enemy.

None of the studies have found an organized, statewide, interest group with the primary objective of *opposing* increases in state aid for the schools. Bailey and his associates found in New England that the opposition consisted of business groups, representatives of rural localism, and conservative politicians and citizens concerned about any policy to increase state taxes substantially. State aid to education is usually such a large percentage of total state expenditures that any significant increase in education assistance will arouse opposition from some groups. But standing or *ad hoc* organizations do not function primarily for the purpose of holding down school costs to the state. To be against public education is not considered a viable or desirable political strategy. Rather, opposition is expressed in terms of the high, overall, state tax burden or the threat to local autonomy. Increasingly, we hear complaints that no one knows the output likely to result from increases in state aid to education. An increase in teachers' salaries through more state aid does not necessarily cause higher student achievement or better pupil attitudes. The opponents' arguments are expressed in terms of a skepticism that more money will result in their definition of "better education."

These interest groups, then, bear similarity to their counterparts at the local level seen in earlier chapters. The same educational demands expressing felt needs are there, and many of the same groups are speaking. What may be different, however, is the existence of more or less permanent coalitions of education interests. These merit a closer look.

Patterns in State Educational Politics

In most states at various points in history, the interest groups favoring state assistance have formed temporary coalitions and in some cases long standing alliances. These coalitions may develop into permanent organizations, may be *ad hoc,* one-time affairs, or may be the strategic devices of the SDE. The aim is to aggregate political resources so as to maximize influence for the same bill or issue. The strategy is usually to achieve consensus among the various interest groups outside of the maneuvering of the state legislature. In effect, the coalition modifies competing programs and compromises values so that a united demand is presented to the legislature and governor. In this way the coalitions are performing one of the functions of political parties.[36]

Who comprises these alliances? The core membership is usually the state's teachers and school boards associations, school administrator groups (including county superintendents and principals), and the state PTA. In some states, such as Colorado and Pennsylvania, these are the only members. In other states the base is broader, including business groups, the American Association of University Women, the American Legion, etc. Working in the background are often "educational academics" in universities, who help chart the goals, prepare detailed analytical information, and draft the legislation. There are also episodic actors (governors or key legislators), who join the coalition or alliance for some special issue but who are not primarily concerned with education. The SDE frequently provides support within the conversion process itself.

Under such a coalition the school boards no longer contend in public that the teachers' demands are exorbitant, nor do the teachers charge openly that the boards and administrators are budget-cutting managers. Value differences are submerged, as are the conflicting needs of different organizational constituencies. Opponents to increased school aid find it impossible to divide the "experts" and thereby help defeat them. One cannot help being impressed by the results of these coalitions in terms of the increased financial support they secure for everyone involved. New York and Illinois have even established separate organizations — the New York State Industrial Conference Board and the Illinois School Problems Commission — that speak for all the major education interest groups.

In effect, the monolithic coalition enhances the schoolman's image as a nonpartisan, objective expert advocating improved programs for the children of the state. The totality of the profession is seen as being in agreement on the needs of the children rather than as warring factions with each group out to enhance its special interest. The image presented to the legislature is consistent with the "above politics" image that schoolmen found so effective at the local level. The locus of political compromise and accommodation occurs outside the legislature in the coalition itself.[37] The agreed-upon bills are then introduced by sympathetic legislators.

So far, we have reviewed political studies of only eleven states — and only four of these had such monolithic coalitions. Another pattern emerges in the New England states, which are dominated by a strong tradition of localism. The participants in the political process represent their school districts first of all.[38] There is a pervading attitude of provincialism, jealousy, and freedom from outside controls, including those of the state government. Each district wants to guard its independence, thereby militating against any coalition formation. Some superintendents emerge as more important than others in the eyes of state policy makers, but their influence has been more effective in preventing passage of state controls. As one might expect, localism has not been a successful formula for increasing substantially the percentage of state financial aid.

The state of Michigan presents a third political pattern — one that is probably closer to future developments than the monolithic coalitions.[39] Here the various education interest groups cannot agree on a common policy proposal, so each approaches the legislature and governor in open conflict with competing proposals of other groups. Any compromise must take place *within* the conversion process, and not before. The arguments among competing teachers, administrators, and board members do not generate an image of educational experts "above politics." Legislative stalemates are frequently the result, although state politicians gain a healthy respect for the pressure tactics of these groups.

Michigan's political pattern has resulted from the inability of the profession to agree on common goals. Its militant teacher groups were leaders in the field of collective bargaining. As long as financial resources are increasing for everyone in large amounts, coalitions can stay together. But any redistribution of existing resources or favoritism for one group strains the coalition and enhances the role of the governor and legislature in compromising or ignoring competing claims of education groups.

Given the trends of teacher militancy and the demands of cities for a larger share of state aid, the outlook for coalitions in many states is hazardous. An interesting pattern may be developing where all education interest groups in a big city may agree on a salary package and then inform the state it must help the city schools to meet the total cost. This is backed by the threat to close the schools if the state will not meet their demands. On the other hand, organizations such as the Texas State Teachers Association show that a united profession and its allies can continue to reach agreements before demands are presented to the state legislature and the governor.

Iannaccone has drawn together some of these data in a typology based on these varied state educational politics. In Table 7.4, the four types are listed along the top. The first, "Disparate," typifies New England, where the various interest groups cannot agree because local considerations are primary. Consequently, the lobby power of any state interest group is limited to preventing undesirable education legislation, while the legislature

Table 7.4 Typology of Interest Group Linkage Structures Correlated to Legislative Effects and Appraisal

		Types of Interest Group		
Correlates	I Disparate (locally based)	II Monolithic (state-wide)	III Fragmented (state-wide)	IV Syndical (state-wide)
Lobby power				
Prevention	Yes	Yes	Mixed yes and no	Yes
Initiation	No	Yes	Mixed yes and no	Yes
Legislator sentiment	Warm and paternal to teachers	Warm, undifferentiated	Differentiated: critical to administrators; warm to teachers	Warm, not critical
Locus of accommodation	Legislature	Apex of monolith	Legislature	The group of syndics

Source: Laurence Iannaccone, *Politics in Education* (New York: Center for Applied Research in Education, 1967), 57.

assumes the major role in accommodating the conflicting values of the interest groups. The "Monolithic" pattern results in both positive and negative lobby power. It removes the political compromise function from the legislator and places it in the deliberations of the monolithic interest group during its legislative package discussion. The "Fragmented" pattern is exemplified by Michigan and California. Among other things it causes a critical viewpoint by legislators toward the squabbling school administration.

The Illinois School Problems Commission (SPC) provides the only instance among the states studied of a "Syndical" pattern. This organizational pattern is linked to the legislature, but the link is a formal governmental unit. The SPC is a creation of the legislature; indeed, ten of its seventeen members are legislators; five are appointed by the governor. Although the major interest groups are included, SPC must be treated as its own government rather than as extra-governmental in character. Its stated objectives are to conserve legislative time and assist in legislative planning for education. Consequently, SPC brings educators and legislators into close agreement and facilitates mutual respect. It also helps to insure favorable legislation on its primary recommendations.

A 1968 four-state study of lobbying by Zeigler and Baer move us away from lobby-legislature relationships to a consideration of what this relationship provides in the way of sources of influence and information. Table 7.5 indicates that education groups are viewed as powerful because of their large membership and the "sacred cow" nature of public education. However, the efforts of their lobbyists are *not* perceived as a major source of power. This finding is congruent with Iannaccone's analysis — education groups are most effective if they are united, thus bringing the full weight of their large membership into the legislative arena. Certainly it is not the large number of education lobbyist contacts that consistently has an impact on favorable legislative consideration. Indeed, Table 7.6 reinforces the success of the coalition strategy in showing that colleagues are the most frequent source of legislators' information about education. Coalitions can more easily rely on key legislators to assist in lobbying other members after an education package is agreed upon prior to legislative consideration.

Table 7.6 also provides insight into the important differences among states in education policy making. The four states illustrate the strength of interest groups in the absence of strong political parties. Thus, political parties, which in Oregon are undisciplined, exert little influence on the votes of legislators. However, notice the particularly strong position of education lobbyists in Oregon compared to that of party leaders. In the strong party states of Massachusetts and North Carolina, education lobbyists do not rank as high compared to other interest groups or to party leaders.

Table 7.5 *Reasons Offered for Power of Labor and Education Groups*

	Massachusetts		North Carolina		Oregon		Utah	
	Legislators	*Lobbyists*	*Legislators*	*Lobbyists*	*Legislators*	*Lobbyists*	*Legislators*	*Lobbyists*
Education								
Large membership	42%	20%	44%	39%	37%	32%	32%	35%
Lobbying effort	15	13	21	21	27	15	39	29
"Sacred cow"	34	54	24	33	25	36	13	22
Labor[a]								
Economic power	11	18			23	16	16	19
Large membership	67	62			58	62	41	55
Lobbying effort	14	16			12	14	38	25

Source: Harmon Zeigler and Michael Baer, *Lobbying* (Belmont, Calif.: Wadsworth, 1969), 195.
[a]North Carolina excluded because of lack of labor lobbyists.

Table 7.6   Legislators' Sources of Information About Education[a]

	Massa-chusetts (N = 244)	North Carolina (N = 164)	Oregon (N = 84)	Utah (N = 90)
Colleagues	82%	87%	81%	84%
Education lobbyists	33	43	58	44
Business leaders	30	53	38	39
Government officials	31	53	45	37
Party leaders	32	31	19	38

Source: Harmon Zeigler and Michael Baer, *Lobbying* (Belmont, Calif.: Wadsworth, 1969), 195, 117.
[a]Total percentages exceed 100 because of multiple responses.

IMPACT OF POLITICAL CULTURE ON THE CONVERSION PROCESS

Such patterns typify the variety of state politics in education. Implicit in these typologies is the assumption that state political systems develop distinctive attributes that influence the conversion process. That assumption has recently excited interest in the potential explanatory force of a state's political culture. We use "political culture" here in Verba's conception as "the system of empirical beliefs, expressive symbols, and values which defines the situation in which political action takes place." [40]

If "the situation," as Patterson has noted, is the American state, this state "political culture may be said to regulate — provide limits and op-portunities for — the want conversion process in a political system, and thus affect the frequency, intensity and quality of demand input." These value inputs would include the distinctive way a state's people feel toward their political authorities, their criteria for the goals of their political system in the state, and their patterns of political loyalty and commitment. The qualities that shape the state's politics, then, may also affect its educational politics. If the states are relatively independent political systems with dis-tinctive political cultures, it would follow that their policy outputs should differ in distinctive ways. Although Patterson demonstrates wide differenti-ation among states in this respect, he does not deal with school attitudes; nor is this done in a recent study showing increasing attitudinal divergence among American regions.[41] Studies of the politics of different regions, be-ginning with Key's *Southern Politics,* pay almost no attention to educational politics, particularly to how the culture may affect distinctively the manner in which that politics is played.[42]

The Political Culture of State Schools

In educational politics we are particularly interested in the impact of po-litical culture on state-local relations. The state does not operate public schools directly except for such special populations as handicapped children. Consequently, the state role has been to provide financial support and exert control over local districts. "Localism" in state politics indicates a cultural difference that the local districts feel can only be protected by pursuing a policy of isolation and freedom from state control. These localists know state money usually brings with it state standards and regulations.

In New England, localism has been pronounced ever since the beginning of public support for education.[43] Schoolman and legislator alike viewed the growth of state control as pernicious, so they considered hometown benefit the prime criterion for assessing proposed legislation. Perhaps this localism is derived in larger part from hatred of the English royal governor, but the attitude persisted because localism became a vested interest. As we have noted, localism tends to impede the state political coalitions of school professionals and depresses the growth of state financial support.

But it also affects the attitudes and behavior of state education administrators. An ongoing study of state administration of federal education funds highlights localism's importance for federal-state-local relations when it notes of one state:

> The Massachusetts State Education Agency has not generally seen its role as one of using its discretionary power to maximize aims through the establishment of high quality standards for programs in the local education agency, neither demanding sophisticated methods for program development, careful operating procedures, tough criteria for program proposal review, nor careful evaluation requirements. In short, the Massachusetts State Department in allocating federal funds and administering federal programs has, in effect, generally transmitted to the local educational agencies the discretionary powers which the federal government and federal legislation gave it.
>
> Briefly, where federal mandate requires the Massachusetts State Department to exercise control over [local] programs and specifies in detail the nature and/or form of such control, the . . . Department has complied with federal regulations. Otherwise it has not availed itself of the discretion available to it.[44]

History has clearly imposed a special cast on Southern schools.[45] Effective public education systems did not exist in this region until after the Civil War, and then they were instituted statewide, with Northerners in control. Also, at that time Southern local governments were financially prostrate and hence unable to assume the financial burden of starting public schools. As a consequence, the South has evolved a "centerist" political culture. As Table 7.1 records, almost all Southern states are those with very high proportions of state contributions to local schools. They have also used statewide textbook adoptions and stipulated other curriculum requirements not common in New England.

Diversity of political culture *within* a single state might also have a substantial impact on state policies. The most noticeable of these is the difference between cities and rural areas, for as Elazar has noted,

> cities frequently represent aggregations of population harboring political cultures that differ from the aggregations living in the surrounding areas. It is quite likely . . . that in every state there are a few cities, dominated by a political culture alien to that of the state as a whole, which will come into conflict with the state on a variety of issues. The entire question is greatly aggravated when a state itself is divided among two political cultures whereby the cities of the minority political culture must champion a sectional as well as a local interest against state officials dimly aware that there are fundamental differences of interest involved.[46]

One sign of this cultural force is seen in education policy making in several states affected by the different orientations of the city and rural interests. The big cities have as their major resource a bloc of urban legislators who, when unified, are able to bargain and negotiate with outstate legislators for city legislative priorities. Masters and his associates found a political pattern in several Midwest states whereby rural-urban cleavage was depressed by such a bargain among area delegations.[47] There is substantial evidence, however, that in most large states the city school districts have not banded together to lobby for urban legislation.[48]

Again, history has shaped this intrastate differentiation. The early superiority of urban schools to those in rural areas resulted frequently in relatively less state financial aid for cities. It also produced freedom from state control for urban schools, such as exemptions from state standards or provisions, clearly a special type of state regulation.[49] SDE personnel, on the other hand, were overwhelmingly from districts outside the cities.

Now that the cities are no longer in a favored financial situation, a new urban lobby is growing in many states to change the present state aid pattern, which favors noncity districts. Indeed, the state aid formulas, originally devised primarily to bring rural areas up to minimum standards, by 1960 also favored suburbs relative to the cities. On a per student basis, the *cities* of thirty-five SMSA's averaged $124.92 in aid from the state in 1960; the *suburbs* received $165.54, a difference of $40.62 for every student. A Ford study of five major states for later fiscal years 1965 through 1968 showed clearly that federal funds were being allocated disproportionately to nonmetropolitan schools. Except in New York, where the heavy weight of poor brought in special federal funds, old allocation rules worked against the use of federal money to assist a critical urban problem.[50] It has been against such system-imposed disparities that some urban schools are now moving, seeking new conversion techniques. In New York, for instance, the six biggest cities, forming their own coalition, now provide an urban-oriented legislative program to overcome this situation. Such an intercity alliance is still rare, however, suggesting a difference in needs and wants — or in political sophistication — among urban school systems.

A comparative analysis of state education politics must also consider the differences in general governmental variables. In some states like California, the legislature has a professional staff and the inclination to exercise considerable oversight of the SDE's implementation of federal and state statutes. In Texas, on the other hand, the legislature has little professional staff and is content to leave administration to the "educational experts" in the Texas Education Agency. In Michigan, the pervasive conflict between the two major political parties and the interests that support them determines a great deal of the educational program.[51] There, each party presents clear-cut alternatives that are reflected in the day-to-day operations of state government. By contrast, viewpoints of political parties are not an important factor in educational policy making in Missouri, where the enthusiasm of the governor for education is crucial in determining the growth of financial aid. In some states, however, the governor can item-veto the education appropriation; in others, the legislature ignores the governor's budget and submits its own from a joint committee.[52]

Recent macroanalytic studies have attempted to sort out the relative impact upon public policy in city and state of these governmental constraints compared to socio-economic conditions.[53] Much to the surprise of political scientists, the bulk of findings in the first wave of research, particularly that led by Dye, showed the governmental and political factors much less capable of explaining interstate and intercity differences than could the economic. Whether parties were competitive or not, the legislature malapportioned or not, the local government centralized or not, the governor having more or less power — in these and many other specific measures of the political culture, Dye found far less impact on policy, as measured by expenditures or performance. Thus in school policy, sizable simple correlations between the states' school policy measures, methods of selecting top school officials, and gubernatorial power suddenly disappeared when levels of economic development among the states were controlled. In short, this finding concluded that it was these levels — urbanization, industrialization, etc. — that more directly affected the volume and kinds of school outputs.

In the recurrent dialectic of really alive scholarship, this was not to be the final word, however. In the late 1960's, other scholars, using different correlation techniques and policy indicators, found that political arrangements did make a difference. Instead of looking simply at a state's per capita expenditure for schools, for example, the new refinement in macroanalysis looked at how state monies were redistributed to local governments, or at the proportions of money that different governments contributed to a policy objective. This conceptual debate, augmented by another over statistical techniques, led by 1970 to the realization that a state's political culture contributed to its policy profile some force independent of existing economic conditions.

The latter played some role in explaining policy outcomes, of course. Mississippi's poor schools, with their bottom-of-the-barrel economic base, could never elevate their rank very high among the states by any conceivable local political arangement. But the political culture that shaped those schools was more significant in explaining why they were so wretched. Political ideas about a dangerous federal government fended off outside school assistance after the Civil War and in our own time.

An illustration of this interstate variation that suggests the independent force of culture is seen in the process of diffusion of new programs. The data are seen in Walker's comparison of innovation by twenty states in a number of policies, including education.[54] Although the study was exploratory and the indicators of "innovation" debatable, the work is highly suggestive. He concluded that decision makers are likely to adopt new programs "when they become convinced that their state is relatively deprived, or that some need exists to which other states in their league have already responded." Professional and political leaders in the states find out about new programs through interstate communication networks, including professional associations of state administrators. Emerging from this study is a regional system of emulation and competition based on geographical contiguity and on a state's location in the specialized set of communication channels through which innovations flow. We know very little, however, about the pattern or system of interactions among professional associations, federal officials, interest groups, and political leaders in setting the agenda of innovations for a state.

A study of educational politics in Missouri confirms this innovation thesis. Although Missouri in 1959 ranked eighteenth in per capita income, it ranked only thirty-eighth in per capita expenditure. The Missouri State Teachers Association operated as the focal point of a monolithic state coalition of education interest groups. They chose to "get what they can with a minimum of agitation or conflict rather than attempting broader public campaigns in behalf of larger objectives." [55] This strategy was in large part based on the "league" Missouri chose to play in. Accordingly, the officials of MSTA "are fully conscious of the gap between the Missouri school aid level and that of, say, neighboring Illinois," but they were quick to point out "that by comparison with other neighboring states — Arkansas, Oklahoma, or Nebraska, for example — Missouri's record is much more impressive." [56] It appears that Missouri's education leaders were emulating and competing with the poorer, not the richer, states as reference groups for their aspirations.

The Regional Culture of School Politics

An interesting pattern may be reflected in all this. While states differ with one another in political culture, they also show significant clustering in their attributes of conversion and output. One form of clustering is the rural-urban division within the state and its impact upon policy. Another form of clustering is in the governmental structures and processes employed. Moreover, it may be that such clusterings constitute different sets, which also differ along a still larger dimension. One such dimension could be the factor of regionalism. The analysis of regional policy outputs should demonstrate distinctive clusterings if a regional "culture" does exist. Macroanalysis studies during the 1960's suggest the potential utility of the culture concept. The analytical model employed here conceives of demands as economic or political indicators of life in a region, and of outputs as measured by public policies. The latter are often indicated by expenditures per capita for a given policy or some other allocational measure.

Thus, in Table 7.7 we find Sharkansky's data for regional clusters of expenditures for all programs in general and for education in particular. The labels in the left column take into account different ways of clustering

Table 7.7 *Regional Expenditures for Total and School Purposes as a Percentage of National Means*

			Expenditures			
			Per capita		Per $1,000 of personal income	
			Total	Education	Total	Education
North			.93	.82	.80	.69
New England			.99	.65	.92	.61
Mid-Atlantic	North		.95	.99	.72	.75
Great Lakes	and		.85	.84	.75	.74
Northeast	East		.93	.69	.82	.61
Northcentral			.89	.83	.83	.76
Plains			.92	.82	.89	.78
Transmississippi			1.10	1.16	1.05	1.09
Mountains	West		1.18	1.24	1.17	1.20
Far West			1.33	1.46	1.04	1.16
Transplains			1.24	1.40	1.16	1.29
Southwest			1.08	1.33	1.19	1.45
Southeast	South		.92	.98	1.18	1.26
South			.96	1.03	1.12	1.20

Source: Abstracted from Ira Sharkansky, *Regionalism in American Politics* (Indianapolis: Bobbs-Merrill, 1970), 154–55.

regions, while the numerical measures are ratios of regional to national economic figures. Regional distinctions, sometimes on the order of two to one, are seen here. Using the per capita ratio, there is a wide gap between the Far West and New England; on the other ratio, a similar gap is shown for the Southwest and the Northeast and New England. Although not shown here, Sharkansky also demonstrates that other measures of educational output show similar regional differences. The South rates lowest in rate of school completion, for example, and in success on national exams, but highest on programs receiving federal support — school lunches, vocational education, and vocational rehabilitation. In poor states, then, the federal resources are used inordinately to close the gap between local resources and needs.[57]

Another place where regional clustering might occur is in electoral behavior on local school referenda. This is a virtually untapped data source, so what follows is only suggestive of research lines requiring fuller exploration. The assumption is that if political culture operates, it should be seen in variation among the states in the rate of supporting school financial referenda, and these variations should cluster regionally. Further, we should find the effect of distinctive structural requirements in these elections, e.g., whether 50 percent or more than 50 percent is required for passage. Such requirements should be a manifestation of distinctive attitudes about the political system and should affect outputs in distinctive regional patterns. There is much evidence that such requirements have affected other aspects of this nation's political life, e.g., in urban voting laws and turnout rate, white suffrage restrictions and black voting, and nonpartisanship laws and party activity.[58]

Our measures here are not subtle, but they will carry the point. We first defined subregions as the Census Bureau does; these were clustered by using the median approval of school bond measures for each year,* and further, we separated states by the legal minimum majority required for passage. Three states require no voter approval (Alabama, Hawaii, and Indiana), twelve require an extraordinary majority, and thirty-five require a simple majority; this is even more complicated by the fact that a vote is not required on all bond measures in all states. We distinguished the large- from the simple-majority states to determine whether structural devices (conceived as reflecting political cultures) affect the conversion outputs. Finally, it may well be the case that the frequency with which bond elections arise within a state implies another phase of political culture. We hypothesized that the greater the demands by the school systems upon the multiple electorates of a state, the lesser will be the approval rate, because

---

* The median was used instead of the mean because some states in a group had unusually large numbers of referenda, whereas their neighbors had very few.

too-frequent appeal to the electorate diminishes citizen's diffuse support for schools.

Tables 7.8 and 7.9 bring to bear upon these propositions the relevant data, both raw and refined. The differentiating influence of the size of majority required is not strongly supported; the data are suggestive but not persuasive. Notice in Table 7.9 the marginal totals on the right side, which compare within each major region those states with a simple versus a high majority requirement. Over the period 1961–1969, the difference was small but in the direction hypothesized in the North East, North Central, and South. In specific years in these three regions, there are larger and smaller differences, but there are also years when the median percentage of bond approvals in high majority states was *greater* than in simple majority states: the North East in 1961, 1963, and 1968; the North Central in 1966 and 1968; the South in 1968. But in the Western region the difference is impressively large, consistent, and in the direction hypothesized; in no year are the data reversed as in the other regions. The data are not shown, but within the two Western subregions the same consistent pattern is found over the years; the subregional patterns elsewhere also reflect the parent region.

The differentiating impact of the high vote requirement is particularly severe in California in local bond elections, as Table 7.8 shows. A two-thirds majority rule has meant that in the last two decades only about one-half or less of the local bonds have passed compared to the results if only a simple majority had been required. Thus in 1966–67, only 29 percent of the bond monies sought were approved, whereas 82 percent would have passed with a simple majority.[59]

One important conclusion to be drawn from the study of this rule's impact is that the national impression of voter discontent with school bond issues may be exaggerated. As Scott and Hamilton recently concluded, "It is the two-thirds requirement that is responsible for almost all of the defeats [in California] — and for the appearance of discord. Although the requirement makes it seem so, the local councils and the voters are not out of step."[60] That conclusion reminds us that environmental stress may arise not merely from the inadequacies of the political system's outputs in failing to meet wants. It may also arise from systemic conversion procedures that constrain or block input demands.

Yet referenda support has changed over the years. The bottom double row of "totals" in Table 7.9 shows that in both types of states these bond approvals peaked in 1964–65 and then sharply declined in parallel. As Table 7.8 reveals, this pattern emerges dramatically in every region, subregion, and indeed, almost every state reported by the Office of Education.[61] The decline is particularly sharp in the North Central and South; Michigan, Ohio, and Wisconsin fell from approval rates of 60–70 percent

Table 7.8   School Bond Referenda Passage Ratios by Region and Passage Requirements, 1961–68[a]

Passage requirement	1961	1962	1963	1964	1965	1966	1967	1968	Median percent of passed	Median number of referenda
None										
Ala. ESC-South	—	—	—	—	—	—	—	—		
Haw. Pac-West	—	—	—	—	—	—	—	—		
Ind. ENC-NC	—	2/2	2/2	2/2	—	—	—	—		
Over 50 percent										
Calif. Pac-W	115/171	160/245	156/252	153/235	92/166	46/91	57/110	39/111	58.6	172
Ida. Mt-W	11/17	8/15	9/9	9/18	13/20	2/4	10/15	3/4	64.8	13
Iowa WNC-NC	50/79	38/100	38/72	46/76	48/75	57/92	57/85	54/88	62.9	83
Ken. ESC-S	3/3	1/1	—	1/1	1/1	—	—	0/1	100.0	1
Mass. NE-NE	20/20	11/12	27/30	16/20	13/16	12/12	9/11	6/8	85.6	16
Mo. WNC-NC	14/16	26/27	18/20	24/28	10/12	14/19	34/56	7/23	84.5	25
N.H. NE-NE	5/6	7/7	8/9	11/11	5/5	2/5	5/6	2/2	94.4	6
N.Y. MA-NE	36/51	77/110	116/161	84/119	65/81	39/55	24/34	5/16	70.6	78
Okla WSC-S	20/25	87/101	105/120	67/81	63/80	52/69	66/78	36/49	79.4	75
S.D. WNC-NC	16/24	14/23	15/26	17/25	14/21	16/30	10/17	9/17	59.9	30
Wash. Pac-W	16/18	42/59	23/34	55/70	39/47	45/54	53/72	16/21	77.4	47
W.Va. SA-S	1/3	0/3	2/8	4/6	3/6	0/1	3/7	3/3	38.1	5
Total	307/433	471/703	517/731	487/690	356/530	285/432	328/551	170/343	67.1	

[a] Regional symbols are as follows (in the table, the subregion is given first):
NE: Northeast; NE: New England; MA: Middle Atlantic; S: South;
ESC: East South Central; WSC: West South Central; SA: South Atlantic;
NC: North Central; ENC: East NC; WNC: West NC; W: West;
MT: Mountain; Pac: Pacific

Table 7.8 (cont.)

Passage requirement	1961	1962	1963	1964	1965	1966	1967	1968	Median percent passed	Median number of referenda
50 percent only										
Alaska Pac-W	1/1	3/5	4/4	1/1	6/6	5/6	2/3	1/1	100.0	3
Ariz. Mt-W	21/24	23/28	17/19	21/22	5/5	5/6	10/16	7/9	85.4	16
Ark. WSC-S	39/39	71/71	31/35	60/68	50/58	50/58	64/77	39/45	87.4	56
Colo. Mt-W	27/35	160/245	19/21	15/27	20/27	10/18	17/23	9/15	69.6	24[b]
Conn. NE-NE	10/11	24/25	17/17	36/36	21/22	18/22	15/16	13/15	94.6	21
Dela. SA-S	6/6	2/2	3/3	6/9	3/4	3/3	4/6	0/1	87.5	4
Fla. SA-S	2/2	1/2	6/6	2/2	–	2/6	3/5	1/2	80.0	4
Ga. SA-S	4/4	10/11	10/10	6/7	2/2	4/7	7/9	4/8	88.3	7
Ill. ENC-NC	95/134	117/157	94/139	105/120	109/135	119/151	118/182	95/146	72.7	145
Kans. WNC-NC	11/12	16/25	4/5	5/5	7/8	28/59	30/54	4/5	80.0	22
La. WSC-S	4/4	21/24	37/38	30/31	19/19	16/17	13/16	3/4	90.8	18
Me. NE-NE	3/3	4/4	6/7	3/3	4/6	4/5	5/6	3/5	85.5	5
Md. SA-S	–	4/4	–	2/3	–	2/2	2/3	2/2	100.0	3
Mich. ENC-NC	49/71	73/108	94/142	99/139	93/129	72/123	56/98	41/105	66.9	115
Minn. WNC-NC	44/67	48/71	64/85	56/86	70/108	52/91	69/91	48/90	65.4	88
Miss. ESC-S	5/6	17/23	13/16	15/19	8/13	4/6	5/9	2/4	70.3	11
Mont. Mt-W	10/13	17/19	15/19	28/35	13/19	3/5	6/6	2/2	79.5	15
Nebr. WNC-NC	37/57	41/59	31/49	35/52	22/28	23/33	29/33	30/39	69.7	44
Nev. Mt-W	2/2	5/5	2/2	2/3	1/2	1/1	–	1/1	100.0	2
N.J. MA-NE	54/73	7/7	79/115	74/92	46/69	73/108	61/91	67/113	68.1	91
N.M. Mt-W	12/13	15/17	21/33	14/15	14/14	6/7	18/19	5/5	94.0	14
N.C. SA-S	2/2	7/9	11/13	7/8	5/6	4/5	1/3	2/4	81.6	6

[b]Exclusive of the 1962 anomaly.

Table 7.8 (cont.)

Passage requirement	1961	1962	1963	1964	1965	1966	1967	1968	Median percent passed	Median number of referenda
N.D. WNC-NC	15/28	28/45	24/47	94/156	22/34	12/26	14/27	3/9	52.7	31
Ohio ENC-NC	102/176	77/128	105/171	94/156	127/213	66/125	103/170	46/125	59.9	163
Ore. Pac-W	33/42	46/61	30/46	46/56	30/40	31/45	25/43	8/13	72.0	44
Penna. MA-NE	2/2	4/4	4/5	4/4	1/1	1/1	3/3	4/6	100.0	4
R.I. NE-NE	3/4	9/10	11/13	13/13	8/10	13/14	4/4	4/6	87.3	10
S.C. SA-S	–	1/1	1/1	4/4	1/1	–	–	1/1	100.0	1
Tenn. ESC-S	2/3	4/4	–	8/9	12/15	–	1/2	1/1	84.9	4
Tex WSC-S	103/127	153/180	161/186	163/204	126/154	123/171	107/142	98/141	80.5	162
Utah Mt-W	4/6	4/4	10/10	5/5	3/3	3/3	2/3	–	100.0	4
Vt. NE-NE	6/8	5/8	9/16	12/15	10/12	15/19	11/20	15/23	70.1	16
Va. SA-S	3/4	10/12	7/8	5/5	4/8	4/7	6/10	3/6	67.5	8
Wisc. ENC-NC	10/11	26/42	29/40	28/38	27/34	21/38	33/54	19/44	67.3	40
Wyc. Mt-W	6/9	8/11	12/17	7/9	10/10	3/4	10/14	1/2	72.0	9
Total	727/999	1061/1430	981/1327	1105/1457	898/1215	796/1188	854/1258	586/998	71.0	

Table 7.9 *Median Regional Differences in Successful Bond Elections by Approval Vote Required, 1961–69*

	1961	1962	1963	1964	1965	1966	1967	1968	Total
North East[a]	83.3	91.7	88.9	80.0	81.3	70.9	81.8	75.0	81.5
North East	82.9	98.0	82.3	100.0	81.6	80.9	88.5	65.9	82.6
North Central[a]	66.7	60.9	57.7	68.0	66.7	62.0	60.7	52.9	61.5
North Central	67.3	65.8	66.9	69.2	75.3	56.2	60.8	48.2	66.3
South[a]	80.0	86.1	56.2	82.7	78.8	37.7	63.7	73.5	81.4
South	100.0	89.2	93.0	88.2	82.5	75.9	66.7	59.7	85.3
West[a]	67.3	65.3	67.6	65.1	65.0	50.5	66.7	75.0	66.0
West	78.6	82.1	90.5	82.1	100.0	83.3	69.0	88.9	82.7
Total[a]	68.7	70.6	67.6	74.6	80.0	62.0	67.1	57.2	
Total	81.1	83.3	85.1	86.3	80.0	75.0	66.7	65.1	

Source: National Center for Education Statistics, U.S. Office of Education, "Bond Sales for Public School Purposes," annual reports.
[a]States with extraordinary majority required.

to around 40 percent in 1968–69. Also in that year, Kentucky and Delaware voters failed to pass *any* of the few attempted. In this we see evidence of a secular shift, a national mood of retrenchment refracted by each region and state regardless of constraints upon conversion or of variations in political culture. That mood is intensified if measured by the amount of money passed. Sources used for the tables above show that the proportion of approved bonds, based on the par dollar value, was even lower each year than the proportion of referenda approved. In 1969, for example, only 43.6 percent of the par value in dollars was approved.

In sum, it does make a difference in every region whether the majority required is 50 percent or higher, but except for the West, the difference is not impressive. Table 7.9 contains thirty-two intraregional pairs comparing differing constraints upon the political system. In only six cases was the hypothesis *not* supported, but in another nine cases the difference was less than 5 percent. So, for almost half (fifteen of thirty-two pairs), the difference is far from persuasive that this constraint upon input demands is significant.

It might be argued, however, that the differentiating effect of the constraint is muzzled by the artificiality of the measure of "region" utilized. After all, the Census Bureau "region" combines such unlikely sets as California and Alaska, New York and Vermont, Michigan and South Dakota, Florida and Mississippi. If this argument is correct, we should determine whether the states themselves — a much more recognizable culture — cluster along relevant dimensions of referenda approval. Table 7.10 indicates the clusters that emerge when we relate the frequency of approval to the frequency of elections, as suggested by an earlier hypothesis.

We find the largest block, in the upper right hand corner, to be characterized by few annual referenda but high support for them. In the lower left, however, frequent-election states also demonstrate lower approval rates. States clustered in these two corners visually support the hypothesis that frequency of approval is inversely related to frequency of elections, but it is true in only a minority of states. The correlation coefficient of the two variables (median number of elections and median approval percentage) is −.06 for all 47 states, −.16 for those requiring only the simple majority to pass, and −.30 for those requiring a large majority. The sign is in the direction of the hypothesis — increasing the number of bond elections *will* accompany a decreased acceptance rate — but the size of the association is hardly convincing except for large-majority states.

Further, little evidence emerges in Table 7.11 of a regional pattern. Southern states do have few bond elections, but Southern approval is spread over a wide range; West Virginia's annual median acceptance rate over this period was only 38.1 percent. However, other regional patterns are missing. While larger states tend to have more referenda, Pennsylvania is a great exception, averaging only 3.6 a year, compared with California,

Table 7.10 *Distribution of States on Bond Elections by Annual Median Approval Rate and Median Number of Referenda, 1961–69*

Median number of elections	Median approval percentage					Total states
	Under 60	60–69	70–79	80–89	90–100	
0–9	W.Va.[a]	Fla., Va.	—	Ga., Me., N.C., Tenn.	Alaska, Del., Md., Nev., Pa., S.C., Ut., Ky.,[a] N.H.[a]	16
10–19	—	Idaho[a]	Miss., Vt., Wyo.	Ariz., Kans., Mont., Mass.,[a] R.I.	La., N.M.	11
20–49	N.D.	Wisc., S.D.[a]	Colo., Nebr., Ore.	Mo.[a]	Conn.	8
50–99	—	Minn., N.J., Iowa[a]	N.Y.,[a] Wash.[a]	Ark., Okla.[a]	—	7
100 and over	Calif.[a]	Mich., Ohio	Ill.	Tex.	—	5
Total states	3	10	9	13	12	47
State percentage[a]	66.7	30	22.2	23.1	16.7	

Source: See Table 7.9.
[a]States with extraordinary majority required.

*Table 7.11   Regional Medians of Frequency of Approval
and Bond Elections, 1961–69*

	Northeast	South	North Central	West
Percent approved				
Total	86	85	67	78
50% only	86	86	67	85
50% and over	86	79	63	65
Number of referenda				
Total	16	6	44	14
50% only	13	6	66	14
50% and over	16	5	30	47

Ohio, and Texas at over 162 each. Although they usually have many referenda, support among these big states varies widely. California's support was 58.6 percent (with its two-thirds rule) and Ohio's 59.9 percent (requiring only a simple majority); yet Texas's support was high at 80.5 percent. A similar variation appears among states alike in their *small* population. Such scattering suggests the existence of distinctive state, but not regional, political cultures; Table 7.11 shows this clearly for all regions but the West. States alike in one quality — population size — show different electoral behaviors, ranging from few to many elections and from high to low support.

Aside from this scatter effect, the most salient aspect of Tables 7.10 and 7.11 is the lack of distinction (except in the West) between the states requiring a simple and those requiring a high majority vote to pass. The large-majority states are scattered, from low support in West Virginia to high support in Kentucky and New Hampshire (100 and 94.4 percents). Even the Southern bloc has deviants in Arkansas and Texas. Yet the relationship between the constraint of a large majority required to approve and the actual approval rate is far from weak. The constraint's effect should be to reduce the conversion rate; among states where it exists, the rate of approval should be low, but where it does not, the rate should be high. The last row of Table 7.10 shows that the constraint does affect conversion. There is a regularly declining proportion of states requiring large majorities as one moves into higher approval rates; the decline is from 66.7 to 16.7 percent. But when states are clustered regionally, the differential effect washes out, except in the West.

CONCLUSION

Several conclusions about the role of states in educational politics seem evident from the data of this chapter. Differing political practices, reflect ing different political visions of our highly varied and individual population, suggest the independent force of political culture in explaining policy differences among states and regions. From the highly centralized politics of Hawaii, reflecting its royalist origins, to the highly decentralized politics of New England — also reflecting royalist origins but of a different nature — there exists a wide range of roles for the states in the conversion process. The influence of educational lobbies and parties varies, as do the weight of governors on outputs, the interaction between interest group and legislature, and the force of direct democracy. Basic to such variety, of course, is that same individualism and pragmatism noted in an earlier chapter as central to the American political character.

Yet in the midst of such profusion, there are some commonalities. The constitutional histories of the states are similar in requiring *some* influence by state government in local school policy, and throughout our history that influence has increased dramatically from the days of the traveling schoolmarm. All states are alike in being the object of increased political demands about school policies — curriculum, training of professionals, finances, and so on. All find expansion in their state school staffs, in their interaction with the local districts, and in their involvement with federal programs. As pressure increases to remove the financial burden from the back of the local district, the state role is bound to increase. That pressure is seen currently in the increasing defeat of tax referenda, in demands for the states to increase their financial aids, in court challenges in 1970 against the inequalities of state equalization programs, and in discussion about the state take-over of *all* local school financing.[62]

Not the least of the forces reshaping the role of the state in American educational policy have been public and private nationalizing developments. Federal law, whether from Congress or the Supreme Court, has drastically altered that role after World War II; in the case of the Elementary and Secondary Education Act of 1965, the impact has occurred in a matter of only a few years. Private pressures operate to the same end, whether in national assessment programs, curriculum modification campaigns, or other professional goals. These nationalizing trends can best be understood only in the actual processes of policy making and administration, so we turn in the next three chapters to such details for illustration. While these trends have impact on local school districts, they also impinge on the state's role. The differentiating influence of political cultures may diffuse and refract these trends, but all policies of school governance are altered or expanded by them. In the matters of federal aid to education, desegregation, and curriculum policies, then, we believe this interplay of variety and commonality may be seen in a period when the American school system underwent significant shifts.

PART TWO

Three Policy-making Areas in Public Education

An output of the political system — whether statute, administrative order, or school board resolution — is rarely permanent. Nor is any output self-executing, for how, or even whether, it is executed is a function of numerous intervening variables — the attitudes and resources of its opponents and supporters, the energy with which political authorities seek compliance, and so on. Thus an output arrives in the cold world like an infant, alive with infinite possibilities. In another sense, law is a memo to the future; as Emerson put it:

> The law is only a memorandum. We are superstitious, and esteem the statute somewhat: so much life as it has in the character of living men is its force. The statute stands there to say, Yesterday we agreed so and so, but how feel ye this article today? Our statute is a currency which we stamp with our own portrait: it soon becomes unrecognizable, and in process of time will return to the mint.[1]

The theoretical assumption of the next three chapters is put well in those words, for we seek to show how policy outputs, whether from Congress, the Supreme Court, or local school systems, take on flesh and blood in the process of their administration. In the main we ignore the input and conversion phases on which, as we shall show, the literature is already abundant. Instead we seek to learn what happens after "Congress Makes a Law" or the courts issue an order.

Each of these is taken as a political decision at one point in time — "Yesterday we agreed so and so." That decision will affect differentially the values and resources of its supporters and opponents, who, interacting with the decision, will advance different interpretations of its administration. These create stress, which leads in turn to new wants and demands that impinge upon the administrators' efforts and to which they must respond. These demands provide information to political authorities that is used to judge the need for new adaptations to stress — "but how feel ye this article today?" At one point in time, then, stands the output, and somewhere ahead in that dim future lies the final disposition — an outcome. This, however, may well necessitate a recycling of the conversion process — "and in process of time will return to the mint."

In this concept of the policy process, this input-conversion-output-outcome is generated by that part of the feedback loop running between output and income (see p. 149). That loop is powerful in its consequences, providing information for authorities and citizens alike, provoking discontent about the law's effect, promoting support either for output or the total political system — and it thus makes possible the regeneration of the cycle. Feedback requires a communications system that allows for a two-way flow of information, wants, and demands. These channels are conceived in such forms as telephone calls, letters, investigations, media coverage, confrontation between administrators and administrated — and all those manifest ways Americans have for enhancing or inhibiting the role of law in their individualist lives.

The dynamism of this process in the United States is made greater by the fact that we operate within a *federal* system. This is no distinct compartmentalization of sovereignties and powers among three levels of nation, state, and locality, but an interlocked pattern of cooperation and conflict. In Grodzin's phrase, it is not a three-layer cake but a marble cake. When a systems framework is imposed upon the mosaic of subsystems constituting federalism, the policy flow may be represented symbolically as in Figure II.1.

At the beginning, arbitrarily labeled Time 1A, a sequence of stress-conversion-output is conceived as transpiring through the national political system. *School Outputs 1* refers to the resulting policy set that is transmitted for administration at Time 1B to the *State School System*. This forms a somewhat different *Stress Pattern 2,* the difference as well as similarities indicated by the 1, 2, designation of Demands and Supports. The result is *School Outputs 1, 2,* the numerals indicating that the national policy has been transmuted by state inputs and withinputs into a somewhat different form.

At Time 1C, state outputs are administered upon the *Local School System* (direct federal-local system relations can exist also), constituting the altered *Stress Pattern 3* and another combination of transmuted and yet similar demands and supports (1,2,3). These may be decisions on curriculum, attendance, zoning, salary improvements, racial composition of

Figure II.1   Intergovernmental Relations in a Systems Framework

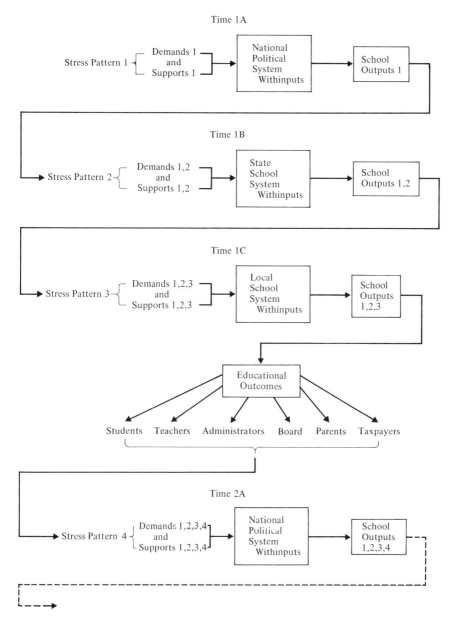

faculties, budget allocations, etc. This policy set is then administered so as to achieve some kind of *Educational Outcome* for those who interact with local schools — students, teachers, etc.

The outcomes may change greatly or not at all the educational stress that precipitated the policy-making process originally. Does the output of federal aid, for example, when it finally gets down to those it is designed to affect, actually achieve the desired outcome, e.g., more qualified teachers of science or language, more students better prepared to start school or express their ideas? These outcomes may in turn generate yet another set of stresses, e.g., defects in administrative techniques, insufficient resources being employed, or unattainable goals. As a consequence of such feedback, then, at some future time (Time 2A) the whole process is recycled.

Before we go into detail about feedback, an illustration of these general conceptions may be useful. During the Cold War phase of American foreign policy, many Americans were seized with the notion that the Russians in their foreign ventures and space developments were "ahead of us." Much of this sense of stress focused upon deficiencies in our supplies of particular technical skills. Our diplomats were seen as lacking language skills in the countries where they represented us, and Soviet "leads" in the "space race" pointed up a purported gap in scientists.

Much of this general distress was given sharp focus when the USSR suddenly put a satellite into space orbit in 1957. This general stress crystallized in the sudden appearance of demands to "do something" about this condition. The media and Congress were filled with varied indications of unhappiness that a nation we conceived of as composed of peasants and outhouses had put scientific hardware into space.

Out of these stress-generated demands, Congress passed the National Defense Education Act of 1958. Funds were provided to encourage students to adopt a teaching career in science, math, or foreign language, and to increase the number of teachers in general, an occupation then considerably undersupplied. Loans provided to students would be "forgiven" if the graduates taught in the selected field or worked in the worst — or "disadvantaged" — schools. Thus this output, which greatly increased federal participation in education (directly in college, indirectly in public schools), used the economic motive to induce a social change.

As this input interacted with the national environment, and particularly with that of the school system, what were the effects? A carefully drawn study in 1971 by Russell, using different kinds of data, is most instructive. He found no special effect for this law in its aim of increasing the total teacher supply, although he found significant differences in another aim, multiplying teachers of science, math, and language. But the "forgiveness" feature of the law had had little effect upon these students' career choices, nor had it moved them in larger numbers into "disadvantaged" institutions.

The reason was that few were motivated in such decisions by money alone. Certainly the law had not caused a measurable difference in the quality of teaching.

One stark datum on the inutility of the monetary motive in this career is that, despite the $1.3 billion authorized for loans, only $94.8 million were spent for the "forgiveness" feature, and only $30 million of that will be cancelled in future years by students doing what the act was primarily designed for. In short, as Russell concluded, "This nation's initial major attempt at manpower planning has not been an effective vehicle to affect significantly the quantity, quality, distribution, or retention of prospective teachers." [2]

In this illustration of feedback, we have a startling case of an output conceived with one set of means and objectives failing in part because it misjudged why people made certain decisions that the act was drawn to change. Moreover, whether schools wanted or could afford a sudden supply of teachers specially trained in these areas was a highly variable quality in a highly variable federal system. The outcome, then, fell far short of the output because of institutional and personal factors intervening in a complex federal society. The mix of demands at the national level was not that at the state or local level, and equally mixed were the felt stresses. The feedback, through such information as that provided by Russell a decade later, could suggest the need to reshape the old law. But by 1970, the oversupply of teachers in most fields would force the recycling in totally different directions — not toward increasing but toward decreasing or protecting the number in existence.

While systems analysis contributes to our understanding of this complex process, its utility does not end there. If sufficient data can be provided to describe what happens for many of the jurisdictions symbolized in Figure II.1, it may then become possible to develop some predictive theoretical statements for testing. What we propose to do, however, is to examine only three public policies against this theoretical framework — the Elementary and Secondary Education Act of 1965, school desegregation in the South, and curriculum innovation. Each provides an output from a different level of the federal system or a different kind of political authority.

All demonstrate, however, what is implicit in Figure II.1. There exist, both vertically within the federal system or horizontally within any of its levels, sets of resistors and transmitters. Many of these have been indicated in earlier chapters. They block or bolster the transformation of outputs into what policy makers had in mind originally. Almost visible here is the underlying pulse of American individualism operating at the multiple access points of federalism to protect and promote individual and group interests.

In these three policies, then, we are pursuing also some of the basic questions that Easton raised about the feedback process — the concept that binds the coming chapters:

> We would need to know, for example, what kind of information typically returns to the authorities along the feedback loop and the extent to which it is accurate, false, or distorted. To what degree do time leads and lags, the number of feedback channels, the length of these as transmission belts and their variety, influence the type of information fed back? To what extent is accuracy dependent upon the perceptual apparatus of the authorities and the way in which it may be influenced by ideology, prejudice, indifference, or lack of ability to obtain and interpret information? . . . We would also need to inquire into the decision rules guiding the retrieval of information from the collective memory banks in which past experience is stored.[3]

8 ESEA and Intergovernmental Relations

The Elementary and Secondary Education Act of 1965 is a wide-ranging piece of legislation that, six years after passage, requires a book for comprehensive treatment. Indeed, several volumes have been written on its passage and initial implementation.[1] Our objectives here, however, are to analyze the last three years of the act (1968–71) in terms of (1) the feedback conflict over its objectives and (2) the political interactions involved in a federal-state-local system for delivering educational programs to the classroom level.

ESEA was five years old in September, 1970, but as Halperin observed, it is hard to imagine where any birthday candles are burning:

> Not among the ranks of federal budget makers and top policy makers, many of whom seem to doubt the act is "cost effective." Not among educators, many of whom accept its funds but complain of excessive red tape and bureaucracy in order to obtain relatively little federal money. Not among the embittered parents of ghetto children, most of whom have seen precious little change for the better in the quality of their children's education. Not even among the Congressional liberals who were the Act's most dedicated advocates, but who are now embarrassed by the critics and seem unable to counter with dramatic success stories made possible by ESEA.[2]

In short, the feedback from five years of ESEA has been heavily laced with sweeping indictments, specific recommendations for change, and a crossfire of conflicting values over ways to improve the original bill. In the process, ESEA has been the focus of numerous investigations, published works, and lobby campaigns.[3] Congressional amendments or revised ad-

153

ministrative regulations may satisfy many critics for a time, but this only leads to another cycle of implementation, feedback, and substantive change.

THE LAW AS OUTPUT

A substantial amount of feedback over subsequent policy adjustment was assured by the special conditions of ESEA's hurried passage. Participants in its birth still recall vividly the periodic waves of near panic that accompanied the precedent-shattering eighty-nine-day passage. Rumors persisted that some key educational group was departing the coalition or that the church-state compromise was breaking up. Its quick passage led to a congressional quip that ESEA should be renamed "The Railroad Act of 1965." Doubts about the effectiveness of its provisions had to be deferred until the principle of federal aid to education was established.

Main Provisions

Title I of ESEA is by far the largest financial component (over $1.4 billion in 1970) and the one surrounded by the most political controversy and feedback. The purpose of this program (as outlined in Public Law 89-10) is "to provide financial assistance . . . to local educational agencies serving areas with concentrations of children from low-income families to expand and improve their educational programs [to meet] the special educational needs of educationally deprived children." The central thrust of the law, then, was to aid low-income children. When first signed, it required the use of two poverty indicators in its fund-distribution formula: (1) the number of children aged five through seventeen from families with an annual income of less than $2,000 (based on the 1960 census); (2) the number of children aged five through seventeen from families with incomes exceeding $2,000 in the form of aid to families with dependent children (AFDC) under Title IV of the Social Security Act.

The United States Commissioner of Education, as well as state and local education agencies, have responsibilities for administering the Title I program. We will merely summarize these.

The United States Office of Education
1. develops and disseminates regulations, guidelines, and other materials regarding the approval of Title I projects
2. reviews and assesses the progress under Title I throughout the nation

State Education Agencies
1. approve proposed local projects in accordance with federal regulations and guidelines
2. assist local educational agencies in the development of projects
3. submit state evaluative report to USOE

Local Education Agencies
1. identify the educationally deprived children in the areas where there are high concentrations of low-income families and determine their special educational needs
2. develop and implement approved projects to fulfill the intent of Title I [4]

But ESEA did not deal only with children. Title I also provided 1 percent of its $1.3 billion for state agencies to administer the program, and Title V allocated $30 million to strengthen the general administrative capacity of state agencies. In effect, as noted earlier, ESEA included a deliberate policy of underwriting the growth and reorientation of state departments of education, which had traditionally been independent of, and, in part, antagonistic to, an increase in federal administrative control of education. As we shall see, Title I was based on a creative tension between federal administrators, who wield general guidelines for local categorical programs, and SDE's with sole power to approve specific local project proposals.[5]

The Objectives of Title I

The feedback after Title I's passage has been in substantial part based on the broad mandate of legislation that engendered a wide range of expectations. Unlike 1970, when about $1.4 billion were appropriated for Title I, the problem facing the bill's authors in 1964 was how to get *any* kind of major school aid bill enacted. Bendiner's analysis of the failure of numerous school aid bills over the years concluded that federal aid "had been beaten down in every way known to parliamentary man." [6] Although after World War II large education bills passed the Senate seven times and the House twice, the president as late as 1964 had never received a large federal aid bill.

In short, the primary task of the 1964 legislative strategists, who set the original goals for Title I, was to devise a politically viable bill. They had to overcome somehow the enormous and traditional congressional issue divisions: state aid to religion, desegregation, and "equitable" distribution of funds among states and localities. Andrew Biemiller, chief lobbyist for the powerful AFL-CIO, stated the viewpoint of the early ESEA backers:

> Let's get started . . . and get a bill through here, and begin to get some money into our school systems where we now know it is badly needed, and then we can take another look and get closer to the goal that both you and I want, and we make no bones about it that we want a general education bill.[7]

This process of "taking another look" has been the underlying force behind the conflicting feedback over Title I objectives ever since its passage.

Obviously, after the year of passage the prime objective of political viability and establishing the principle of federal aid to the schools would recede.

The second priority of ESEA framers was to begin reform of the entire fabric of American education through giving first priority to new programs for the needs of "disadvantaged children." In 1965, there were few people in or out of Washington who did not feel that the educational system needed more dollars for the poor and that it took dollars to stimulate innovation.* ESEA designers also wanted Title I to accomplish some of the financial equalization embodied in unsuccessful general aid bills, especially for the financially pressed rural South and central cities in the North and West. Educators and local politicians warmly embraced the bill, in part because of its potential for tax relief.

Two other objectives of the Title I framers were more diverse — strengthening federal-state relations by building up SDE's and speeding the pace of school desegregation in the South. Hundreds of Southern school districts would receive an increment of 30 percent to their total operating budget. This was to be the "sugar solvent" that was designed to melt Southern resistance to quick desegregation in order not to forfeit the windfall funds. This desegregation focus did bow to states rights, however, through the financial subsidies (partly under Title V) and the important decision-making role accorded SDE's. Thus, these agencies received 1 percent of the $1.3 billion for Title I as an administrative allowance and to encourage their oversight of local program proposals. The bulk of state aid is still distributed through an automatic formula, but Title I empowered state officials under general federal regulations to make program and methodological decisions. In short, thus reinforced, the SDE would have more programmatic control over federal funds than over money raised within the state.

The inclusion of all these policy objectives in a single, categorical, aid proposal was designed to speed congressional affirmation, but it also meant that the resulting program could not be homogeneous. The diverse objectives also reflected what we have shown in earlier chapters, the array of interests and decentralized power centers in the American polity.[8] Our emphasis here is on a major point. Given the compromises, the interested parties in the feedback stage could not be expected to agree on the ordering of priorities in the original act. Additional priorities were bound to emerge as the funds had an impact at the local level. In effect, although much of the feedback has included "evaluations" of the act's performance, these evaluators' perspectives and criteria were influenced by their particular ordering of policy objectives.

* This point is stressed repeatedly in the congressional hearings, committee reports, and floor debates on ESEA in 1965 and subsequent years when the act has been renewed (1966, 1967, and 1969).

For instance, feedback demands for changes in the legislation have been galvanized by those who support an evaluative measurement of how much the Title I students improved their ability and achievement in reading and math. During consideration of the initial 1964 bill, Senator Robert Kennedy stated that he had little confidence in the ability or motivation of educators to serve the poor. He stressed that most Title I money would be going to the very schools that had proven least effective in teaching the poor.[9] Even Senator Kennedy's critics agreed there was a lack of proven techniques in 1965 for evaluating the impact of compensatory education for children. Consequently, one of the few amendments specified the development of "effective procedures, including provision for appropriate objective measurements of educational achievement . . . for evaluating at least annually the effectiveness of the programs in meeting the special educational needs of culturally deprived children." But to evaluate whether a program that reaches over nine million children "works" on the single dimension of achievement-test scores is to ignore the multitude of other political objectives in Title I.

The defenders of Title I contend that a program seeking broad social change should not be evaluated mainly in terms of pupil achievement. They point to such consequences as the fiscal equalization impact of Title I and the concern it has generated among educators all over the nation for the disadvantaged child. Before turning to this issue, however, it is worthwhile exploring the specific feedback mechanisms, including the effects of the "systems analysts' " measures of educational output.

THE POLITICS OF TITLE I PROJECT APPROVAL

Educational Attainment as Feedback

A number of evaluation studies with a primary focus on achievement have attempted to assess the national impact of Title I.[10] On the whole, these studies have found *no significant change* in the achievement scores of Title I children. It is not our objective here to analyze the methodology or tests employed. The predominant view, however, from all existing knowledge is that the impact of Title I on pupil achievement is at best unclear or very slight.[11] Part of the problem appeared to the critics to be a national, average, per pupil expenditure from Title I of only about $120. Evaluators reasoned that such small amounts, added to a 1970 total per pupil expenditure of $885, could not be expected to bring about substantial changes in achievement for children who had been having great difficulty.

This feedback on pupil achievement was addressed to a minor extent to Congress, but the principal federal consumers of such findings were the budget decision makers within the office of the president and in HEW. In view of the enormous financial requirements for Vietnam, the resulting responses of these agencies were twofold. One, the Office of Education and the states should require more explicit educational criteria and project standards before local applications are approved. Two, the federal allocation for Title I and compensatory education in general should be held at the 1966 level until evaluations of pupil attainment were more conclusive and encouraging. Because of the high rate of inflation, the latter policy meant that the 1970 appropriation of over $1.4 billion for Title I is, in real purchasing power, actually less than its initial appropriation in 1966.

At the same time that federal budget makers were concerned about the feedback on educational attainment, they also were skeptical about the ability of SDE's to ensure that local project applications met the legal stricture of having "sufficient size, scope and quality to give reasonable promise of substantial progress." This concern highlights the conflicting policy desires in our federal-state-local educational delivery system. Federalism in education has developed a presumption that each level of government must retain inviolate its own sphere of responsibility and activity. Actually, as we have noted frequently, these supposedly autonomous levels of educational government interact symbiotically in a system of mutual obligation and dependence.[12] Federal and state governments are dependent on local governments to operate the schools — a function whose centralization most Americans deem undesirable. Federal policy makers thus support the popular value of "local control of schools" verbally, but as in the case of Title I, prefer to provide categorical grants to push national priorities that may transcend the priorities of particular states or localities. With federal funds come policy controls through the requirements for eligibility and accountability. On the other hand, states and localities try to get federal funds with as few requirements as possible.

The feedback on educational attainment, which led federal policy makers to the conclusion that more federal direction was needed, was resisted by many states and localities. Officials in the latter did not hesitate to contact their congressmen or such Washington-based lobbyists as Edgar Fuller, who represented the chief state school officers.[13] As we shall see, however, Congress was more responsive to the feedback on another objective of Title I — the equitable allocation of funds among the states.

But the federal administrative leaders were deeply concerned about the feedback showing low program effectiveness. In March, 1968, Commissioner of Education Harold Howe sent out revised federal guidelines to the SDE's for their use in reviewing local Title I applications. His letter (Title I Program Guide #48) embodied many of the implications of the information provided by feedback to that date.

> As yet we do not have all the answers we would like to have about the effectiveness of local Title I programs. It appears evident that Title I

> programs are more effective when: (a) Title I expenditures are concentrated rather than spread; (b) not just one, but a comprehensive group of services is provided; . . . (c) services are maintained over an extended period of time; (d) services are integrated into a total school program that includes new approaches. . . .

A key change was Howe's interpretation of "criteria" in the federal statute as requiring SDE's to make an *affirmative finding* on the above issues and to specifically delineate factors to be considered for a *finding*. Prior to this, USOE guidelines had urged the states to follow federal advice but had not required affirmative findings before a local project could be approved.

Federal Aid Politics in Texas and California

Before this federal policy statement could become a policy outcome it had to be transmitted to and enforced by SDE's in local school districts. Such a transmission process feeds back new inputs of information to higher authorities, of course. In this, the performance of the states varies enormously, often depending, as we saw in the last chapter, on the particular state political culture. In order better to grasp the varied politics of such intergovernmental relations, it is worthwhile comparing the differential reaction of two states to Commissioner Howe's revised 1968 criteria.[14]

In California the pattern of political influence resulted in a divorce of Title I control from the state superintendent, Max Rafferty, and the hegemony of an independent Advisory Commission on Compensatory Education dominated by an activist administrator, Wilson Riles. The administrative structure for Title I was specified by the California legislature in large part to help implement the educational philosophy of Riles and to shield the program from the influence of Superintendent Rafferty.

State legislative leaders saw Rafferty as a political rival who did not share their viewpoint on educational policy. So they created an eleven-member advisory commission, including four legislators, which appointed a chief administrator who reported directly to it and the state board. Rafferty was bypassed in this chain of administrative control. The legislature contended it wanted to insure that federal and state compensatory programs were not "absorbed and lost" in the California SDE. Riles, the state director of compensatory education, who had significant influence on appointments to this new advisory commission, owed a good part of his own administrative appointment to his relationship with Senator Eugene MacAteer, the sponsor of the bill to remove control from Rafferty.

At the outset, Riles's philosophy indicated that he would not shrink from a tough stance on federal priorities and program quality:

> I've been around [the California Education Department] for eight years. What usually happens is that the district sends its budget man up. He is concerned only with how to get dollars, not with methods or

programs. If this is to be a program operation, we must have mechanisms to ensure that when they come for money, we can nail them. We make them start with identifying the target area, the most pressing needs of youngsters, strategies and program to meet those needs and how to evaluate results. *Then* we talk in terms of how much funding is needed to carry out their objectives. My viewpoint is that this is not just money to help districts build buildings or buy projectors; it is to meet the needs of deprived children.[15]

Thus it was that the California Division of Compensatory Education had the political support and independence to implement Commissioner Howe's more stringent program approval requirement. Indeed, California had used most of the 1968 USOE criteria even *before* Washington was convinced it needed to make changes. Local districts in California met solid resistance on all political fronts when they objected to rigid and extensive project approval mandates. As one SDE administrator explained:

The local agencies took their complaints to Riles and the Advisory Commission who rarely disagreed on the need to enforce the guidelines. They would then appeal to the ultimate authority, the State Board of Education. Once the State Board voted 10 to 0 against a large city district using a lot of Title I money to build high schools, the word got out all over the state that it was useless to appeal to the State Board. They were viewed as being 100% behind Riles and his staff. After all, they had strongly supported Riles for the appointment to head the Division of Compensatory Education.[16]

In California, then, a powerful coalition was formed to implement federal guidelines. The state legislature did not intercede on program or project decisions after establishing an implementation structure "independent of the traditional state administrators." The SDE staff even sent out their own state Title I guidelines, contending that "the Federal guidelines were too vague and confusing." The state's more explicit guidelines contained more criteria for local project approval than those sent by Commissioner Howe in March, 1968. For example, they specified that Title I projects could only be implemented in elementary schools. The involvement of the governor's office in these programs and the allocative restrictions imposed by the state were minimal. Governor Edmund "Pat" Brown appointed state board of education members who supported Riles in numerous ways, but their direct involvement was nonexistent.* The political situation under Governor Brown and State Superintendent Rafferty was summarized this way:

The Superintendent would make a proposal; the Board, usually the President, would strongly (in some cases, angrily) criticize the Super-

---

* Indeed, the state superintendent, elected on a statewide ticket, has never been considered under the governor's administrative direction or part of his cabinet.

intendent, the major newspapers would give broad, front page coverage to the controversies, some local parent or political groups would issue statements for or against positions taken by participants. . . . The reaction of the Board publicly was one of unity, but privately, a minority was extremely disturbed.

The Speaker of the Assembly [Jesse Unruh] saw the Superintendent as a threat to Democratic party hegemony in the State and vigorously attacked him for a long period of time during the year. The Speaker's attack was for the purpose of getting the Superintendent out in the open from behind his shield of non-partisanship when he was obviously running for governor. . . . The Governor was in the painful position of seeing his political friends on the Board of Education in a furious fight with a Superintendent who represented his political rivals and was, in fact, a potential candidate against him, yet he had to maintain a cautious neutrality.[17]

The administrators of Title I in California were able to steer clear of these continual controversies, however, because of their independent organizations. Brown's successor, Ronald Reagan, has for different reasons also elected to remain uninvolved in Title I administration, regarding it as a "welfare program."

No sharper contrast with this state-federal cooperation can be made than in Texas, where Title I political and administrative situations have followed a quite different course. Implementation of federal regulations and guidelines has been slower to reflect Washington's desires; yet this conforms to traditional Texas administrative and political realities. In 1970, Title I provided $98 million to California and $70 million to Texas for grants to local schools. Although the Texas SDE has received over 69 percent of its total 1970 administrative budget from federal sources, it has been no more than a reluctant partner in the Title I program.

The Texas Education Agency (TEA) has carefully nurtured an image of being "above politics" and of not being pressured by the kind of statewide political figures active in California. The same state superintendent, J. W. Edgar, has served since 1948, when he was first appointed by a reconstituted state board. The 1948 act reorganizing the state administration of education in Texas was explicitly designed to depoliticize the operation of TEA.[18] Texas legislators decided that by electing the state board they could stop the election of the state superintendent, who, prior to 1948, had used patronage and political stumping of the state to win votes. Commissioner Edgar's strategy was to change TEA's political image by ending the overt favoritism of his predecessor to rural areas, where the majority of the voters were. In that change, Edgar's tactics have included appointing prestigious and respected persons to key staff positions and extensive use of local school advisory groups before state policies are set. His administration has led over the years to independence from gubernatorial and legislative influence on federal aid allocation. Unlike Rafferty, Edgar's image does not engender any concern about his political ambitions among state political figures. This substantial TEA independence from state political forces is coupled, however, with a traditional deference for local control of education, especially when potentially objectionable federal aid strictures are involved.[19]

The ambivalence of Texans toward federal aid is also an important factor in the delivery of federal programs through the state government to the local school level. Indeed, in the context of Texas political history, the phrase *federal aid* borders on the obscene.[20] Traditionally, Texans in or seeking political power follow the "states rights" line, stressing a diminution of federal power and the virtues of home-grown government. This value tends to restrict the strings that either the federal or state governments can attach to funds destined for local agencies. This philosophy, however, has not impeded a large flow of federal funds into Texas, but it has kept the distribution of federal aid from becoming an election, or even a visible, issue.

The Texas Title I staff in an interview with one of the authors expressed their administrative policy in this manner:

> Our job is not to make decisions concerning how effective a particular component is; this is a local decision. Our job is to see if the program meets the federal requirements. If a school district's Title I program does meet the legal requirements, then we have an obligation to fund the program. We do not feel that we are in any position to dictate particular methodologies to schools. The state department might encourage local school districts to choose one of the USOE recommended "best practices," but local agencies should be allowed to do something else, if they can justify that something else.

The California and Texas political cultures thus influenced what programs emerged at the local level. The California SDE specified that Title I projects must not group or "track" children if it led to segregation. Also, they must include components for language development and mathematics, parent involvement, nutrition/health, inservice training, and intergroup relations. The TEA decided to leave such matters to local determination and not to require much of anything in the applications. It stuck to this stance despite the charge of the National Advisory Council on Title I in its 1966 annual report that "for the most part, however, projects are piecemeal fragmented efforts at remediation or vaguely directed enrichment."

TEA did not even send out Commissioner Howe's program guidelines of March, 1968, for over a year after they were received. The dissemination of these guidelines came only after USOE had threatened to cut off

federal funds to Mississippi because of its failure to follow federal requirements. At that point, TEA became concerned about this new enforcement
policy and changed its application review substantially. Now, although
specific federal regulations and guidelines are checked, local judgments on
program content and priorities are rarely questioned. As a TEA evaluator
observed: "We don't collect evaluation data on program strategy any more.
If the Title I administrators are not interested in what reading programs are
effective, then why should we collect that kind of evaluation information?"

In short, this analysis of two states' reaction to the consequences of
feedback about Title I highlights the different politics in intergovernmental
education programs. In part, a state's response is shaped by the traditional
values of the state as a whole toward local control. Other factors are the
administrative culture of a state — its habitual strategies, information
sources, etc. — as well as the self-interest values of the state Title I administrators. But the personal values of the administrator were either constrained or liberated by political support from other school political
authorities — the state superintendent, state board, legislature, and governor's office. In California, the Title I administrator identified with Washington's viewpoint on compensatory education program design, and had an
independent political base to implement it. In Texas, traditional viewpoints
toward intergovernmental relationships set boundaries around the state's
role toward local districts.

This differential state response to the 1968 guidelines led to more feedback information and subsequently a set of revised federal guidelines and
project approval criteria. Indeed, one of the first major alternatives of
Commissioner Howe's successor, James Allen, was to convene a large task
force to devise new federal-state Title I policies that would enhance the
effectiveness of local projects. This action was preceded, however, by the
investigation outlined in the next section.

Another Round of Feedback

The discouraging feedback on Title I pupil attainment and the subsequent
program design changes discussed above were followed by a series of investigatory reports by civil rights organizations focusing on Title I's objective of providing more education dollars for poor children. Investigators
contended that pupil achievement gains could not be expected to occur,
because maladministration had resulted in unintended funding patterns. The
flow of dollars did not insure that poor children really had had more spent
on their education than their wealthy colleagues. The investigators' hopes
were that "by bringing to light some of the more flagrant misuses of Title
I funds . . . a concerted and continuing effort will ensue to help poor
children get what the nation promised when the act was passed." [21] Indeed,
they felt that Title I never had a chance to bring about achievement gains,

and consequently, the systems analysts were using the wrong evaluative yardsticks. All this arose because the money was being spent for general aid and diverted from the special educational needs of disadvantaged children.

Civil rights groups were equally concerned with another objective of Title I's legislative framers — its supposed stimulus to racial integration. Their investigation charged that in many Southern districts Title I had caused the opposite. It provided the needed financial support to keep open black schools that were about to be closed because of lack of local finances to maintain a dual school system.

For example, Armand Derfner, representing the Lawyers Constitutional Defense Committee, charged that in Mississippi

> just in the last few years, when there has been some pressure to equal-ize, the state has been enabled by the use of Title I funds to keep pour-ing state and local money in the white schools. . . . They have suddenly gotten this $30 to $40 million a year from Title I money which they can put into the black schools and claim they are equaliz-ing. But that is not what Title I is supposed to do and that is not what the act was intended to do.
>
> We think that . . . Title I has been used in Mississippi to allow the state to continue discriminating and to continue the practices that have gone on so many years and to fail to make any attempt to equalize the schools.[22]

The NAACP Legal Defense Fund charged, for example, that a South Carolina school district, using Title I money to construct new classrooms at an all-black elementary school, justified it as a way to decrease teacher load. But this black school continued to have the highest pupil-teacher ratio of any school in the county system.[23]

The investigators' attention, however, was also brought to the wide disparities in school expenditures within Northern cities. Expenditures per pupil in Washington, D.C., ranged from $393.97 in one elementary school to $600.96 in an elementary school serving a high-income area. They rea-soned that Title I might only be providing poor children with as much per pupil money as the wealthier children received — but this did not follow the framers' intent of *more* total dollars per pupil for the *neediest* students. This feedback resulted in a specific demand for "comparability." This would require a federal law or regulation providing that *state and local* funds for education be distributed equitably among all the schools of a district *before* a district was eligible for Title I money. This demand met a sympathetic reception within the Nixon administration, and about a year after the investigatory reports cited here, acting Commissioner Terrel Bell issued new comparability guidelines. A Department of HEW Task Force was also instructed to devise guidelines to overcome the negative incentives for desegregation in Title I implementation. Yet at this writing, the comparability guidelines had been watered down considerably after protests by professional education groups, so they may not accomplish the objectives of the civil rights investigators.

Congress and Title I Feedback

We have just shown the administrative changes resulting from feedback about compensatory education program design and the allocation of ESEA funds among schools *within* a district. Congress has also mandated a wide range of changes in the original Title I legislation based on various kinds of feedback. It has displayed a particular concern with yet another of Title I objectives — interstate equalization through channeling federal funds to low-income states and cities. Indeed, the recent political support of Title I has rested more on its success as an equalizing financial vehicle among states than as a proven instrument of educational improvement. While the systems analysts and behavioral engineers found a receptive and interested executive-branch audience for studies of pupil achievement data, Congress was listening to state and local officials who complained about not receiving a fair share of the federal financial pie.

Congress then considered the Title I allocation formula and its impact on state finances, under education committee chairmen Rep. Carl Perkins of Kentucky and Sen. Lister Hill of Alabama.[24] Various alternatives were considered for increasing the allocation floor from $2,000 to $3,000 or for changing the payment rate for each disadvantaged child from 50 percent to 60 or 75 percent of the state average per pupil expenditure. These reviews were influenced by ties between the environment and political authorities. Both chairmen were from nonurban states, for example, so neither responded to a big-city constituency. Their states also had very low per pupil expenditures and per capita incomes compared to the national average.[25] A computer simulation revealed that the financially poor Southern states would benefit the most from increasing the Title I payment to one-half the *national* average per pupil expenditure instead of the much lower figure of one-half the *state* average used in the original legislation.

But the Democratic administration made no proposal to change Title I in this direction, as it was more interested in funneling money into big cities, not the heavily rural South. However, Congressman Perkins (D-Ken.) and Rep. Sam Gibbons (D-Fla.) teamed with Senator Hill (D-Ala.) and Sen. Ralph Yarborough (D-Tex.) to provide formidable support on the congressional education committees for the option of one-half the national average. They attracted support from Rep. Albert Quie (R-Minn.), the leader of the Republicans in the House comittee. Quie favored the change on the basis of "equity" for the poorer states, since Minnesota with its high per pupil expenditures had too little to gain. This coalition was influential enough to push the amendment through Congress. Opposition from high income and expenditure states never materialized. Congressmen from these districts were successful at a later date in adding to ESEA those students who lived in public housing units, most of which exist primarily in urban areas.

As 1971 opened, the cycle was ready to move again. The Nixon administration was seeking to abolish categorical grants of the type in ESEA and move to revenue sharing. Here, funds would go directly to state and local governments. More significantly, all schools — not merely poor ones — would be eligible for funds.

THE POLITICS OF OTHER TITLE I OBJECTIVES

Legal Assistance Pressures

One of the chief aims of the Johnson administration's poverty program was to establish a variety of private, nonprofit organizations to challenge authoritative institutions such as local schools and federal bureaucracies.[26] While the cornerstone of the Johnson poverty program — community action agencies — has never been an important source of Title I feedback, the lesser-known legal-assistance arm of the Office of Economic Opportunity has. OEO has funded free legal services to indigents at Neighborhood Legal Service offices. These centers are located in poverty areas, ordinarily in conjunction with the community action agencies of which they are a component. In addition to providing lawyers to poor people with legal problems, they have also encouraged law reform through test cases and legislation.

In recent years this legal assistance network has become increasingly active in suing governments at all levels for their administration of Title I. The results of these suits generate changes in a specific district or state and also provide feedback on general policy problems to federal lobbyists or policy makers. A Center for Law and Education at Harvard has served as a national information service in strategies and legal grounds for Title I suits.[27] Many of these suits have a broader intent, as this excerpt from a Center report indicates.

> Aside from the informational aspects of Title I litigation, the threat of a law suit, if well-timed, may give the poor bargaining power to affect program changes — even though those changes may be unrelated to the legal basis of the suit. The trauma of litigation, the inconvenience of depositions, the fear of adverse publicity, and the costs of defense may well make school administrators more amenable to making concessions. . . .
>
> Another reason to adopt a Title I litigation strategy is that a law suit might well compel state and local educational agencies to adopt

regular procedures for the review and approval of Title I project application. Often there is a mystical and secretive process for channeling Title I proposals through a bureaucratic power structure, a process which remains unknown to . . . children, the parents, and the community.[28]

Suits are brought in behalf of parents or children in a wide range of complaints against Title I programs, including lack of local compliance with the 1968 program criteria. As the excerpt indicated, a suit's objective may be, in part, to galvanize a local interest group to lobby the school system for changes in the Title I program emphasis. In short, these Title I lawyers see as a prime objective the stimulation of a parent and student constituency for Title I that has a genuine decision-making role in formulation of its projects. They see these laymen offering alternative educational values to the professional educators who have controlled the program at all levels of government.[29] Because lawsuits are a convenient and effective device for ensuring that schoolmen will pay attention to parent viewpoints, they provide citizens with new political resources for educational bargaining. Title I thereby creates a new set of inputs for local schools by its funding of a new and independent base of power for the formerly powerless.

Title I as a Welfare Program: The Providence Case

One of the less-publicized objectives of Title I was its potential for providing various welfare services to poor children, and original USOE guidelines and publicity featured this flexibility. The act contained enough latitude to provide health, clothing, and food, the rationale being that it was impossible for children to learn if they did not have adequate health or nutrition. In some cases, school children have been kept home in the winter because the family lacked warm clothes or even shoes. In the initial years of Title I, several Southern states spent large sums of money on school breakfast/lunch programs and on basic medical care. Indeed, the National Advisory Council on Education of Disadvantaged Children early stressed that educators should give more attention to the welfare components.

Notwithstanding the reluctance of some boards of education to assume the unfamiliar task of feeding and clothing the poor, the solution to these social problems should be funded by Title I in order that impoverished children may respond productively to the school's primary mission of teaching and learning.[30]

Schoolmen in many districts reacted with the claim that Title I funds were already insufficient to provide teachers and other educational services in the depth or scale required to affect pupil performance. If these funds were to be diverted to make up the large deficiencies of welfare payments, enormous sums of education money would be needed to maintain welfare families at a minimum standard of living in several states. USOE reacted with a decision that local judgments could best decide these priorities. Some states, such as California, thereafter did require a health and nutrition component in almost all local projects.

Evaluation of this use of funds was murky. If a school district did choose to use much Title I money for food, clothing, and health, this could be having a significant impact, but it would probably not be measured by the achievement tests used by evaluators having only cognitive objectives in mind. Again we see that the evaluator's criteria can determine a large part of judgments about whether a federal-state program "works" or not.

By 1970 the feedback process involving interest groups and local citizens resulted in a concerted campaign to channel more Title I funds to welfare objectives. Events in Providence, Rhode Island, crystallized discontent of the poor over this provision's administration, offering a brief but clear illustration of recycling of the conversion process as a result of feedback protest. George Wiley, the president of the National Welfare Rights Organization, had been interested in Title I as a source of clothing money to supplement inadequate welfare budgets. Members of NWRO were on the parent advisory board for the Title I program in Providence. These parents, representing welfare recipients, demanded that Title I provide direct clothing grants of $48 to each Providence child on AFDC, regardless of whether he participated in a Title I program or could document a particular clothing need. The Providence school district at first resisted the proposal, then expressed sympathy for it, and referred the issue to the Rhode Island SDE.[31]

Here, it met a cold reception. The SDE contended that it must be demonstrated that the absence of clothing funds was a specific impediment to educational attainment and then that these monies were integrated with a Title I academic program. State officials estimated that Wiley's clothing policy would consume $1.5 million of Rhode Island's $4 million Title I allocation. Viewing clothing as a welfare problem, they stressed that the Welfare Department could never pay for the teachers who must be relieved of their duties if clothing payments were increased. As one state official emphasized, "We did not want to see good academic programs wiped out by clothing payments." Wiley's demands, however, made just before the fall, 1970, elections, did elicit considerable sympathy from Rhode Island's Democratic governor and Providence's Democratic mayor. The SDE, however, felt it was insulated from control by these political officials because of the federal requirements.

The NWRO also engaged the help, funded by Harvard's Center for Law and Education, of Title I lawyers from the OEO. Although these lawyers assisted parents in documenting their need for clothing, the suit did not involve the clothing issue alone. This staff prepared a sixty-two count lawsuit charging SDE with everything from misappropriation of federal money to not enforcing adequate evaluation of local Title I programs. Protest politics takes other forms than litigation, however. The SDE building had twelve bomb scares and one fire, while the Rhode Island Title I coordinator was placed under twenty-four-hour police protection after welfare mothers staged numerous demonstrations in his office.

Because the SDE firmly believed it was acting within the USOE guidelines and legal mandates, the issue was bound to end up in Washington. As the beleaguered Rhode Island Title I coordinator observed, "This is not a state-run program when we get into a question of entirely new program approval criteria." USOE had already been made aware of the issue through welfare demonstrations in Norfolk, Virginia, New York City, and Cleveland (where the mothers demanded $100 per child for clothing). Rhode Island had to wait several months, however, before finding out whether USOE would support its stand and vindicate its opposition to the governor. Within USOE, the Title I administrators viewed the NWRO clothing demands as possibly leading to vast diversions of education money. In their view the basic integrity of the Title I effort was threatened. NWRO supporters charged, however, that USOE opposed clothing because the government wanted to ensure that the money continued to flow into the pockets of education professionals and not to poor people.

In September, 1970, acting United States Commissioner of Education Terrel H. Bell "clarified" the federal guidelines on clothing by essentially affirming the position of the Rhode Island SDE and the traditional viewpoint of USOE's Title I career administrators. Bell declared that Title I "is an educational program, not a welfare program" and that clothing may be paid for from Title I only in "emergency situations." The USOE guideline specified that no direct payment could be made to any child or parent, either by a school district or through a welfare agency, and that no predetermined amount should be set for clothing payments.[32]

The part of the decision that incensed NWRO particularly was Bell's directive that local districts could not spend any more money in the future for clothing than they had in past years. Wiley called this a "restrictive and punitive action against poor people" and charged that local clothing programs, brought about by pressure from local welfare groups, were being abandoned. An undaunted Wiley took the issue to his White House contacts and to Bell's superior, Secretary of HEW Eliot Richardson. His hope was that Richardson would see the embarrassing publicity that the welfare mothers could attract better than the acting commissioner of education, who was a temporary career appointee. As one Washington lawyer supporting NWRO remarked, "Those welfare ladies are very skillful at making a bureaucrat look like an ass." The issue also cut across two of the large bureaucracies under Richardson's stewardship — welfare and education — which might differ on the priority of clothing.

Secretary Richardson, like his successor, Robert Finch, met regularly with representatives of NWRO. When they raised the Title I clothing demand, he agreed that he could not see the justification for limiting future clothing expenditures to the level established in past years. He also remained unconvinced that Title I's legislative history, as USOE asserted, limited the general magnitude of expenditures for clothing. Consequently, he overruled USOE regulations that had limited clothing payments to the level of the previous years.

This ruling was communicated through the federal system to the Rhode Island SDE and finally to the Title I parent advisory group in Providence. In effect, HEW had set new boundaries within which local political bargaining would take place. The Rhode Island groups worked out a Title I project of $48 for each child who was in the *existing* Title I program and whose teacher or social worker indicated in his records that the specific child needed clothing. Direct grants to parents were not included in Rhode Island as the HEW regulation stated. Facilitating the agreement was the sixty-two count lawsuit that the welfare parents were mounting against the Providence school district and the SDE. The Rhode Island Title I coordinator, however, said the policy cycle would begin again because Title I administrators from several states planned to appeal Richardson's decision to the Congress after the 1970 elections.

SUMMARY

This review of political feedback and policy making highlights the interaction at every point in our federal system of stress arising from a program that reflects conflicting values. The intergovernmental effects detailed here flesh out the framework of analysis diagrammed in the introduction to Part Two. Federalism imposes a distinctive pattern on these interactions that is seen in the many access points it offers to the multiple interests of the school system.

The initial decisions of federal administrators and congressmen in 1965 set off stress among different individuals and interest groups at the state and local level who favored one of Title I's many goals over another. This stress created demands, some of which entered the policy process at the local level (e.g., clothing in Providence), and then became outputs and demands for state and federal officials to administer and cope with. In other cases, the political decisions of local authorities generated demands that went initially to federal policy makers, who then attempted to implement the proposed reform through state and local education officials — thus Commissioner Howe's program requirements. The response depended in significant part upon the particular political tradition and culture in the state or local district. In recent years, however, lay political actors and interest groups not affiliated with any level of government or historic influence base have become increasingly active in generating stress and articulating wants so that their educational demands are communicated to policy makers.

But as we emphasized, those who hold official education positions are not passive transmitters of demands, which they send along as outputs. They have values and attitudes that shape their viewpoint about and responsiveness to the demands. If they place a high value on local control, then they will not be receptive to many demands for more detailed and rigid federal regulations. If they do not see an important role for poverty-stricken parents in shaping the priority and substance of Title I education programs, they are likely to resist the establishment of parent advisory councils.

Further, the direction of Title I was shaped by the fact that the vast majority of the long-term administrators at all levels of government were socialized into the public-school-administration norms and professional outlook. Consequently, there is a common value basis for reaching agreements among administrators at all levels of the federal system. The growing constituency of poor parents, however, cannot be accommodated within these professional value confines. More, they increasingly are learning how to develop and use new resources against these restraints. The future outlook is for even greater stress between professional educators and groups representing low-income parents.

This section also highlights the difference between a policy output and outcome. A legal requirement in the statute or an administrative stricture in the federal regulations is conceived of as a policy output. But if state and local education officials are antagonistic to these legal mandates, they can prevent them from becoming outcomes merely by not enforcing them. Or by their own means and in response to their own values, they may transform outputs into outcomes unanticipated — even undesired — by the authorities originally producing them. It is not enough to provide information about the output to have it be received, accepted, and acted on. Information on federal requirements can be disseminated widely, for example, but it would take an army of auditors and program analysts to check on compliance in 19,300 local school districts.

In effect, the American federal system has built-in checks on "federal control of education." These checks can widen or narrow the gap between output and outcome. At each level below Washington are local authorities who can offer resistance to "federal control." They also have allies in

Washington, they share administrative norms of professionalism, they are linked to peers at other system levels, and they can fight from the high ground of localism that has meant so much in American history. If federal control takes place, it does so under two conditions — by massive federal enforcement pressure or by local acquiescence in national goals. The former is rare in our history because of its costs for everyone in the system, as epitomized by the Civil War. The latter is more characteristic of federal-state relations, but there is a cost factor here, too. Federal goals embodied in outputs must be compromised, creating a larger or smaller gap between output and outcome.

The next chapter shows both federal pressure and compromise, and the costs each required.

9   Southern School Desegregation

The previous policy outcome has one quality possibly unnoticed in the analysis. Teachers, parents, board members, administrators, and ethnic groups may well disagree over the direction or even pace of the program, but all share implicitly the notion that federal aid to local schools is desirable. The primary reason for this, of course, is that the program is essentially supportive of the goals that these participants have in common. Subsidy of schooling is the hallmark of ESEA, although that law necessarily led to regulation of schoolmen. Subsidy and regulation are interwoven in many intergovernmental programs, of course, and both involve allocation of resources. We have seen the two aspects operating when all participants support the basic goal of the output. What occurs, however, when they do not because the output's regulatory aspect dominates its subsidy aspect?

Because local schools do not get all that they want in life, it is well to understand their politics when compelled by the superior power of intervening authority to change old and favored ways. Many examples of this might be noted, particularly in the enlarged role of the state in school policy in this century, e.g., directives on budgets and audits, teacher certification, curricula, student attendance, health and safety, administrators' responsibilities, and taxation. In California, these run to numerous volumes of 2300 pages.

Instead of these, however, we choose as an illustration of such regulation the most publicized case in our time — the pressures by Washington for Southern school desegregation. A generation or more ago it would have been better illustrated by the school consolidation movement; the arguments over values in both cases have a surprising similarity. Our purpose in this selection is to demonstrate aspects of the schools as a political sys-

173

tem: the difficulties of intergovernmental relations in a federal system, the clash of values in a pluralistic society, and the evolving nature of the American creed. Much of this we have seen in the previous policy, of course. But what is emphasized here is the reaction of local school systems to the thrust of outside regulation and in particular to the role of the judiciary, as distinct from administrators.

At first thought, courts seem an unlikely adjunct of schools and, for the naive, an unlikely adjunct of politics. But the history of education has been shaped by important court decisions on the duties and responsibilities of school components; even though trivial, the right of students not to have their hair cut is only the latest of many such contributions. At a more significant level, the United States Supreme Court has been directly involved in the question of religion in our schools: Bible reading, required prayers, flag salutes, transportation and other expenses of parochial students, etc. Court involvement can be as direct — but narrow — as whether schools can be prohibited from teaching German, or as indirect — and extensive — as whether schools can be segregated by race. Schoolmen may react by massive noncompliance, as with the Bible and prayer decisions, but to be indifferent is very difficult.[1]

Court involvement in such matters surprises only those who view the bench as a political eunuch. Contemporary analysts of the judiciary emphasize not merely its behavior but the values that its behavior implements. Judges are political because they must choose between competing values brought before them in conflict. As early as 1840, Alexis de Tocqueville was noting that "scarcely any political question arises in the United States that is not resolved, sooner or later, into a judicial question." The reason is that when men differ in the political arenas, one site where that contest may be transferred is the courtroom. As we shall see, the form and rules of such contests may differ from those in other sites. But they are still essentially political because contenders seek the authority of the political system to justify and command the distribution of resources — such as rights and property — that each deems desirable. The allocation of resources that follows from a court mandate can be as effective in reality as that which issues from a legislature.[2]

What, then, are the relationships between the judiciary, as part of the political system of the state, and the political system of the school? What are the constraints and strengths in this relationship? What is the form of accommodation and conflict in the input, conversion, feedback, and outcome phases of the political process here? How does federalism filter (Easton would say "shape") the outcome? What values are reflected among participants? These are the questions we pursue as we illuminate national efforts after midcentury to expand the American creed to include those excluded from it since Jamestown.

THE JUDICIARY AS A POLITICAL SUBSYSTEM

In our perspective, the judiciary shares attributes of a system in Eastonian terms, although it is also a subsystem of the larger political system. Like other such subsystems — legislatures, agencies, and executives — the judiciary's environment presents it with demands which it may convert into outputs; these interact with the environment to be transformed in time into outcomes and thus generate later inputs to the court. The relationships indicated in Figure II.1 thus apply to the courts also. This assumes no distinct boundaries of the judicial subsystem marking it off from others. Instead, we assume it interacts with legislative and executive subsystems continuously, as well as with private systems in the social environment. In this view, as Schubert notes, the important action is not in the courtroom but is outside "in the interplay between judicial, legislative and executive systems, and between national and state judicial systems; and in the effect of judicial decisions upon society and the economy, and vice versa." [3]

That environment within which judges operate marches constantly into their chambers, sometimes unobtrusively and sometimes loudly. For example, a historical constitutional framework imposes certain constraints upon the selection of judges and their procedures, and these forces from the past shape who is made a judge and what he does. Professional canons have their effect on who is selected or even considered; institutional traditions require procedures that shape the pace and division of labor. Further, the partisanship of extramural party life, which has affected a judge's recruitment as well as his deliberations in our past, is not without influence even today.[4] Changes in the social order outside the chambers bring changes inside to the courts' issues, structures, and attitudes.[5]

The value conflict thrust into the court seeks authoritative allocation of resources to implement those values. For this reason, courts — and particularly the United States Supreme Court — have a manifest function of resolving conflict. Such allocational decisions have an impact — not always favorable — on all branches of the national government and at all levels of the federal system. This task of conflict resolution performs latent functions for the values underlying the conflict. Thus, the Supreme Court legitimizes national policies and the values they reflect. Conversely, such action serves to illegitimize policies and values favored by some. The trick, of course, is for the Court to do this in a way that does not decrease support for the courts as an institution while assuring that their decisions are accepted.

Further, the Supreme Court must maintain some kind of balance with other national subsystems so as to reduce potential conflict among their respective policy decisions. In the process, the judiciary provides signals to litigants, general public, and political subsystems and their actors (including their own local courts) as to the policy-value outputs it will reinforce. The issuance of such signals is not the same as their acceptance, however. So the Court through its history has had to balance itself carefully at key intersections of a nationally separated government, a federally divided nation, and a diverse population. Yet judicial policy making has shown more consistency than the preceding might imply. Whether at the trial or appellate level, distinguishable behavioral processes are commonly at work: initiation of controversies, accommodation via out-of-court settlement, persuasion of judge or jury, decision making, implementation of decisions, and their reconsideration.

All of this is understandable as a facet of systems analysis. Inputs for the judicial subsystem are evident as reflections of environmental demands. Their form and presentation differ for this subsystem, however. The lobbyist gives way to the lawyer, buttonholing to law review articles, and publicity campaigns to litigants' briefs.[6] The demands are presented formally, dealing with matters of logic and legal precedent. The political authority to whom all this is addressed operates within a matrix of constraints, including its own values aroused by the issues. Recent research stresses the independent role of such values in the conversion process; outputs are seen as a function of the interplay of judicial values within the social process of court procedures, all of this with political consequences for the environment.[7] In this view, legal precedents are only partially controlling, and only when judicial values agree. But when the issue is new or has new applications, then the psychological impact of values on the bench exerts an independent force as an explanation of judicial outcomes.

However such decisions are derived, they constitute outputs for society. They are something more than a statement of which litigant won and lost. Rather, they instruct a larger circle as to the value norms that the judicial subsystem seeks to impose upon the environment. At different periods in our history, the norms of political, social, and economic freedom have assumed different judicial priorities. Most recently, the economic norms have seemed least important to the Supreme Court, the political next, whereas the social — particularly civic equality — have dominated the era of Chief Justice Earl Warren. We will shortly turn to one of these.

The final need is to understand the impact of judicial outputs on society. While the Court may signal authoritative norms, what if no one notices, or if noticing, defies them, or if obeying, misinterprets them? When the Court confirms what is widely accepted already, as with its nineteenth-century opposition to polygamy, output and outcome are similar, for compliance is very high. When, however, the Court innovates in accepted norms, some gap between output and outcome is to be expected, and compliance will be less than complete.

The conditions under which the judiciary can innovate, as Schubert has defined them, are very constraining. Given a majority of justices favoring a change, a national majority in similar agreement, and the chances that the Court's decision would not hurt it in other policy areas, then innovation would be forthcoming. But these combinations have not existed often in our history, and indeed, they have not in other political subsystems. Such an absence accounts for much of the inertia and procrastination in facing emergent demands in the American political system. If the Court moves when the maximum conditions do not exist, considerable dissonance arises from other political subsystems. Then the Court is said to lack "self-restraint" and is accused of being "activist."

More importantly, when that output does generate dissonance, the feedback will show evasion of the original decisions. So it was in the Dred Scott case in 1857, and so it was in the case of *Brown vs. the Board of Education of Topeka* in 1954. Not until the Court was joined by a national majority and by other elements of the national political system was there compliance with the Court's insistence on the social norm of racial equality in the education of children.

INPUT AND CONVERSION
IN THE *BROWN* CASES

Such a conceptualization of the judicial process is illuminated in each stage of the 1954 *Brown* case.[8] We begin with environmental forces prior to the decision that generated stress and the resulting demands. A major constraint on this decision was a constitutional principle derived from *Plessy vs. Ferguson* in 1896 that separation of the races was not a denial of equality; one justice had dissented bitterly that "our Constitution is color blind and neither knows nor tolerates classes among citizens." This decision must be seen as part of a set of Southern forces capping the Reconstruction and separating Negroes from any form of power.[9] For over a half century, this decision legitimized a "separate but equal" condition for all blacks in all aspects of a white-controlled Southern society.

In the 1930's, though, small indicators of change, if not of mind, then of emphasis, appeared in the Court. Over a ten-year period it increasingly insisted upon a meaningful equality in the quantity of facilities, even though still separate, in Southern law schools. This quantitative emphasis was joined in 1950 with insistence upon qualitative measures of equality, raising the interesting possibility that mere separation itself was a barrier to a qualitative equality, a foreshadowing of the *Brown* decision in 1954.[10]

That hint set off a Southern reaction of energetically improving Negro schools, sometimes spending more on them than on white schools.

It was out of this constitutional and social milieu that cases arose in Kansas, Delaware, the District of Columbia, South Carolina, and Virginia that challenged segregation, not merely in law schools or colleges, but at the very base of Southern education — the primary and secondary public schools. The challenge could not rest fully on legal precedents, for there were none. Instead, social science evidence was introduced at the trial-court level to support the charge that segregation had deep qualitative, psychological consequences for Negroes that were not erased by quantitatively equal facilities. The Delaware courts actually agreed with the Negro challenge, although only on grounds that a quantitative inequality existed in fact. But over several years all these cases wended their separate ways to the Supreme Court, which announced in June, 1952, that it would hear them in the 1952–53 term. Thus after years of effort, the main legal spokesman for Negro rights, the National Association for the Advancement of Colored People, had through its legal arm brought squarely to the highest court a challenge against the "separate but equal" doctrine of *Plessy vs. Ferguson*.[11]

But the NAACP was not alone in this contest, or in providing inputs to the Court, for many other actors were involved directly or indirectly. Some twenty-four *amici curiae* filed briefs, nineteen of which supported the NAACP — e.g., the ACLU, the CIO, etc. One of these was from the United States solicitor general; although the federal government was not a party to the case, both Presidents Truman and Eisenhower (whose terms overlapped the argument before the Court) felt a federal interest was involved. However, this brief did not call for overturning the "separate but equal" doctrine but attacked only quantitative inequality.

These inputs were focused in oral arguments for three intense days in December, 1952. For the Negro cause it was insisted that the Fourteenth Amendment's "equal protection of the law" guarantee extended to school segregation, that school conditions had changed since 1896 when public schools were few; now the inequality was widespread, and segregation created a qualitative damage. On the other hand, counterdemands from the states emphasized that courts must not overturn established concepts of law if the legal system is to provide certainty in men's lives, that school segregation affected as many as twenty-one states (seventeen required it), and that white resistance to abolition of segregation would damage the school system for all.

The conflicting press of these arguments was powerful, for the Court could not make up its mind. No decision was handed down that term, but instead the participants were asked in June, 1953, for additional answers in the next term to questions obviously disturbing the justices on the

Fourteenth Amendment framers' intent and how desegregation might be implemented. Some months of curious scholarship followed, as each side sought to use history and constitutional law to shape the decision desired.[12] The federal government, when asked to contribute its views, was divided, because some Republicans in the new Eisenhower administration wanted to build a party base in the South. Its final presentation equivocated on abolishing desegregation, but the attorney general, when asked in oral argument, did support its abolition.[13] Other participants in the December, 1953, reargument offered answers supporting their assertions. The advice on implementation was not so clearly drawn, however.

Again, decision was delayed, this time until May, 1954, but when it came it was unequivocal. School segregation, even where facilities were equal, deprived children of equal educational opportunities and hence was unconstitutional. History threw little clear light on what the intent of the framers of the Fourteenth Amendment had been in this respect, but certainly the scope and importance of education had changed since then. Separation of children in this important aspect of their lives "generates a feeling of inferiority as to their status in the community that may affect their hearts and minds in a way unlikely ever to be undone." While such psychological knowledge may not have been available in 1896, it was today, so its weight should not be denied. Nullifying the *Plessy vs. Ferguson* edict, the Court wrote that "we conclude that in the field of public education the doctrine of 'separate but equal' has no place. Separate educational facilities are inherently unequal." As to the implementation of this opinion, new arguments were again requested from the federal and state governments for the fall of 1954.

Few opinions in Court history have had such dramatic impact upon American institutions, and yet the document was brief, the language clear, and the legal jargon missing. Few previous cases were cited, but instead the Court made reference to scholarly studies on the history of education and the psychological effects of segregation upon children. Most important, however, and remarkable given the controversy involved, the decision was unanimous. Only the justices know the factors that moved each to this common stand, for not all of them were of a mind when the case began.[14] As major reasons for arriving at unanimity, some outsiders cite the effective persuasion of the new chief justice, Earl Warren, others the broad nature of the wording, and yet others the argument that precedent may be changed when preceding conditions in the environment have changed.

Whatever its content and origin, the decision was still only an affirmation of social norms, even though buttressed by interpretation of the Constitution. Implementation was another matter, which required new decisions about strategies of enforcement. Almost a year later, the Court laid down the enforcement guidelines in what can be called *Brown II*.[15] It was no sweeping set of deadlines, but a call for "all deliberate speed" by Southern schools to desegregate under administration of local federal district courts *after* Negroes had brought suits in a school district. The work should begin promptly, delays had to be justified by the districts, and local hostility was not a justification. However, little substantive guideline was provided for the district courts as to what constituted desegregation or to what was meant by "all deliberate speed" (*deliberate* can mean both "intentional" and "slow").

Some facets of this conversion process are of great consequence for what followed in the next decade, particularly the delay of the Court in reaching any decision and its unwillingness to require prompt desegregation. It seems that some justices, perhaps all, were concerned with how they could effect any abolition of desegregation. Although they supported social equality, they were uncertain that the nation, and particularly the South, was prepared to accept it. In that condition, then, procrastination could be seen as a strategy that might hurdle the horns of the dilemma.[16] The Court could not then be assured of full support from any other major component of the political system, as the total political context of enforcement was not yet favorable. The procrastination strategy, however, offered time not only for shaping that context but for the Court's norms to be discussed and accepted by those to whom it would apply. As we shall see, however, the strategy did little to bring about Southern school desegregation; output and outcome were to be totally opposed.

FEEDBACK TO THE *BROWN* DECISIONS

In the year between *Brown I* and *II,* Southern reaction was muted; just after *Brown II* some Southern leaders and press actually expressed relief that it had not been worse. But the blunt comment of Senator James O. Eastland better expressed what was to transpire: "The South will not abide by, or obey, this legislative decision by a political court." [17]

The Variety of Resistive Feedback

Although feedback was to be generally negative, the degree and instruments of its resistance were quite varied. Thus, it is now forgotten that feedback from the Border States was positive, for during the next decade an immense amount of desegregation took place there. In the states immediately bordering the Deep South, however, compliance was considerably less. But in the Southern heartland, compliance was almost nil — indeed, in Mississippi nothing at all happened. The patterns of this feedback ran from prompt and full compliance when *Brown I* was first announced — even before *Brown II* — to partial and delayed acquiescence, and on to a total and persistent — even contemptuous — refusal to comply that was aimed at undermining the authority of the Supreme Court.

The total resistance in the Deep South is best accounted for by a social structure so thoroughly imbued with segregationist values that the new Court norms found no access there. This is what Southern spokesmen said and what scholars confirmed. It was not merely that the South was segregationist; its many subsystems were equally homogeneous on other values as well.[18] Governors and other state officials reflected in their resistance a regional public clearly of a similar mind.[19] Federal district judges, creatures of their regional culture but also part of the judicial subsystem they were sworn to support, were torn different ways. Those least tied to the dominant culture were most supportive of the Court;[20] consequently, authoritative actions of the Southern judiciary ranged from constant support of *Brown I* and *II* to evasion or outright refusal of support. The resistance set by many of these authoritative figures in the Deep South was mirrored by that of the region's schoolmen, police, lawyers, clergy, and businessmen.[21]

The instruments of resistance clearly demonstrated the ingenuity of Americans in protecting their individualism. At one end of the continuum of resistance was a stark record of outright violence. In the four years of 1955–58 alone, observers recorded at least 225 acts of violence against private liberties and public peace: six Negroes were killed, twenty-nine persons shot (eighteen Negro), forty-four beaten, five stabbed; homes were bombed (thirty), burned (eight), shot into (fifteen), and stoned (seven); and schools and churches were bombed or burned.[22] At the other end was the instrument of the statute, rich in variety but single in purpose — to maintain school segregation. Table 9.1 encapsulates what was a broad and deep defensive reaction in this form.

Many local laws provided alternative means of keeping the races separate but on ostensibly nonracial grounds. Thus, pupil placement laws created complicated nonracial criteria by which school boards assigned students, with the outcome that separation was still maintained. Some states provided for the closing of schools threatened with desegregation, although this tactic was used sparingly.[23] Too, school funds could be withheld if desegregation threatened, and private schools could be established with state monies. Further, the NAACP was attacked by laws designed to hinder its effectiveness as the agent most responsible for bringing litigation. All of these defensive statutes in their time collapsed under court orders, which called them evasions of the purpose of *Brown I* and *II*. But for at least a decade in the Deep South, although less in the surrounding states, they were major barriers against transforming the Court's output into any new outcome.

This response was echoed, if not stimulated, by the region's spokesmen in Congress. Their most publicized effort was a 1956 "Declaration of Constitutional Principles," quickly labeled the "Southern Manifesto." This accused the Court of abusing its power, of usurping the power of Con-

Table 9.1 Major Legislation on School Desegregation in 17 Southern and Border States, Plus District of Columbia[a]

Legislation	Ala.	Ark.	Del.	D.C.[b]	Fla.	Ga.	Ky.	La.	Md.	Miss.	Mo.	N.C.	Okla.	S.C.	Tenn.	Tex.	Va.	W.Va.
Anti-NAACP/Barratry	X	X			X	X		X		X				X	X	X	X	
Closure of Schools Permitted	X	X			X	X		X		X				X		X	X	
Compulsory Attendance Amended or Repealed	X	X			X	X		X		X				X	X	X	X	
Emergency Powers to Officials					X	X		X				X					X	
Freedom of Choice – Seg./Deseg.	X	X	X		X	X		X				X	X		X[c]	X	X	X
Human Rights Commissions			X	X			X		X		X							
Interposition/Protest	X	X			X	X		X		X				X	X		X	
Legal Defense Authorized	X	X			X	X		X		X				X	X	X	X	
Limitations of Federal Powers Proposed	X	X			X	X		X		X							X	
Private Schools: Authorized/Encouraged	X	X			X	X		X		X				X			X	
Property Sold/Leased to	X	X			X	X		X		X				X			X	X
Pupil Assignment	X	X			X	X		X		X		X		X	X	X	X	
Racial Designations: Removed											X	X						X
Required	X	X					X	X	X	X	X	X	X	X	X	X	X	X
Scholarships Out-of-State	X		X		X	X		X		X		X		X	X	X	X	
Segregation by Sex	X	X[c]			X	X		X		X				X	X	X[c]	X	
Segregation Committees	X	X			X	X		X		X					X			
Sovereignty Commissions	X																	
State Constitutional Provision for Public Schools Removed	X									X				X				
Teachers: Tenure/Removal	X				X	X		X				X		X			X	
Protected in Private School	X	X				X		X		X							X	
Tuition Grants to Schools/Students	X	X			X	X		X		X		X		X			X	
Withheld Aid to Deseg. Schools	X	X						X						X		X	X	

Source: Southern Education Reporting Service, in Reed Sarratt, The Ordeal of Segregation: The First Decade (New York: Harper & Row, 1966), 363.

[a] The table indicates types of legislation passed, not the number. One bill often included several features; several bills might duplicate each other.
[b] D.C. Board of Commissioners.
[c] Appointed without legislation.

gress, and of encroaching upon the rights of states to control education as they judged best. It commended "those states which have declared the intention to resist enforced integration by any lawful means," a clear signal for mobilizing Southern resistance to the law. Most Southern congressmen signed it; of those who did not, two were defeated and one almost lost.[24]

But these national regional spokesmen had more than words at their disposal. They used the considerable power that has regularly accrued to their tenure in Congress to block any assistance for the Court and to use investigating committees to denigrate the total effort. As an example of the last, the District of Columbia school system was presented as a particular chamber of horrors; Southern congressmen received and magnified every complaint they could find in the very schools they themselves were responsible for. Further, the greatest number of bills ever introduced in our history to curb the Court's powers came in 1955–57.[25] Efforts in 1957 and 1960 to authorize the attorney general to bring desegregation suits were blocked, leaving it to Negro parents and the NAACP to shoulder the entire burden, as they had for many decades.[26] Later, President Kennedy's 1963 civil-rights bill was being stymied by Southern opposition when he was assassinated. But thereafter, although Southern Senators fought grimly, their cause became lost in the popular reaction to Kennedy's death and the national publicity occasioned by protests in the South itself.

Variations in Outcomes

Thus, from the poorest rural school in Mississippi to the United States Senate, a whole battery of devices was aimed at delaying implementation of *Brown I* and *II*.[27] The Deep South could find an encouraging analogue in the North's efforts at control that had failed after the Civil War. The weapons of delay and obstruction that had served the Confederate Army so well, and that had also borne fruit in the Reconstruction, were quickly and effectively used. Yet noncompliance varied according to subregional culture, with the result that Mississippi was not typical.

We may see these Southern reactions along a range of compliance, recognizing that a given district might skip many of the following:

1. *Voluntary noncompliance,* i.e., close the schools entirely rather than comply, e.g., Prince Edward County, Va.; although many Southern states passed such laws, closure was rare.

2. *Involuntary minimal compliance*
   a. Refuse voluntary compliance and ignore threat of litigation, e.g., Miss.
   b. Notice *Brown I* and *II* only when Negroes bring suit.
   c. Defend suit by supporting state over national law ("interposition"

was popular for a time) or by denying the legitimacy of the Court to rule in the matter.

d. Appeal all adverse decisions and otherwise put off change by recourse to every delay built into legal procedure.

e. When higher court upholds Negro claim, adopt minimal adjustment to his claim by

(1) granting claim only to specific Negro litigant and not to class of segregated Negroes.

(2) interposing alternative methods of student placement (e.g., pupil placement, freedom of choice, gerrymandering) that desegregate only a few.

3. *Involuntary token compliance,* i.e., steps 2a–2c but desegregate after first adverse decision; yet use alternative that desegregates the least.

4. *Involuntary moderate compliance,* i.e., same as 3 but made wider plan for desegregation without, however, effecting it on a compulsory basis.

5. *Voluntary minimal compliance,* i.e., move before threat of litigation, with compliance only minimal.

6. *Voluntary compliance,* i.e., providing full compliance without threat of litigation.

We cannot know how Southern districts distributed themselves across these feedback responses, but we can summarize the possibilities. In Figure 9.1 we find eight broad categories along the two dimensions of the pro-

Figure 9.1   Typology of Southern School District Compliance with Brown *Decision: Willingness to Comply*

Percent of students desegregated	Involuntary	Voluntary
None	Mississippi Deep South districts	
Minimum	Token districts	
Moderate	Border districts	
Maximum		Districts farthest from Mississippi

portion of students desegregated and of the willingness to comply in the district. In general, Deep South districts were in the upper left cells, those in the immediate Border States in the "involuntary" or "voluntary moderate" cell, and those farthest from Mississippi in the "voluntary maximum" cell.

Certainly on a state-by-state basis we can see this propinquity factor operating. In Table 9.2, the states are distinguished subregionally and by their proportion of desegregation in districts and students. This dramatic differential in compliance ranges from Mississippi's stance of "Never!" to the District of Columbia's "Now!" After a decade of effort at judicial enforcement, 1 of 2 black students in the upper South attended a desegregated school, but only 1 in 45 in the middle South and a microscopic 1 in 750 in the Deep South did so. For the whole region, these efforts of a decade found only a little better than 1 in 3 districts desegregated; only 1 in 11 black students attended desegregated schools.

The pace of desegregation differs subregionally, as the Border States moved quickly, particularly in urban schools. Here, between *Brown I* and *II*,

Table 9.2   Status of Southern School Desegregation, 1963–64

Subregion and states	Districts desegregated[a]	Negroes in desegregated schools
Border	92.4%	54.8%
Delaware	100.0	56.5
District of Columbia	100.0	83.8
Kentucky	98.6	54.4
Maryland	100.0	47.8
Missouri	95.6	42.1
Oklahoma	81.7	28.0
West Virginia	100.0	58.2
Token tier	26.5	2.26
Arkansas	5.7	.33
Florida	23.9	1.53
North Carolina	23.4	.54
Tennessee	31.5	2.72
Texas	29.3	5.52
Virginia	43.0	1.63
Deep South	1.77	0.13
Alabama	3.51	.007
Georgia	2.21	.052
Louisiana	3.00	.602
Mississippi	0.00	.000
South Carolina	.92	.003
Total region	37.3	9.3

Source: Adapted from Staff Report, *Public Education* (Washington, D.C.: Government Printing Office, 1964), 287–92.
[a]Only for districts containing both races.

156 districts desegregated and a year later 70 percent had complied; in five years about 45 percent of the Negro students were in desegregated schools. In the Token Tier of states, all began desegregation in the first five years and, except for Virginia, did so voluntarily. But the pace was slow and faltering, accompanied by massive resistance in Virginia, including closing down one county's schools, and by the governor's armed refusal in Arkansas. The somewhat faster pace of Texas and its large weight in numbers makes the subregion's total rate of compliance artificially large.

In the Deep South, almost nothing changed in response to this judicial policy output. The minimal compliance seen in Table 9.2 is actually somewhat elevated because of the unusually large number of black students desegregated in Louisiana (1814). More normal for the heart of the Old Confederacy was Alabama with twenty-one students, South Carolina with nine, and Mississippi with its rigid zero. By the end of this era, only 11 of the 620 districts in the subregion had even begun desegregation, and all but two of these (both in Georgia) did so only under a direct court order.[28]

Judicial and Public Response
to Resistive Feedback

As these differential outcomes developed, the Supreme Court was silent. In the face of this civil disobedience, what it did not say is as important as what it did say. While a national storm began building around its calm chambers, the Court offered no defense or detailed explanation of the ideal it had proclaimed. Discussion ensued all over the nation, as Southern resistance was met increasingly by civil-rights protests, and both were fastened in the spotlight of national news media. Litigation provoked discussion among whites who had never considered, and blacks who had never raised, the possibility that segregation violated a basic value in the American creed.

But the Court itself issued few opinions on the feedback of resistance. For a decade it mostly restrained itself to *per curiam* decisions tersely upholding without opinion the lower court enforcement of the *Brown* decrees. Between 1955 and 1958 it did not discuss desegregation at all, simply declining to review such cases. The Court broke its silence in 1958 only for the sensational Constitutional crisis surrounding the Little Rock case. Here it took the chance to reaffirm the principle of *Brown I* and *II* and to assert its continuing unanimity in the matter. But it said very little directly about the details of the segregation plan for Little Rock.[29] For the next five years the Court resumed its silence, merely declining to review Southern challenges, whether brought by whites or blacks. It next broke that silence in 1963 in an opinion that struck down a blatant evasion scheme, while powerfully complaining about delay nine years after *Brown I*.[30]

This decade of silent Court reaction can be seen as part of the procrastination strategy mentioned earlier, giving the political context of the environment the time to reshape itself to support the Court-endorsed social norm. By not getting involved with details of numerous plans in diverse communities, the Court may have diverted some of the lightning then flashing about the Southern countryside.[31] Further, by affirming only occasionally, unanimously, and on the level of fundamental principle, it served as a teacher of norms to the public beyond the South.[32]

Whether because of or despite this strategy, as the first decade of its use ended the Court was supported in the *Brown* decision by at least a majority of Americans and by almost three-quarters of non-Southerners, as seen in the national polls of Table 9.3. The turbulent events of Little Rock in September, 1957, were associated with some reduction in support; Southern support, particularly by whites, remained low and stable. But whites outside the South and blacks inside it provided support that began and remained high.

However, views of the *Court* are not the same thing as views on the *principle* for which that body acted, namely, that students of both races should go to school together. We could expect strong support of this by blacks, but it is more important to know the effect on white attitudes if there is any substance to the concept of the socialization function of the Court. Figure 9.2 shows evidence consonant with the concept, as measured by poll responses of white Americans to the question of whether races should attend schools together.

Whites in both North and South reflect a changing national view from 1942, when not even one-third of all whites favored school desegregation, to 1963, when almost two-thirds did. Among Northern whites, the shift was from 2 in 5 to almost 2 in 3 and finally to almost 3 in 4. Even Southern whites showed some effects; in 1942, 1 in 50 approved but two decades

*Table 9.3   Percent Approving of Supreme Court Decision
on School Desegregation*

	National	Non-South	South	White: South	Negro: South
1954	54	64	24	–	–
1955	56	68	20	–	–
1956	57	71	22	16	53
1957: January	63	74	27	–	–
1957: October	59	–	23	15[a]	69[a]
1959	59	72	22	–	–
1961	62	–	24	–	–

Source: Polls reported in Hazel G. Erskine, "The Polls: Race Relations," *Public Opinion Quarterly*, 26 (1962), 140.
[a]November, 1957, polls.

Figure 9.2   *Percentage Agreement That Black and White Children Should Attend School Together*

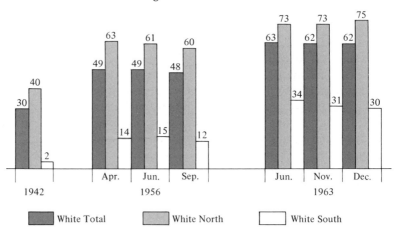

Source: Paul B. Sheatsley, "White Attitudes Toward the Negro," *Daedalus,* 95 (1966), 219.

later about 1 in 3 did. By 1963, the whole nation stood where only Northern whites had stood seven years earlier, and the Southern whites stood in 1963 where the nation had stood in 1942. This is clearly a shift of no small proportions, much of it, particularly in the South, rather sizable in the years after *Brown I* and *II.* Southerners might reject the Court's decision, but many *were* accepting its normative message.

The exact role played by the Court in this transformation is not clear, of course. Other events were operating in the environment that had some influence in this direction. The numbers of Americans educated has changed since 1942, a fact having direct bearing on increasing tolerance. Americans were moving about inside their nation in great numbers after World War II, being exposed to new ideas and closer racial contact.[33] The characteristics of a community's population and political system are other factors that could affect the degree and rate of desegregation. Dye found that by 1960 cities both North and South differed regularly in the socio-economic and political factors associated with segregation, although the proportion of black students everywhere was directly related to this practice.[34]

Yet, as potential explanations of these changes there were also the publicized events of this decade that centered around what the *Brown* cases had begun: highly visible conflict in schools in Prince Edward County; Clinton, Tenn.; Little Rock; and Oxford, Miss.; national legislation on civil rights in 1957 and 1960; sit-ins, "freedom rides," and a March on Washington, etc. And at all these places were the national media, transmitting to the nation — and to the South — not merely what was transpiring but how it fit into a new consciousness about black rights.

In little of this did the hand of the Court appear directly, but in all of it was the indirect influence of the forces it had set in motion by the *Brown* decisions. At least the resistant Southerners had no doubt that the Court was the *bête noire*. That body figured large in its total condemnation of all the change in process; a highly popular book in the region described the evils that flowed from the *Black Monday* when the Court had issued *Brown I*.[35]

SYSTEMS APPLICATIONS TO
THE 1964 CIVIL RIGHTS ACT

Conversion and Output

It was against such Southern obstructionism that the Civil Rights Act of 1964 was to move. The year before its passage was the most dramatic in the history of this country's efforts to realize the value of equality for its black citizens.[36] The conversion process that led to the 1964 Act transpired in a thunderstorm of sensational events in the streets of obscure Southern towns, in Dallas, in the offices of the White House, and in the chambers of Congress — all fed continuously to an American public generally supportive of the change. An enormous coalition of libertarian interest groups was linked directly with executive and legislative cohorts to succeed finally in overriding Southern bastions of congressional power. In this moral and political struggle, an enormous change occurred in the stance of the federal government vis-à-vis American — and particularly Southern — blacks. Despite setbacks and hesitancies of political authorities since then and in the future, the position of that minority will never again be what it had been. What it will be, however, is a story not yet written.

The core of the 1964 Act for our purposes appears in Title VI:

> No person in the United States shall, on the ground of race, color, or national origin, be excluded from participation in, be denied the benefits of, or be subjected to discrimination under any program or activity receiving Federal financial assistance.

By this wording, the cutoff of federal funds suddenly became a weapon against long-stalled school desegregation. It was augmented by the authorization of federal enforcement power, both in the Health, Education, and Welfare and the Justice Departments. Through its Office of Civil Rights, HEW administered the cutoff program, and Justice, through its Civil Rights Division, initiated litigation against discriminating school districts. The Court itself suddenly became more active with more frequent and sweeping opinions.

Against this battery of new forces, Southern schoolmen's power was reduced considerably, but they still retained large resources of delay and evasion. Unlike the ESEA output reviewed earlier, there was *no* state enforcement of a federal policy in desegregation matters in the Deep South. Washington's enforcement efforts were in the main made directly against local districts. What might seem an uneven contest was equalized because the resources of the state governments reinforced local district noncompliance. Under ESEA, the states wanted to control the subsidy, sometimes in keeping with Washington's guidelines, sometimes — perhaps often — in accordance with state wishes, and sometimes as local districts wished. But here, states wanted nothing to do with desegregation — unless it was to prevent enforcement of the law. In that difference lies an essential distinction between subsidy and regulatory policies.

Feedback in the Johnson Years

A brief review of these contending elements will demonstrate how their interactions advanced desegregation farther than opponents deemed desirable but less than supporters hoped. The feedback to this law was influenced by several conflicting strains in the enforcement process. As a rough measure of these strains, we can place Southern segregationists at one extreme fighting off any change, the Supreme Court and civil-rights groups pushing at the other extreme for full and prompt compliance, and the federal administrative agencies working somewhere in the center of these opposing pressures. The center's location fluctuated with the pressures of Southern congressmen to block or attenuate any federal enforcement, with the will of presidential enforcement, and with the courts' changing opinions on acceptable desegregation plans. By 1970, this push-pull process had accomplished far more desegregation in the Deep South than seemed possible a few years earlier. But it had also brought into play forms of resistance not evident earlier, particularly in the rural South and urban North.

The pivotal position of the administrative enforcers is quite clear. From the first days when the 1964 Act was handed to HEW, its agents (at first law professors travelling to Washington) moved into a complex matrix of local pressures transmitted through powerful congressmen and modulated by their own uncertainties about how to proceed.[37] They had to impose.guidelines for administering these provisions upon a mosaic of school systems for which no single formula made sense. The first guidelines were delayed for almost a year and were revised in successive years, a mark of the difficulty of administering this school complex.

From 1965 on, these guidelines concentrated greater weight upon the Southern segregationists when the fund cutoff penalty came to have significant meaning with passage of ESEA. Southerners had not fought the cutoff provision very hard when the 1964 Act was being shaped, as they were more concerned with public accommodations provisions. Federal monies, not very extensive before 1965, thereafter reached the enormous proportions shown in the previous chapter. To a Southern educational system already well below national levels, ESEA money meant the possibility of quantum jumps in educational quality — and particularly for black students. The threat, in short, became very large and very real, so that Southern efforts were moved by a concern not only to evade desegregation but to do so without losing money. On the other hand, HEW was given a statute with undeniable national majority support that could threaten cutoffs of funds sorely needed, and, under Lyndon Johnson, the pressure of a president earnestly supporting Southern desegregation. In the first years after 1965, HEW moved quickly into hundreds of school districts with effects we will shortly note.

In that movement, the Supreme Court played an increasingly demanding role. Despite a silence broken only rarely in the previous decade, it handed down three important school decisions in the 1965 term; in one, *Rogers vs. Paul,* it treated the details of a district desegregation plan, ordering prompt admission of black children to a high school. At the district and particularly appellate court levels, decisions increasingly overturned desegregation plans on the grounds that they were evasions. Whereas these courts earlier had accepted pupil placement and "freedom of choice" plans because they were not evasions on their face, in the late 1960's they repeatedly found them invalid because the result had only been to continue segregation.

The justices were quite consistent about several points. First, the elimination of racial schools was the guiding star. In the *Jefferson County* case, Appellate Judge Minor Wisdom put quite clearly the purpose of the law and of any plan evaluated under it; it was to "bring about an integrated, unitary school system in which there are no Negro schools and no white schools — just schools." The second consistency was that the judges had little willingness to condone delay any longer. In this same case, Wisdom expressed such judicial exasperation; "The clock has ticked the last tick for tokenism and delay in the name of deliberate speed." [38]

The end of the Southern delay engendered by *Brown II* may have come in the Supreme Court's terse, two-page opinion in the *Holmes County* decision of October, 1969. Continued segregation "is no longer permissible," it said, and "the obligation of every school district is to terminate dual school systems at once and to operate now and hereafter only unitary schools." They must "begin immediately to operate as unitary school systems." Moreover, any further effort at litigation over desegregation is foreclosed until that unitary condition is achieved. Thus, the kind of decree that many had called for fifteen years earlier now emerged, and if compliance be merely a matter of the proper wording of a judicial decree, the job should be done.[39]

The joining of HEW to the Supreme Court in the enforcement of school desegregation shaped the role of that agency, for in general, the judiciary led it in standards of the permissible and the expected. The justices' standards set general policy guidelines — sometimes by denying the suitability of a specific desegregation plan — that were difficult for the agency to evade. Moreover, this judicial pressure provided national administrators with a shield against Southern congressional pressures to move slowly — if at all. With the Johnson and Court pressure to move quickly, the HEW and Justice Departments were able to fend off Southern pressures. But if desegregation pressure from either of those sources faltered, the Southern power in Congress would be much harder to hold in check.

Feedback in the Nixon Years

That pivotal position of HEW and Justice was illuminated by the coming to office of Richard M. Nixon. The yearning to build the Republican party's strength in the South, which we earlier noted had affected Eisenhower's stance on civil rights in the 1950's, came to the fore again. Southerners felt they had received signals from Nixon as candidate in the 1968 campaign that the pace of desegregation would be slowed if not stopped.[40] And in the first year of his administration, they felt they had received signals to that effect from Nixon as president. For over a year, his top officials suggested indirectly that a reconsideration was under way on the question of pace.

More direct actions seemed to validate the reality of this shift. Soon upon entering office, Nixon called for a delay in fund cutoffs for a few schools; when the schools failed to meet guidelines, however, the cutoffs were reimposed in all but the one case that had met them.[41] But thereafter fund cutoffs almost disappeared as an enforcement technique. In the fall of 1969, the Justice Department's top officials counseled delay in enforcing stricter plans in thirty-one Mississippi districts. This occasioned a splash of publicity over the government's opposing the NAACP for the first time in school litigation, over the Civil Rights Division lawyers' rebellion against the attorney general's reluctance, and over the eventual firing of the division director.[42]

President Nixon finally laid down his desegregation policy in March, 1970. He denounced racial segregation in schools and their facilities as this practice existed in the South, but declared that Northern segregation, based on *de facto* circumstances of housing patterns, was to be treated differently. Although *de jure* segregation was to be eliminated, it required "an area of flexibility — a 'rule of reason' . . . in which school boards, acting in good faith, can formulate plans of desegregation which best suit the needs of their own localities." On the other hand, *de facto* segregation "is undesirable but is not generally held to violate the Constitution." He had strong reservations about past school policy "which demands too much of our schools," for "there are limits to the amount of government coercion that can reasonably be used." An example of a policy that exceeded this limit was school busing, which he firmly opposed.[43]

This policy statement gave desegregationists far less than they had known under Johnson, and was also probably less than Southerners had hoped for. Yet it did fit a highly differentiated school system, suggesting that different causes for the same effect require different methods for changing the effect. It did affirm, as Eisenhower never had, the moral correctness of the Court's decisions about the unconstitutionality of segregation. It did agree that segregation, when *de jure,* must be "eliminated totally." This was some cheer for desegregationists. But it also gave prime weight in making such changes to local school boards' judgments; it asserted the primacy of the neighborhood school as the basis of our educational system; it announced that if both kinds of segregation existed only the *de jure* need be remedied, and it cautioned that although Washington would provide federal advice if needed, it was not to go beyond "requirements of law" in imposing its judgment on local schools. All these items contained equal good cheer for segregationists.

Yet the policy shared one element of all compromises — it did not really make everyone happy. Southern segregationists felt misled, although as we shall see, they did enjoy some slackening of the pace set in the Johnson years. Desegregationists in the North and South felt deeply hindered, although as we shall see, the enforcement did not stop. Possibly the group most pleased were Northern segregationists, who felt relief that the enforcement power was not to be turned in their direction in any meaningful way. Nixon's displeasure at school busing had most meaning in their region, as so little of this involved the South.[44]

The criticism from desegregationists was extensive and bitter. The Southern Regional Council illustrated private group counter-pressures in its itemized condemnation of post-1968 "federal retreat" and "fourteen years of failure." [45] The United States Commission on Civil Rights illustrated governmental pressures by its critical surveys of each stage of the desegregation after the 1964 law. Its 1966–67 survey could report "results . . . both heartening and discouraging." The report in September, 1969, however, was a thorough-going attack on the Nixon policy for employing a "numbers game" of statistics seeking to prove that the administration was enforcing desegregation.[46] Finding Southern resistance still extensive, it concluded that without strong law enforcement nothing would change. State and local officials were still recalcitrant and evasive. Their wide use of "freedom of choice" plans put the burden on black families to initiate desegregation instead of requiring affirmative action by school officials themselves.

Enforcement Outcomes: Local

The value of the 1964 Act, with its emphasis upon federal administrative rather than private individual power, seems obvious if judged by the outcome of enforcement. Thus, the microscopic desegregation recorded in Table 9.2 for the Deep South in the 1963–64 school year, where only private action was available, had grown considerably by 1968–69 under the federal thrust. In percentage terms, the later desegregation rates were: Alabama 7.4, Georgia 14.2, Louisiana 8.8, Mississippi (where none had existed) 7.1, North Carolina 27.8, South Carolina 14.9, and Virginia 25.7. However, as noted in the Commission on Civil Rights criticisms above, reliance upon litigation instead of administrative enforcement would mean a decrease in desegregated districts. In every Southern state, the use of guidelines had led to more desegregated districts than had the use of litigation; the commission reported that the latter had desegregated only 9.4 percent of the districts, whereas guidelines had desegregated 21.0 percent. With massive documentation, the commission argued that the undermining of administrative enforcement left the action up to a much weaker organ, the local courts, whose biases and ineffective orders had been clearly demonstrated in the decade after *Brown II*.

Even if we grant much of this criticism, it does not follow that Southern desegregation had stopped. In states of the Confederacy, the proportion of black *students* in formerly all-white schools (the reverse is a rarity) had been less than 1 percent in 1962–63 and a year later just past 1 percent. By 1964–65 it had doubled to 2.25 percent, but a year later — the first full year of Title VI — it reached 6 percent. In 1966–67 there was a relatively great increase to 17 percent, a year later to over 20 percent, and in 1969–70 the figure was estimated at 40 percent. The figures for school *districts* desegregated have always been higher; HEW reported more than 97 percent in the fall of 1970. Here, though, "desegregation" might mean for any one district that only several blacks were in white schools.[47]

In the Nixon years, these figures continued to grow, although the creation of private schools to drain off the bitterest segregationists makes such data uncertain. Too, despite the administration's reluctance to push stronger desegregation in 31 Mississippi school districts, those districts complied with court orders in early 1970 with an ease that surprised the press — and possibly Mississippians themselves. Further, the first reactions of both races at the change was relief that it had not hurt as much as feared. Press reports and more careful opinion surveys found extensive accommodation to new roles by parents, students, and faculty of both races. However, not all accommodated, for many whites rushed off to hastily devised private schools. But their financial support was too limited for them to survive for long, and efforts at state subsidy were nullified by federal court decisions in May, 1970.[48]

At a pace once believed impossible by friend and foe alike, then, Southern school districts were moving into a desegregated stance. They had a distance yet to go to achieve the Court goal of a unitary school system.

While complaining bitterly at the successful attack on cherished values, they were, nevertheless, moving. In the process, not only behavior but also attitudes changed. By mid-1969, almost one-half of white Southern parents would not object to sending their children to a school where half were black; 78 percent would not object if there were just a "few" blacks. However, six years earlier 61 percent had *opposed* having their children in school with that "few," and 78 percent opposed if the schools were half black.[49]

Outside the South appeared other signs of popular support of the Court's socialization efforts. By mid-1970, only 15 percent of Americans reported favoring *de jure* segregation, although 61 percent supported the *de facto* kind. Polled on their support of the Court order in early 1970 requiring that districts in Mississippi and Tennessee desegregate at once, although 40 percent of a national sample disapproved, 48 percent approved; 12 percent were unsure. But wide regional and status variations existed in this approval, which enlisted only 8 percent among whites in the Deep South. Higher-status whites gave majority support; lower-status whites gave majority opposition. But by the end of 1970, Southern attitudes were in the midst of abrupt change. Whether because desegregation has not been as bad as feared, or because whites were still evading it in classrooms, they were more nearly divided on the question of desegregation without further delay. A 42–43 percent split of approval-disapproval of a Supreme Court decision to this effect reflected this shift.[50]

Whether viewed in terms of the participants in, or observers of, the federal action, by 1970 a major reversal in American opinion had transpired — at least as it applied to one form of segregation. As Orfield noted of the efforts by HEW to apply its guidelines,

> It has been a strange sort of revolution. There has been only isolated violence, and few people outside the South knew anything significant was happening. There have been no manifestoes, but only dry bureaucratic documents. Instead of charismatic figures, the leaders have been a small group of civil servants.[51]

Enforcement Outcomes: National

But historic change also took place both in the practices of federalism and in a new priority to old values. Thus, the federal fund-cutoff provision was a departure from traditional intergovernmental relations. Historically, we have rejected national controls for their frustration of our individualistic localism. Enforcing fund-cutoff provisions in the past have not worked because of the political backlash for federal officials who tried it. That is, national cutoffs were regularly followed by political attacks on "federal bureaucrats," attacks that could weaken support for the program's financing in later years and weaken local cooperation in other programs. Active enforcement of Title VI, therefore, was a major change in American federalism. The negative feedback from cutoffs, which led to President Nixon's drastic reduction — if not cessation — in use of this instrument, illustrates the strength of the political tradition traced here. Another president might have ignored this feedback, but, after all, it had played some part in putting him into office in the first place.

Another historic shift occasioned by Title VI and these Court decisions was to place Washington squarely in the conversion processes of local education. Local control of schooling, as noted earlier, has been part of the foundation of American public policy. The federal government had been involved locally in the past, as we have noted, but all this was supportive of local education, not regulative. Title VI, however, was clearly supportive of another norm — equality — which sharply confronted local norms of white supremacy. Obviously, law supportive of one group and its norms is seen as regulative by another.

The Court had been quite clear about which norm it chose, but other national political authorities were divided. President Eisenhower never endorsed the Court's norm or sought statutes to implement it; Kennedy made a few more efforts, although without securing a statute.[52] As we have seen, the efforts of Johnson and Nixon produced quite different paces of enforcement. Even with the backing of the 1964 Act, administrative agencies had to reorient themselves to an entirely new set of values. For all its century-long history, the United States Office of Education had been an instrument of *local* education forces, serving them primarily in a supportive capacity. But under Title VI, as Orfield observed, it "was caught in a conflict between equality and localism [and was] expected to force local officials to recognize the rights of Negro children but do nothing else to threaten the tradition of local dominance." [53] The cooperative methods of earlier supportive policies achieved nothing in the Deep South, of course; only the threat of cutoff moved these districts. In the process, the feedback from enforcement of Title VI, as well as of ESEA, marked drastic changes in that "tradition of local dominance." But behind all this was the pressure of the Court.

THE JUDICIARY IN THE POLITICAL SYSTEM

We return to the singular role of the Court in this policy process. In Easton's terms, it sought a *regime change,* an alteration of the basic norms or principles by which the political system operates. The value of equality had existed for some time in the American creed but without effective meaning in the lives of black, Southern citizens. From *Brown I* and *II* onward, however, the Court worked to change that condition, thereby revitalizing a norm for this minority. Such legitimization was conducted

under a strategy of procrastination, possibly for fear of undermining its
authority in this and other cases. As Krislov has noted,

> In stressing the continuity of its moral authority even at the risk of
> foregoing a victory, the Court follows the pattern of other institutions
> like the Catholic Church, which instills respect through its moral stand-
> ing rather than through the imposition of sanctions. The Court, like the
> Church, has not sought to challenge and test the limits of its power,
> preferring to display the impression of power.[54]

Has the Supreme Court's "moral authority" in the political system been
damaged by its decisions on civil rights matters over the last two decades?
It seems unlikely. We have noted previously the popular support of Court
decisions and the even greater support of their specific norms. From a national survey by Murphy and Tanenhaus in 1964 and 1966, it is clear that
such support is highly differentiated by the kind of policy in view.[55] More
important, many if not most Americans know little of the Court's work and
constitutional role; little better than 1 in 4 are so knowledgeable, and these
are generally well-educated and politically attentive Americans.

If we distinguish between specific and diffuse support for the Court (that
is, popular judgment on its specific issue outputs or on its general im-
partiality and competence), as we see in Table 9.4 there seems to exist
more diffuse than specific support. That is, many persons critical of specific Court actions still support the Court in its institutional capacity; 9.6
percent gave strong to moderate specific support but 37 percent were in
that range on diffuse support. There was some congruity, however, as those
positive on one kind of support were also positive on the other, and those
negative clustered similarly. The boxed figures of 69 percent and 42 percent show the reinforcing influence of the two classes of support. Yet even
many of those negative because of some specific Court decision did continue to render diffuse support.

Finally and most evident in Table 9.4, large numbers of citizens were
unclassifiable because they knew little about specific Court outputs (53.8
percent); even at the more generalized level of diffuse support, 29.4 percent had no opinion about the Court's role. Indeed, if we ask what proportion perceives the Court at all, knows its proper task, and has judgments
about its specific and general activity, almost 3 in 4 citizens are *excluded*.
Of these knowledgeable opinion holders remaining, most are positive in diffuse support, but they represent only about 1 in 8 of all Americans.[56]

The preceding suggests that the Court, as it interacted with the federal
political system in these years, did not cause dissolution of its support,
although we know little about what level of support it enjoyed before 1954.
Public acceptance of Southern school desegregation increased, even among
Southern whites, over these years. Public evaluation of the Court in this

Table 9.4 Specific vs. Diffuse Support of the Supreme Court by Percentages, 1966ᵃ

Specific support	Diffuse support						Total sample
	Strong pos.	Mod. pos.	Pro/Con	Mod. neg.	Strong neg.	Unclassifiable	
Strong positive	69	15	12	—	—	4	2.6 = 100%
Moderate positive	56	13	13	4	3	11	7.0
Pro/Con (divided)	34	18	28	8	10	4	5.0
Moderate negative	18	16	19	20	17	9	19.2
Strong negative	12	13	11	18	42	4	12.5
Unclassifiable	14	19	8	9	2	49	53.8
Total sample	19.9	17.1	11.9	11.4	10.3	29.4 =	100.0%

Source: Walter F. Murphy and Joseph Tanenhaus, "Mapping of Some Prerequisites for Court Legitimation of Regime Changes," *Law and Society Review*, 11 (1968), recalculated from data in Table 9, 377.

ᵃFigures within the lines are to be read along the rows, each row totaling 100 percent. Figures outside the lines represent the proportion of that row or column in the total sample of 1291 persons.

process is vague because so few are aware of what the Court does in general or in specific. Yet among those with knowledge and opinions, support outweighed opposition, particularly among those most active in the conversion process.[57] However, such data do not tell us much about the success of the strategy of procrastination. Obviously, we have no alternative strategy whose effectiveness in the social environment we can judge. Certainly national opinion, an invaluable ally in a democracy, was not as supportive of desegregation in 1954 as it was to become later, suggesting it might not have adapted as easily if a quicker strategy had been employed. It seems certain that enforcement of the 1964 Act began in a climate of opinion quite supportive because of events traceable to *Brown I and II.*

One might better judge the efficacy of this strategy by asking what forces the Court *could* have rallied to its side in 1954 if it had called for prompt desegregation. Congress, particularly in its bastions manned by powerful Southern chairmen, was of little help. Not for three years after *Brown I* could Congress manage a civil rights law, and at that it was a weak effort that did nothing for school desegregation. President Eisenhower was distinctly unsympathetic to the Court's norm, although he would defend the institution if it faced outright disobedience, as in Little Rock. The lower federal courts in the region most affected were, in some cases, downright hostile to the *Brown* decision; the enforcement difficulties these judges could create contributed to a null effect in the Deep South for a decade. Political parties could not coalesce on the matter, as each had some interest in either supporting or opposing Eisenhower or in attracting Southern voters.[58] In short, it is difficult to see how greater and speedier compliance could have been achieved by alternative strategies, given this lineup of negative or neutral forces in the political system.[59]

The dimensions of the system interactions described in this chapter suggest many of the political aspects of the judiciary as an authoritative allocator of values and resources. Within its own political system, the Supreme Court used numerous methods to keep lower court resources in line with its opinions. In its relationship to other political authorities, the Court has insisted without deviation upon a normative goal, imposing on presidency, agencies, and legislature an unceasing pressure. Indeed, after 1964, HEW's work was directly tied to implementing plans that the Court would accept. In its relationship to the political subsystems of state governments, the Court has permitted delay in implementation without altering its objective; the delay suggests a sensitive awareness of the limits of its own resources. In its relationship to thousands of school districts, each a mini–political system, the Court's willingness to accept delay only encouraged delay, of course. But it also helped build the massive details of segregation that could be used to sensitize public and lawmakers in the future.

In this sense, a strategy is a resource as much as available armament or capital. The Court's strategy had to fit conditions of 1954–55. At that time, it lacked physical resources, it was confronted by hostile or indifferent elements of the larger political system reflecting the social environment, and yet it was seized by a desire for a change in the regime's effective norms. The Court could only borrow on its legitimitizing resource and expend it through a procrastinating strategy until the vague national majority jelled and other elements in the political system fell in line. The Court does not need to use procrastination, however, on every regime change. In the case of reapportionment, the impact was almost invisible to the wide public, although the Court itself had instruments for achieving effective compliance.[60] But in the case of Southern school desegregation, the Court's feedback channels were clogged by white Southerners, who felt deeply on the matter and who had powerful resources of delay and obstructionism. Thus the political conditions in the environment necessitated distinctive judicial responses, another sign of the political quality of the judiciary.

Finally, although this chapter examines the role of the Court's political impact upon schooling, we must not fail to note that *on its own* the Court has been ineffective in imposing a uniform norm upon a pluralistic school system. In Southern desegregation, the data show such a slow Deep South response to *Brown I* and *II* that full compliance would have required another century. Not until a statute backed by a willing Congress, energetic enforcers, and a supportive public came into being did much happen, and even now that region is still resisting. As the nation turns its face north to deal with desegregation there, we can see clear signs of firm resistance to ending *de facto* segregation, particularly if it requires busing. Congress and the presidency (under both Johnson and Nixon) have assumed the same reluctant stance they held in the period after *Brown I* and *II*. Further, in school prayer and Bible-reading decisions, the Court has been ineffective except in those localities where political forces existed to implement them. Where they did not exist, little has changed.[61]

Nor can the Court do everything, even with supportive inputs. We are just beginning to learn that desegregation — an administrative, physical act — is not the same as integration — the emotional and spiritual belief of men. Intervening between these two conditions are group resistance, popular ignorance, communication failures, information overloads, and other dysfunctional aspects of social disorganization. In the sequential process from segregation to integration many facets of social life must be combined to achieve any results. Even with a Court mandate, much must be done to move people. Judicial action can be immensely supportive for desegregationists, of course, but its major function — and we do not belittle it — is to initiate social change. That does not bring total or quick acceptance, provide all resources for the resourceless, teach how to resolve conflict or live with ambiguity, or develop other accommodative skills. Other persons and events must perform these tasks.

In this regard, then, the Court is in the position of Glendower in *Henry IV:* "I can call spirits from the vasty deep."

Hotspur responds, "Why so can I, or so can any man, but will they come when you do call for them?"

But it is also obvious that the Court's call on school segregation did evoke spirits. Possibly the simplest way of gauging the consequences for the Southern school system of the political system of the judiciary is to answer the queries: What if there had never been *Brown vs. Board of Education of Topeka?* What would be the condition of school desegregation in the South today? Both friend and foe of the Court would have to agree that little would be changed. That recognition marks the significant potential of the Court for affecting the educational system. Even on its own, it can at least create a national dialogue about regime norms.

In this way, the unthinkable of yesterday becomes the convention of today. Creating this flexibility of mind is a function that the Court and good teachers share.

10 Curricular Decisions in the Political System

CURRICULAR CRITERIA AND DECISION METHODS

On one subject, the myth of an apolitical education has gone long unchallenged. Both those who practice and those who study it have endorsed the separation of curricular issues from ordinary political processes. Professionals have regarded those decisions as professional matters to be decided on technical grounds by teachers, principals, supervisors, and directors of curriculum. It is this separation of politics from their work that we next explore.

Evidence of the political aspect of curriculum has long been overt. Educators realize, of course, that state legislatures have ultimate authority over curriculum. Indeed, teacher groups work through the legislature to influence laws relating to the subject they teach. Scholars' work on curriculum has also long shown signs of outreach into the political world. In a study of the professional discourse on curriculum, Pilder found that it has reflected most of the major, national, political tensions from 1918 to 1967.[1] When immigration was a national issue, "Americanization" was a curricular issue. When totalitarianism posed a threat to democracy, "education for democratic life" was the concern. When World War II created a shortage of manpower, "manpower training" became an important theme in such writing. When Sputnik shocked the nation, the softness of existing curricula was cited as a major contributor to our national decline.

In the face of such well-known relationships and countless local replications, no experienced educator would deny that demands of the community,

This chapter is a revision of a paper prepared by Michael W. Kirst and Decker F. Walker for The Rand Corporation Seminar Series in Education, 1970. The original paper was published in *Review of Educational Research* (December, 1971).

national or local, affect the curriculum. But in spite of their acknowledgment of this force (which we define as the ultimately political basis of curriculum), educators customarily conceive curricular decisions as nonpolitical, professional matters. Political input from interested citizens has hardly dented that shield. The major concession of schoolmen to citizen pressure for a voice in curricular policy is lay participation on school committees. Even this involves the use of committees only to establish broad goals — which the professional staff feel free to interpret as they see fit. When laymen have participated in more concrete ways, their participation has still been within a framework designed by the school staff. Laymen chosen to exercise this power, usually prestigious figures representing no interest group or other political entity, have rarely been satisfied with the degree to which they were able to deal directly with substantive curricular questions.[2]

One may criticize or applaud the deeply entrenched tradition that curricular decisions are above partisan politics and beyond direct voter participation, but it has helped to bring about an almost total absence of the political viewpoint in curricular research. As a result, the questions of which persons and groups mold the curriculum, in whose interests, and in what way — always important and always relevant *political* questions — have not been asked insistently and incisively. In studies that have asked such questions, the implicit ideal has generally been an impartial, objective, technical *method* of processing data from students, teachers, parents, and scholars so as to determine a single "best" curriculum. However, the distinctively political concepts of conflict and accommodation have seldom been applied in curricular discourse.

Value Bases

Despite adjustments, schools have regarded their curricula as fixed quantities, not to be adjusted in the interest of achieving some goal. The Latin root of the word *curriculum* means "race course," and one virtue of a race course is that it is fixed and standard. For centuries the European curriculum was fixed, bounded by the study of the *trivium* (grammar, logic, rhetoric) and the *quadrivium* (geometry, astronomy, arithmetic, music). Moreover, for most of the last 300 years, the Western curriculum has changed only slowly. For most of those who got any education, it consisted of arithmetic and literacy training in the vernacular, supplemented with Bible study. The intellectual elite, in addition, studied the "disciplines" — higher mathematics, history, national literature, languages, philosophy, and increasingly, the natural sciences. Curriculum changed only slowly, however, and few occasions for political conflict arose.

But the image of the race course has not really been an accurate one for Western curricula since the seventeenth century. In that time the race itself would be a more accurate symbol of the increasingly agitated jockeying for position in the curriculum. First vernacular languages, then physical sciences, then biological sciences, applied sciences, and engineering, and, most recently, the social sciences have successively fought their way into the curriculum at the upper levels of the educational system. Here they have exerted pressure for entry into the curricula of the lower schools. In the lower schools from at least the 1850's, other pressures to include more immediately useful material [3] eventually produced courses in home economics, agricultural and industrial arts, physical education, driver training, and sex education.

These developments have reached their logical (and absurd) conclusion when elementary teachers may be expected to teach, and children to learn, reading, writing, several varieties of arithmetic, geography, spelling, science, economics, music, art, foreign languages and history — at the same time as the children are helped to develop physically, morally, and intellectually, and are molded into good citizens. Furthermore, if the school were to take advantage of the millions of dollars invested in national curriculum development, each of these matters had to be treated independently with specially trained teachers. Things are hardly less chaotic in secondary schools.

All this confusion has provoked conflict over the proper bases for deciding what to teach. Authoritative allocation of resources in these value conflicts is the essence of what we mean by the political process in curricular decision making. Should schools teach those things that are likely to be immediately useful in life outside the school or those things most fundamental to an understanding of organized knowledge? Should they emphasize the development of individuality or the transmission of and conformity to the cultural heritage? So long as men disagree on how to evaluate curriculum, they are bound to quarrel over its composition. The bases for this disagreement can be such things as social class or race.

Over the last several decades, four broad bases for evaluating curricular elements have emerged as salient — tradition, science, community, and individual judgment. These values are bases around which people's preferences tend to congregate, but their conflicting nature creates stress, which generates demands for changes in the existing curriculum. They are neither mutually exclusive nor exhaustive, but they do represent major streams of thought and feeling among curricular constituencies. In short, they are ways of answering Herbert Spencer's question, "What knowledge is of most worth?"

The *appeal to tradition,* exemplified in recent times by the Great Books program and the Council for Basic Education, rests on the assumption that subjects of study that survive the test of time are in the long view most beneficial and therefore should receive the highest priority in the curriculum. The *appeal to science,* the newest and probably the fastest growing basis for curricular decision making, has received strong support from many influential groups, including the United States Office of Education. This appeal rests on the assumption that educational and psychological research will reveal those capabilities whose cultivation is the school's responsibility. In this view, the school curriculum should give first priority to the development of these underlying primary abilities.

The *appeal to community* presupposes that every school is part of a community of association and interest in which reside the ultimate criteria of usefulness, relevance, and benefit of any curricular element. Therefore, those matters that deserve first priority in the curriculum are to be determined by the community, either directly or via its representatives, or by studies of the community. The *appeal to individual judgment* amounts to a skeptical denial of any rational value basis for curriculum making beyond the student's own values, needs, and desires as these are manifested in his own considered judgments. Adherents of this position argue that any basis for curriculum is doomed to failure if it purports to provide only general, impersonal answers to Spencer's question.

Each of these values has its supporters and detractors, who bolster their positions with techniques that we regard as political. Some schools stand primarily, and reasonably consistently, on only one of these bases. The curriculum of St. Johns University is based largely on the appeal to tradition, as are the curricula of a number of private "Latin" schools. Several medical schools have reorganized their curricula along predominantly scientific lines,[4] and experimental programs with a scientific basis are widespread, most visibly in preschool and primary school programs.[5] Many "free" schools and "free" universities across the country, as well as "progressive" or "radical" schools, base their programs on a *particular* community or on the free choices of individual students.[6] But by and large, public school programs are a heterogeneous mixture of these different bases. As such, they reflect the political compromises and diverse values found in any state or local district.

The Decisional Method
of Disjointed Incrementalism

The acceptance of any of these values, when possible, simplifies the curricular problem considerably by providing a limited and well-defined set of criteria for narrowing the bewildering array of curricular choices. But this alone does not resolve the political conflict in curricular policy making. Those who agree that the truths honored in our tradition should shape the curriculum may still disagree over whether certain classics should be taught in the English or Latin translation or in the original Greek. They may argue over whether to include Vergil together with Tacitus and Julius Caesar in a fixed course of study. They may differ over the amount of time to be allotted to the Bible and other more strictly oriented texts. The resolution of such problems requires a decision procedure in addition to a value basis.

The oldest and simplest solution to this problem is to endow an individual or small group with the authority to make these decisions by exercising professional, and presumably expert, judgment. This decision-making body (e.g., a traditional school board) is related to the community that gives it authority and power, just as a government is related to its constituency (e.g., through elections) or the management of a firm to its customers (e.g., through voucher systems). These and other relationships provide the decision makers a degree of autonomy that ranges from absolute responsiveness to virtual independence.

But this only pushes our search one step further. What sort of decision procedures do the curricular decision makers follow? That can best be described by what Lindblom and Braybrooke call a strategy of *disjointed incrementalism,* i.e., a collection of "relatively simple, crude, almost wholly conscious, and public" strategies for decision making, which, "taken together as a mutually reinforcing set . . . constitute a systemic and defensible strategy." [7] The major features of disjointed incrementalism are: (1) acceptance of the broad outlines of the existing situation with only marginal changes contemplated; (2) consideration of only a restricted variety of policy alternatives, excluding those entailing radical change; (3) consideration of only a restricted number of consequences for any given policy; (4) adjustment of objectives to policies as well as vice versa; (5) willingness to reformulate the problem as data become available, and (6) serial analysis and piecemeal alteration rather than a single comprehensive attack. In short, curricular decision makers use pragmatic methods of decision making that result in minimal changes at the margin.

This is no surprise, considering the history of the field, the state of the art of formal decision-making methods, the complexity of the school as a phenomenon, and the paucity of reliable data about the events taking place within the sanctity of the classroom and about their effects on children. The absence of formal decision-making procedures complicates the task of comprehending the political processes in curriculum building, since informal methods are more complex, diffuse, and irregular. Indications are that modern decision tools, such as systems analysis, behavioral objectives, and computer-aided instruction, may begin to be used to decide what to teach.[8] Curricular decision making, however, presents a severe test for any formal decision tool. There is no clear and simple criterion of success like profit or number of enemy dead. Contrast this specificity with such ambiguous school outcomes as "good citizenship."

The newer methods rely on behavioral objectives as criteria of value. That is, the users of each method assume they have been supplied with a complete list of the "behaviors" desired by the school and that all the school's real objectives can be expressed in the form of these behaviors. Dissent on these points is strong, however, and they are vigorously disputed in the professional literature.[9] Indeed, some critics strongly oppose even the attempt to define such criteria, on the grounds that they necessarily leave out the more evanescent benefits of education. It is true that we are hard-pressed to specify the educational benefits of, for example, play for children, even though most of us believe that it has great educational value. Even if we could get wide agreement on operational goals, however, the most significant goals are likely to take a long time to achieve. But the assessment of the beneficial effects stemming from a complex treatment directed toward a distant objective is a presently insoluble technical problem. An even more elemental task is to find satisfactory measures of the subtle effects we want, such as the ability to apply what is learned to unfamiliar situations, the ability to learn new things quickly and surely, and the ability to decide what knowledge is appropriate to a given problem.

In summary, curricular decisions are not based on quantitative decision techniques or even on much objective data. This leaves a great deal of latitude for deliberation and for complicated political processes to resolve conflicts of values among various groups and individuals. As we will see, these value conflicts are resolved through low-profile politics, accompanied by a considerable amount of overt political interaction.

At this point we turn our attention to mapping the political system for curricular policy making and to assessing the influence of the various interest groups and conversion personnel. By *influence* we mean the ability to get others to act, think, or feel as one intends. A superintendent who persuades his board to install the "new math" is exercising political influence on a curricular issue. Political analysis should focus on the question of who has leverage — the capacity of substantial influence on the curricular output of a school system — for those with leverage can make a big difference in the outcome of conflicts over curriculum. Our focus here is on the content of curricular policy rather than the priority that curriculum receives in budget allocations. Our primary concern is with the decisions in the local school system about what to teach children.

A mapping of the political system for curricular policy making in local schools is exceedingly complex. It involves three levels of government, numerous private organizations (including foundations, accrediting associations, national testing agencies, textbook-software companies), and interest groups, such as the John Birch Society or NAACP. In short, it touches on all those components described in earlier chapters. Moreover, there is a configuration of leverage points within a particular local school system, including the teacher, department head, assistant superintendent for instruction, superintendent, and school board. Cutting across all levels of government is the pervasive influence of the mass media, which various celebrities, commentators, interest groups, and journalists use to disseminate their views on curriculum. It would be very helpful if we were able to quantify the amount of influence of each of these and show input-output interactions for just one school system, let alone a representative sample. Unfortunately, this is considerably beyond the state of the art, so we must settle for a less precise political analysis.

INPUTS FROM
TRADITIONAL CURRICULUM SUPPORTERS

From the vantage point of a local public school system, the options for determining curricular content are constrained greatly by outside groups. In our political culture's emphasis on "local control," curriculum is one area where a uniform national standard and substance should ostensibly be avoided. Indeed, federal aid to education was stalled for years, in large part because of a fear that the federal dollar would lead to a uniform national curriculum.[10] This fear notwithstanding, visitors from abroad are usually surprised by the coast-to-coast similarity of the curriculum in American public schools. This has transpired because, in effect, we have granted political influence over curriculum to national, *nongovernmental* agencies that demand a minimum national curricular standard below which few public schools dare to fall. These agencies primarily provide the inputs of specific and diffuse support for a traditional curriculum.

Accrediting and Testing Agencies

A good example of this is the leverage on curriculum that private accrediting associations display. State governments also accredit, of course, but it is the private, regional accrediting organizations that most concern local schoolmen. These agencies define the specific curricular standards and criteria required for their stamp of approval. The largest of the regionals, the North Central Association, uses written reports for its judgments, but others employ site visitors. The accrediting agencies' curricular standards are highly detailed. For instance, a 1965 sample provides that "written criteria be set up for the evaluation and selection of textbooks . . . continuing study be given to offering four years of language [and that] broader use of the audio-lingual approach be explored." [11]

The political influence of the accrediting agency is based on the faith *other* people have in the accreditation. Since loss of accreditation is dreaded by every schoolman, these agencies can bring almost irresistible pressure upon local curricular offerings. Not surprisingly, these agencies often are a force for supporting the traditional curriculum and resisting radical changes.[12] In effect, although accrediting agencies stress *profes-*

sional judgments, they make *value* judgments about what should be taught, and, by their prestige, make basic allocations of decisions on curriculum.

Testing agencies in the United States, also largely in private hands, exert an equally "standardizing" influence on curriculum. The Educational Testing Service, for instance, has an income of about $20 million a year from its tests. Over one million students take the College Boards, and 700 institutions require it. Consequently, local schools do not have a choice as to whether or not they shall offer the dozen subjects covered by these achievement exams. These tests do not entirely determine the detailed content of the curriculum, of course, but they do limit what teachers can spend their time doing. Moreover, national, standardized reading or math tests given in the pre-high-school grades may determine a great deal of the specific content of the reading or math curriculum. The fact that local schools want to look good on these nationally normed tests is the driving force behind testers' influence over some curricular decisions.

Although the testing agency and its panels of expert advisers largely determine the content of the standardized tests used in elementary and junior high schools, in high schools the tests tend to be dictated largely by the colleges and universities. The latter, then, are another major source of inputs for curricular decisions, because the tests follow guidelines laid down by colleges as part of their entrance requirements. Students take a college-preparatory course whose curriculum is determined almost entirely by college entrance requirements. And the prestige accorded to the subjects required for college entrance undoubtedly influences more of the non-college-bound students (probably via their parents) also to take these courses. The alleged tyranny of college entrance requirements over the secondary school curriculum has therefore been a persistent complaint of high schools.

In the late 1930's, the Progressive Education Association sponsored an eight-year study in which students in experimental schools were able to waive the usual unit entrance requirements. The only requirement was a recommendation from their principals. An evaluation of the college performance of these students showed them to be equal to students in similar schools in every respect — and superior in many. Although the design of this study has been criticized, no one has attempted to replicate it, and entrance requirements still remain.[13]

State Law

State departments and boards of education have also had a traditional role in setting and enforcing minimum curricular standards. This role has varied enormously, depending on whether the political culture of the state supported what Elazar called a "centrist" or "localist" policy.[14] We have noted that in New England the local schools enjoy an autonomy from state controls that goes back to the hatred of the English governor, whereas Southern states often centrally mandate textbooks and courses of instruction. However, most states do not mandate the school curriculum to any great extent. A 1966 survey by Conant revealed that although the great majority of the states mandate courses in the dangers of alcohol and narcotics, only half require work in United States history and physical education, and less than half (ranging from 46 percent to 2 percent of the states) require instruction in other specific subjects.[15] Although California and Iowa have over thirty curricular prescriptions, over half the states have fewer than ten. Enforcement of state board mandates on curriculum is very spotty, and local districts with strong views can circumvent the weak enforcement machinery.

A major reason for lack of state mandating is historical and political. It is often the newer subject areas (vocational education, driver training) that have had to use state law in order to gain a secure place in the curriculum. These subjects were introduced into the curriculum after 1920, amid great controversy, whereas mathematics and English never had to use political power to justify their existence in the school curriculum. Consequently, the "standard" subjects are less frequently mandated by state law; it is the "new boys" who have had to go outside local school traditions to gain recognition and power in the curriculum.

For this reason, associations of teachers of special subjects can be very influential at the state level, using their power base to preserve curricular interests. Vocational education, physical education, and home economics teachers use their NEA state affiliate to ensure that their specialties are stressed in the local schools. They are also supported by the manufacturers of the hardware required by the newer courses, e.g., sports equipment and home appliances. The driver-education teachers are a newer state lobby, but they have been so effective that almost all states now mandate driver education.

Ironically, it is the teachers of academic subjects who are usually poorly organized or weakly united at the state level. Because nobody consults them, their influence is minimal, as indicated by the national trend to require less professional training for teaching licenses in physics, math, or history than for home economics or industrial arts.[16] Yet in truth they have little need for such group action when inputs from private agencies, accrediting or college, work so effectively.

The impact on curricular policy of these organizations that set minimum standards and tend to support the *status quo* is summarized by Koerner:

> Suppose a local board, aware of the obsolescence and flaccidity of much that passes for vocational training . . . decides to reduce its program in these areas. In theory this is one of its sovereign rights. In

practice several things occur to change its mind. First, the vocational education lobby goes to work on other members of local government and on the state legislature or state department of education to protect the extensive interests of vocational education teachers. Second, the regional accrediting association comes to the aid of the status quo and makes threatening noises, suggesting and then perhaps demanding, on pain of disaccreditation . . . that the board rescind its decision. Third, the NEA state affiliate "investigates" and through its considerable power "persuades" the board to a different view.[17]

INPUTS OF DEMANDS FOR CHANGE

Operating in the political environment of the local school are several organizations and individuals who provide alternative inputs on curricular matters. The range and nature of their curricular demands are restricted by the minimum standards and requirements discussed in the prior section, but they work away at the margins of the conventional.

Most curricular decisions are made at the local level as a function of external and internal constraints. Thus, outside agencies can only provide alternatives to choose from, but local school boards and schoolmen must take the final steps in deciding what to teach. As we have seen, state officials and the state legislature usually prescribe certain rather broad limits. The power of local officials to select is bounded, however, by the resources available to them, perhaps more severely than by state law. Thus, if ten years ago local schoolmen had wanted to teach a history of America that gave a full or at least realistic place to the black man, they would have had to write the textbook themselves. Some schools attempt such things, but most do not. Teachers do not feel able to do the job, and the board lacks money for released time or research assistants. So until recently, most schools could not opt for integrated history even if they were so inclined. As we noted earlier, it is only now becoming possible for schools to teach a reasonably balanced account of the role of minorities in our history. On a less controversial plane, but for the same causes, until 1960 a school could not offer modern physics unless it was blessed with a truly outstanding teacher.

The bald fact is that most teaching in our schools is and must be done from a textbook or other curricular package. Not trusting teachers to write their own materials, we do not give them the time or money; at the same time, we do insist upon standardization. So long as this is true, the suppliers of these resource materials will have a potentially powerful effect on the curriculum. Both teachers and publishers are motivated toward standardization by the expectation that they will transmit a common culture, as we stressed in Chapter 2.

Publishers

Who supplies these decision resources to local schools? Until ten years ago the unequivocal answer to this question would have been "textbook publishers." But a lot has happened in the interim. Textbook publishing has become part of an enlarged education industry that produces all sorts of printed, electronic, and mechanical devices for classroom use. Also, the federal government, private foundations, and various nonprofit organizations of scholars, teachers, and laymen have taken a more active role in producing curricular materials. Nevertheless, the textbook is still the most widely used piece of educational technology, and textbook publishers are still powerful influences on the curriculum. The Texas Governor's Committee on Public Education in 1969 estimated that 75 percent of a child's classroom and 90 percent of his homework time have been spent using textbooks. Thus, the publisher's control of the content of the textbook is virtual control over the curriculum.

But the power of the textbook publisher is a brittle sort of power that cannot stand up against serious opposition from any large segment of the population. Some publishers still put the unit on evolution in the center of the biology textbook so that the books destined for Southern and Western schools can readily be bound *without* those pages. Sections on "Negro history" were once added in the same way. Publishers cannot (or will not, which amounts to the same thing) stand against the demands of their customers. Nor can publishers spend millions of dollars developing materials for one course in the way the National Science Foundation has supported projects in the sciences and mathematics. In short, in spite of their potential power the publishers have *not* been able to operate as independent agents. Instead, they reflect the conflicting desires of their customers — the local schools and in some areas the state authorities.[18]

Where state adoption prevails, the state department of education seems to exercise considerable leverage. In Texas, the state commissioner nominates members to serve on the State Textbook Committee, and he must approve the books that it recommends. Texas SDE specialists draw up the detailed criteria for the publishers' bids, including the topics to be covered. The selected books are distributed at state expense to every school room, but the same textbook must stay in service for six years. Districts that want to use more modern writing must do so at their own expense.

Federal Government

The federal government has become another very powerful influence on the curriculum in the past decade. Because of the fragmented federal budgeting of monies for curriculum development, it is not possible to determine exactly how much Washington, mainly through the National Science Foundation and the Office of Education, has spent on curriculum development over that decade. The amount approaches $250 million, however, and, rough an estimate as this is, we know the figure is enormous. This money dwarfs all previous curriculum-development efforts by states, regions, localities, and private enterprise. An index of the impact of government-sponsored courses is the fact that over 50 percent of our schools use the new physics and chemistry; 65 percent use the new biology.[19]

It is true, however, that federal agencies have not sponsored the development of controversial curricula. The National Science Foundation specifically perceives its role as one of "course improvement," not new-course creation. Almost all federal money for curriculum development, therefore, has gone to update and improve the existing curriculum. We have new math, new physics, new biology, new social studies and new English — but not psychology, sociology, economics, philosophy, problems of modern living, interpersonal relationships, sex education, or film-making and film-viewing.

But emphasis upon improvement of existing coursework is nevertheless a powerful force. Federal agencies have decided which proposed "improvements" to finance, and they have exerted certain pressures on the staffs of projects they finance, including pressure to state the objectives and to conduct evaluations using these objectives.[20] It is unclear whether federal agencies will continue this pattern or expand their efforts toward genuinely new courses. They could also cut back on their funds for curriculum development in disillusionment over the failure of test results to show definite superiority of the new curricula.

Of course, no one can foresee the path that this federal policy will take in even the next few years. These agencies jumped from virtually no influence to a place of preeminence at one stroke of the pen that signed the National Defense Education Act of 1958 into law. President Nixon has proposed the creation of a National Institute of Education and inaugurated a "right to read" campaign to encourage emphasis upon reading in elementary and junior high schools. "Sesame Street," a nationally televised preschool program, has been produced under the auspices of the Office of Education, among others. Until now, Washington's educational influence has been conservative, but it still has an important potential role for change in its available resources, particularly when the right circumstances arise to enable federal agencies to seize the curricular initiative.

Foundations

Another set of active agents in curriculum making are the foundations — chiefly Ford, Rockefeller, Carnegie, and Kettering. Over the past ten years they have generally undertaken the role of supplementing and balancing — without duplicating — the efforts of the federal government. When Washington was financing only projects in mathematics, science, and foreign languages, the foundations were financing projects in the arts and social sciences. The foundations have also been bolder in funding efforts in non-standard courses, such as psychology, economics, and photography among many others.

All that is known of the policies of the foundations that have supported curriculum development over the past decade are their declarations. We have not been able to locate a single study or evaluation of the foundations' effects on curriculum. We can understand the difficulty of studying this problem, but in view of its importance one might expect at least a case study. Possibly this lack stems from the foundations being relatively new to curriculum development. Possibly, too, the effect is blurred by the fact that foundations must rely on local or state education authorities to accept the new materials or on interest groups to present political demands for change to those authorities. Yet this gap in knowledge of curricular politics is a curious one.

Conventional Sources

Although the two major sources of funds for curricular planning in this country — the federal government and foundations — are relatively new and therefore not fully understood or dependable, there are better known and steadier, if less copious, sources. Professional associations of scientists, engineers, and business and professional men have supported curriculum-development efforts related to their professional interests. They will no doubt continue to do so as long as they can be convinced of the need for new curricula in their special fields. Local school districts provide modest sums for updating their curricula. We have no dependable estimates of the amount spent in this fashion, but the figure must surely be quite small for individual districts. Occasional regional or state-wide curriculum-development projects have been funded well enough and long enough to permit thorough, substantial efforts. The state of New York, through its Board of Regents, has been outstanding in this respect.

Also, of course, private businesses, chiefly textbook publishers in the past, but increasingly amalgams of publishing and electronics firms, spend unknown amounts for curriculum development. These firms harbor vital curriculum expertise, for publishers use their sales organizations to ferret out the likes and dislikes of the schoolmen who buy their books, and they "edit" the book with one eye on this information.[21] Strangely enough, this network of salesmen is the only reasonably dependable, comprehensive mechanism for compiling the preferences and prejudices of local schools on curriculum matters.

Twenty years ago we could have stopped with textbooks in our treatment of the contributions of private firms to curricular decisions. But not any more. Science Research Associates is owned by IBM, Xerox has bought American Educational Publications, GE and Time have formed General Learning, RCA has bought Random House, and CBS has bought Holt, Rinehart and Winston. These firms can produce curricular alternatives in the form of programmed sequences, films, software and hardware for use in computer-aided instruction, and similar devices — all of which have potentially powerful effects on the school curriculum. Note, too, that no other agencies will be able to produce these items. The new notions of performance contracts and vouchers are supported by both federal agencies and private firms, but it is the corporations that will formulate the specific curricular packages and will contract with the local districts that have federal money.

Yet it is likely that curriculum development will be forced to rely chiefly on the traditional sources of money in the next decade. The pressing problems of war and domestic issues — race, environment, and poverty — will leave at best only a moderate priority for educational concerns unrelated to these issues.

Professors

But sources of money are not the only influences on the resources available to the local decision maker. Sources of ideas and expertise are also crucial. The major source of ideas for curricular change has always been the college or university. The last twenty years have seen an intensified reliance on college and university professors in the form of national commissions on curriculum and university-based projects. In most cases, professors have participated as subject-matter experts — as scientists, mathematicians, historians, etc. Only a few psychologists have been employed to advise projects on methods; education faculty generally have not been heavily involved in projects.

University professors do not, of course, constitute anything like a unitary block of opinion on curricular questions. In fact, they have been a major source of much-needed diversity in the once seemingly stagnant curriculum of the American school. Nevertheless, university professors tend to regard education as an entirely intellectual affair, whereas long tradition in this country and, indeed, the Western world, emphasizes moral, physical, and aesthetic concerns. Many of the scholars drawn into the public school curriculum through the federal government's curriculum projects tended to share MIT physicist Jerrold Zacharais' view that "our real problem as a nation was creeping anti-intellectualism from which came many of our educational deficiencies." [22] This value orientation differs significantly from that of the general public, which, if it chose, could reassert the claims of less intellectual matters for attention in the curriculum.

If university faculty do not represent any organized body of opinion, their professional associations sometimes do, and when they do they can be extremely influential. The role of the American Association for the Advancement of Science and the American Institute for Biological Sciences in introducing evolution into biology books over the strong objections of fundamentalist Christians [23] can be influential when they are united and determined. The American Mathematical Society sponsored the School Mathematics Study Group until the Sputnik-induced National Defense Education Act authorized the National Science Foundation to finance it as an independent enterprise.

Too, Turner describes the American Council of Learned Societies as extremely influential in recent revisions of social-studies curricula.[24] The ACLS urged its constituent societies to see what they could do about revising the curriculum in their disciplines. It commissioned nine scholars to investigate the relation between the social sciences and the social studies (eventuating in the influential 1962 report *The Social Studies and the Social Sciences*). It also conducted a survey to determine what the constituent societies were doing about curricular questions; it sponsored a conference of scholars and educators to formulate a K–12 design in the humanities and social sciences; and, finally, it commissioned a study of the present state of the social studies curriculum.

In summary, when a school district faces the problem of putting together a course, it has only three basic choices. The whole problem can be left to individual teachers; groups of teachers can make the plans and teaching materials for the whole school; or materials can be purchased. American public schools increasingly favor the last approach. Therefore, the sources of these materials are, and will probably remain, important determinants of the curriculum. The sources we have identified are the projects financed by the federal government and private foundations, college and university faculties, professional associations, private businesses, and organizations of laymen. But the fact of the matter is that any group with sufficient talent and resources can prepare curricular materials and possibly start a trend that would sweep the school system behind them.

DEMANDS AND SUPPORT
FROM LOCAL COMMUNITY FORCES

In a survey of the force of innovation in education, Pellegrin concluded that

> the greatest stimuli to changes in education originate in sources external to the field. What I have shown is that the sources of innovation lie largely outside the local community, and in most instances outside the education profession.[25]

This statement would appear to apply to curriculum and the organizations and individuals discussed above that provide most of the ideas, alternatives, and value orientations adopted by schoolmen. A good example of this today is the teamwork of corporations and Washington in implementing performance contracts. The role of the local lay community in curricular change, however, appears minimal, for it is primarily actors within the school system who decide whether a break is to be made with the traditional curriculum.

The Lay Public

In earlier chapters we noted the ignorance of the lay public, on education. This may be a major reason why it has only minimal political leverage in its schools. A 1969 Gallup poll shows that the public knows almost nothing about the substance of education and is not involved with broad curricular issues. Most of the information that Americans receive about schools concerns "happenings," or the hard news reported in the media. When asked to tell how they would judge a good school, their criteria were, in order, qualified teachers (vaguely defined by most respondents), discipline, and physical equipment. The "biggest" problem of the public schools they see to be discipline (26 percent); 4 percent ascribe it to the curriculum. Gallup observed that this lack of information does not stem from a lack of public interest:

> When asked specifically what kind of information they would like to have, the answers deal to a large extent with the courses taught — the curriculum — innovations being introduced and why — college requirements — and the like. Significantly, there is great interest in the very areas that most school publicity presently neglects — the content of courses and the educational process versus school operations.[26]

This limited public role undoubtedly stems in large part from Americans accepting the view that curriculum is an issue properly to be settled by professional educators trained in these matters.

Of course, the community does get involved in curricular issues on occasion. We earlier cited Martin's survey of suburban citizens and leaders who focused on curriculum — indeed on most school matters — only episodically — "issues which emerge under unusual or special conditions and shortly subside." [27] Martin and others have concluded that community influence seems most often to be a *negative action,* like defeat of a bond issue, tax increase, or school board member, or the termination of controversial curricular offerings like sex education. On the other hand, Gittell and her associates in a study of six cities concluded that

> innovation can only be achieved as a result of strong community participation with power to compel both new programs and expenditure

increases necessary to finance them. The brief experience in Philadelphia . . . suggests that substantial community involvement provides both the pressure for change and a community atmosphere favorable for obtaining the necessary financing.[28]

Gittell was referring to innovations of all types, and it is not clear to what extent her findings are relevant to curriculum. The distinction is between what Gittell shows can be and what experience shows exists; that is, the public can influence school matters but rarely does so.

All the studies demonstrate, further, that the historic separation between education and general government has left minimal influence to the mayor and the city council over the curriculum.[29] Saxe, in his survey of fifty mayors, noted a traditional "separation of functions" between schoolmen and city officials, epitomized in one mayor's comment that "I do not intend, however, to become involved in school issues such as curricula, busing of students, and matters of that type, since this is clearly the responsibility of another agency." But Saxe notes that "a majority of the mayors cooperating in this survey (20 out of 32 . . .) [are] reconsider[ing] their hands-off attitude."[30]

At the local level, then, curricular decisions have been very much a function of withinputs among school professionals, often within the bureaucracy beneath the superintendent. The formal institutional description would lead one to believe that the school board plays a more decisive role here than the evidence justifies. The limited role of lay control over school matters noted throughout this volume, then, applies also to curriculum. It is useful to explore in detail these withinputs in the conversion process of curricular policy.

School Boards

The limited influence of the school board noted in other policy matters exists here, too. Although value decisions are at their core, curricular decisions require some knowledge of the philosophy and methods of education. Lay school boards, however, usually have no experts or even part-time staff, independent of the school bureaucracy. Too, they can give little time to any school problem, being only part-time officials meeting at night once or twice a week after a full day in other responsible positions. Nor are they usually presented with performance criteria or test data upon which to question the curricular judgments of the superintendent and his staff. Part of this defect arises because curricular proposals rarely are related to measurable objectives and seldom undergo systematic analysis, as we saw in the first section. In general, disjointed incrementalism does not assist a lay board in playing a crucial decision-making role, certainly not in curricular policies.

The method of electing school boards also limits the board's perspective on curriculum. The Gallup poll noted earlier indicates that curricular issues are usually not presented to the voters as election mandates. Moreover, as Salisbury points out, the board has traditionally viewed its representation of wards or ethnic groups in the same way as the superintendent, i.e., it has agreed that:

> regardless of ethnic, racial, religious, economic, or political differences in other areas of urban life, education should not legitimize those differences. Education is a process that must not be differentiated according to section or class, and the city is a *unity* for purposes of the school program.[31]

Consequently, school boards and superintendents have historically resisted a differentiated curriculum for Italians, Irish, blacks, chicanos, and other ethnic, racial, or religious groups.

But increasingly, as the ethnic proportion in urban schools grows ever larger, that resistance is becoming harder to maintain. The "black studies" movement in the late 1960's in the urban North signaled a major break in the traditional power and unified perspective of schoolmen on curricular matters. A similar sign is the adoption of bilingual programs for students of Mexican and Chinese origin, particularly in the California schools.

Superintendents

To date, few studies have distinguished the political influence and leverage that exists within the school bureaucracy. Most have tended to treat the superintendent and his bureaucracy as one actor with similar interests and to compare their unitary role to that of school boards, city officials, community interest groups, and so on. Studies of large school systems have found, however, that the bureaucracy wields substantial influence, with which the superintendent may be in conflict. Yet, guarding curricular decisions as an area of their professional competence, superintendents have been viewed by many analysts as key figures in the innovation process. We noted in Chapter 5 Martin's judgment on his pivotal role within the school and community.[32]

Studies support this concept for some superintendents. Examining curricular innovation in West Virginia and Pennsylvania, Carlson found that the superintendent was the "agricultural extension agent" as well as the "experimental station" for the new math.[33] The superintendents who adopted new curricula interacted frequently with a peer group of other innovative superintendents. In short, a group of professional friends spread the new math to each of the members of the group. Not all were equal in such peer influence, as certain key superintendents were viewed by their colleagues as particularly important advisors and opinion leaders on curriculum. In West Virginia, however, the SDE's advice was often sought. Carlson's data show from another vantage point that superintendents who did *not* adopt curricular reform programs (1) had less formal education, (2) received fewer friendship choices among local superintendents, (3) knew well fewer of their peers, (4) participated in fewer professional meetings, (5) held less prestigious positions, (6) perceived less support from their school boards, and (7) relied more on local sources for advice and information.[34]

These men, therefore, especially the most influential, do not operate in a social vacuum. It is worth noting that the innovations that Carlson explored were developed by the federal government and by foundations. Since then, regional education labs have emerged to try out new curricular ideas, although their influence is yet unknown. Amid these innovative ideas, the superintendent, with his own perception and estimate of professional needs, mediates between outside opportunities for change and the local population.[35]

School Bureaucracy

The superintendent's power may be more potential than real, however. Although he can, if he chooses, block most internal demands for change in official district-wide curricular policy (other than "episodic issues" like sex education), it is not clear, especially in large cities, whether he is closely involved in many important curricular decisions. The key bureaucratic officers appear to be assistant superintendents for instruction and department chairmen who work in committees with groups of teachers.[36] The influence of the principal seems small because, as Pellegrin notes, "He is burdened with such a multitude of managerial activities that it is extremely difficult for him to devote the time and effort required for innovation on a substantial scale." [37] Despite the stress that the principal's formal job description puts on curricular leadership, he also is little more than a middleman between the teacher and the central office for the implementation of curriculum.

Teachers

It may seem somewhat odd to leave the teacher until so near the end of a chapter on curricular policy making. After all, teachers do control the presentation of material within their own classrooms and regulate their own schedules and methods of instruction. Yet studies of curricular innovation at the classroom level find that "teachers seldom suggest distinctly new types of working patterns for themselves." Chesler has noted:

> It is a unique school indeed in which teachers discuss their classroom problems, techniques, and progress with one another and with their

principal. In most schools teachers practice their own methods — rarely hearing, or even caring, if one of their colleagues is experimenting with some new teaching device or technique.[38]

Little of this judgment has been affected by recent teacher militancy. Through collective bargaining, teachers are certainly increasing their control over such "bread and butter" issues as pay, class size, and relief from noninstructional duties. But during the 1960's, their influence or bargaining rarely extended to curriculum. James found that demands from teacher organizations in fourteen cities related only to staff benefits and not to curriculum.[39] It is quite possible, however, that curricular issues will become a concern of teacher negotiations. They are beginning to appear among some contract demands, but as yet these have not been central issues, i.e., those over which a strike might occur. Perhaps as differentiated staffing arrangements bring teachers together over curricular concerns, such issues will receive more attention from their organizations.

Students

As in so many other — if not all — school matters, students come last, because they have no influence in any formal sense over what they learn. This is so obvious a fact that research to establish it would be trivial. Of course, decision makers sometimes take students' views into account, but not usually. Schoolmen's surveys even to assess student opinion are rare.

But students, to the distress of parents and school officials, are voting with their feet on major curricular questions. Enrollment in high school physics is declining at a greater rate since the new physics began to be taught. There is some evidence that the increased interest among students in "free schools" is a reaction to a curriculum over which they have little control and which they see as overly rigid and abstract. This is a matter that needs further study as a subject no longer trivial, for the growth in the 1960's of student discontent with curriculum in colleges may well reach down to secondary schools in the 1970's. The push for "black" studies is already evident there.

Community Demands Summary

This review of the agencies contributing inputs to curricular policy making has been necessarily brief because the input sources have been so numerous. However, their very multiplicity and varied levels work against any simple notion of professionals alone making such decisions. As we show in summary form in Table 10.1, these decisions flow from a matrix of influences, public and private, professional and lay, internal and external to the local system. Further, the mix of influences that determine curriculum in one area may be reshuffled in another. In all, however, the decision is far from nonpolitical.

Table 10.1 *Illustrative Typology of Input Sources for Curricular Decision Making*

	National	State	Local
General legislative	Congress	State legislature	(City councils have no influence.)
Educational legislative	House Committee on Education and Labor	State school board	Local school board
Executive	President	Governor	(Mayor has no influence.)
Administrative	HEW–USOE	State department	School superintendent
Bureaucratic	OE (Bureau of Research); National Science Foundation (Division of Curriculum Improvement)	State department (division of vocational education)	Department chairmen, teachers
Professional association	National testing agencies	Accrediting associations and NEA state subject matter affiliates	County association of superintendents
Other private interests	Foundations and business corporations	Council for basic education	John Birch Society, NAACP

DISTINCTIVE FEATURES OF
CURRICULAR POLICY MAKING

It might be useful as a summarizing device to compare curricular policy making with other types, e.g., economic policy making. In our economic system, everyone's decisions to buy and sell ultimately — albeit minutely — shapes the national economy, just as the decisions of thousands of local boards shape national educational policy. Economic questions are usually considered too complex to permit direct voting, and for this reason some economic decision makers are insulated from the electorate. Those who are not usually confine their economic campaign positions to being against inflation and recession, although they will take stands on particularly heated but specific issues such as the oil depletion allowance or wage-price controls. Similarly, although to a lesser degree, parents are not expected to understand or to vote on the new math or the new social studies. Nor do candidates for election to local school boards normally take campaign stands on general curricular issues, except on particularly heated but specific issues such as sensitivity training and sex education.

But the analogy between economic and curricular policy cannot be carried far. Curricular policy is primarily and traditionally the concern of the states and localities, even though the federal government's role is rapidly expanding. Even when a new curricular policy is determined, it is a long way from implementation. If a policy innovation survives emasculation by the administrative hierarchies of federal, state, and local officials, it still faces a pocket veto by 2 million classroom teachers. As long as teachers consider themselves to be professional agents, with some autonomy in curriculum by virtue of their expertise, policy implementation will be a matter of persuasion rather than dictate. Of course, it is possible that teachers will be replaced by mechanical and electronic devices or at least be so cowed by that possibility as to make them dependable agents of policy. But the increasing unionization of teachers indicates that they will at least have a say in determining the policies they are asked to carry out.

Classroom teachers do not stand alone between policy makers and their goals, however. Numerous agencies such as the College Entrance Examination Board, the national accreditation committees, the scholarly, scientific and professional organizations, as well as specifically educational pressure groups, vie for a voice in curricular policy making. It seems highly unlikely that any one agency, even the federal government, could wrest policy-making autonomy from so many hands.

But the example, given in the introduction to Part II, of American schools' reaction to Sputnik shows that if a national emergency creates sufficient stress, encrusted traditions can be swept aside in one session of the Congress. After the NDEA was passed, money became available in enormous amounts, peer leaders among school professionals encouraged their colleagues, and both interacted toward a mutually reinforcing goal. As a result, it was a rare school without a new math or language training program. Local control seemed to evaporate in the welcome given to money and in the curricular thrust from outside upon willing local schoolmen.

The Sputnik case suggests that, in spite of the difficulties of achieving systematic curricular policy, efforts in this direction are virtually certain to increase. The steadily increasing role of federal and state governments, the increasing tendency of elected officials to speak out on educational questions, the increasing willingness of mass media to publish achievement-test scores of local schools, the recent national assessment program (which will provide detailed information on the educational attainment of American youth), and demands for community control and ethnically approved courses and texts — all portend an increasingly political approach to curricular questions on the part of some of the general public. One observer has noted that "at least in the giant cities, it is academic to debate closer educational-political cooperation. Whether we like it or not, the events of the day will not permit a fragmented approach to education in the city." [40]

This development, whether one anticipates it with eagerness or dread, merits careful attention from students of schools. For American schools may be at the opening of the third stage of our historical curriculum development. We began the Republic with limited variety and poor quality in course content in the preprofessional era of *private free enterprise* in schools. The rise of the profession during the nineteenth century brought standardization and greater variety to curriculum as the colleges imposed their own controls and their influence improved quality. This was a stage of *private nationalization,* whose agents were the professionals of schools and colleges who secured state support for their ideas.

The third curricular policy stage may be more one of a *mixed private and public free enterprise.* Like the others, it arises from stress in the community over what schools are or are not doing, a reaction against the evils of curricular standardization — social blandness and blindness, conformity, lack of popular control. More diversity is a theme underlying these new ideas — vouchers, teaching machines, group teaching, "free" schools, student evaluation, ethnically honest textbooks, and so on.

In the face of this individualistic clamor, schools are both open and closed to curricular innovation. We know of their bureaucratic tendencies so denounced by current critics.[41] Yet we have also shown their potential for openness, which stems from the host of agencies seeking to influence curriculum. The federal government, accrediting associations, and professional scholars provide powerful forces for standardizing established curriculum, but foundations and some schoolmen also provide an innovative impulse.

The composite picture of this policy, then, reveals that curricular tensions exist within the schools because of different value bases and group interests. These tensions generate conflict over how the school system is to allocate its resources, a conflict in which the general public plays only an occasional — and even then peripheral — role. In this larger interplay between the environment and the schools, curricular decisions are outputs emanating from a political system, a process of adjusting to demands by allocational, authoritative decisions of the school.

Viewed in these terms, curricular decision making should give rise to other questions. Whose interests are served by the kinds of decisions made; how are systemwide curricular changes made; and how does this decisional process contribute to the rigidity of the school's political system? These queries are not merely for scholars, reflecting research gaps; they are also for the public to ask and know, for the answers tell them what they are getting in the way of an education.

PART THREE

Political Science and the Study of School Policy

The many facets of American schools that we have explained within a systems framework demonstrate both similarity and variety. Yet we have not considered all school aspects, nor do we plan to. Surely enough has been offered to indicate the political quality of schools, both within their institutional boundaries and as they relate to society. In this chapter, therefore, we wish to return to examine the utility of the framework that has guided our study and to pursue some of the implications of the politicization of schools in recent times. Put differently, how useful is our way of viewing schools and what does it matter that this view finds schools now more political than popularly suspected?

LIMITS AND USES OF THE SYSTEMS ANALYSIS FRAMEWORK

The interrelationship between politics and education is clearly not new, as our discussion in Chapter 2 noted. For as Wolin recently observed, these subjects comprise

two of the oldest, most pondered matters in the recorded history of Western civilization. . . . Shortly after the ancient Greeks discovered philosophy as a self-conscious activity focused upon a complex of "problems," of which politics was one of the most important, they made the same discovery about education: the latter, too, presented problems of which politics was one of the most important.[1]

But disagreement arises over two more general problems. How are politics and education to be viewed, whether conceptually in their empirical existence or preferentially in the world of value? In short, how *do* schools and politics relate to one another as a matter of fact and how *should* they as a matter of value?

In most respects, this book has focused only upon the first, empirical question. But putting an empirical question is no simple matter, for it is an effort open to fallacies in framing — as well as in verifying the question and in estimating the significance of the facts unearthed.[2] Accordingly, it is important to review critically the systems analysis framework that shaped our selection from and our view of the empirical world of American schools. To this point we have uncritically employed its components to organize our data and reflections. Yet it is not without its critics for this and other purposes. Such criticism is extensive, so we must necessarily condense much of it into main arguments. It will thereafter be appropriate to review this framework for any utilities it may still have.

Without too much injustice to the complexity of these criticisms of systems analysis, we suggest that they are basically of two kinds. One set argues that such analysis is ineffective, i.e., it does not or cannot do what it claims as an analytical tool. The second set argues that even if it does meet its claims, it is an undesirable way of thinking about schools — or any other segment of social experience — because of what it implies about the values of man and society. Although it is simplified, we shall use this dual critique of the ineffective and undesirable in what follows.

The Ineffectiveness Critique

Although not all critics of systems analysis charge it with the same kind of ineffectiveness, as a battery they mount a formidable attack.[3] The variants of this attack include the following: all models of reality, including this, are unreal ways of analyzing reality; it is not new; it does not ask the best questions of reality; its concepts are not amenable to measurement; it cannot generate testable hypotheses deducible from its theory; and even its heuristic uses are limited. A brief statement of each criticism and an evaluation of its validity provide the format for this section.

The Anti-Model Critique. The first criticism is not directed particularly at systems analysis but generally at all efforts to construct models as devices to explain reality. The problem is, it is urged, that our thinking about reality cannot precisely fit the object referred to. Just as in the semanticist's famous insight the road map is not the same as the road, so the model is not the reality it purports to describe. Indeed, such thinking is most often shaped by the use of a "prevailing metaphor," which, once introduced, influences subsequent theorization about the reality referent. What transpires, then, is the development of theory *about* reality but not *of* reality. Moreover, efforts to break through by operationalizing the theory and by observing reality usually produce only case studies, but these cannot "test" the full range of the theory and by themselves permit of no generalization. Grant has summarized the dilemma well:

> On the other hand, those employing the systems approach impute to reality meaning which is merely contrived. A complex of interactions is "understood" arbitrarily within the framework of certain generalizations. Judgment of particulars is here given up for the sake of generalization. On the other hand, political scientists preferring the case studies approach have compiled enormous files of descriptive accounts. But no one is willing to say when those files will be sufficiently extensive to justify generalizations based upon them. . . . The desire for generalization is here given up for the sake of judgments about particulars. Whether generalization or particularization be sought after, the meaning of reality is missed. Reality is not simply general or simply particular.[4]

The formulation of this dilemma should not seriously detain us, however, for it is in most respects a false issue. As Landau has noted in a classic statement, "The choice is not between models and no models, but between a critical consciousness of their use and an uncritical acceptance." When thinking about reality, we *do* think in analogies, most often in the process of comparing the perceived but not clearly understood reality with a known and illuminating analogue or metaphor. As Kuhn has shown, much thinking in physical and natural sciences has proceeded along exactly these lines. The utilities are not minor, either; for, in Landau's terms again, "The transfer of meaning from one context to another serves to introduce new modes of thought, new systems of analysis, which profoundly affect the 'received axioms' of the past. A change in image is a change in method." [5]

Certainly it is true that the search for case studies offers far less chance of developing a thorough-going, validated "theory" of reality. Indeed, much effort of this kind partakes of the Baconian fallacy, i.e., the belief that gathering facts without presumptions will lead to the whole truth. Fischer's words state the problem here for the historian, but they have relevance for all social inquiry.

> [The fallacy is the belief that] a historian can operate without the aid of preconceived questions, hypotheses, ideas, assumptions, theories, paradigms [etc.]. He is supposed to go a-wandering in the dark forest of the past, gathering facts like nuts and berries, until he has enough to make a general truth. Then he is to store up his general truths until he has the whole truth. This idea is doubly deficient, for it commits a historian to the pursuit of an impossible object by an impracticable method.
>
> The impracticable method is a simple induction from the particular to the general. It cannot work, because there is an infinity of particulars in the past. . . . There is no practicable limit to the number of

facts which are relevant to even the smallest historical problem. . . .
The impossible object is a quest for the whole truth — a quest which characteristically takes one of three forms. Occasionally, it consists in an attempt to know everything about everything. Sometimes it seeks to learn something about everything. Most often it is a search for everything about something. None of these purposes is remotely realizable. A historian can only hope to know something about something.[6]

A variant of this anti-model criticism, however, has special force. While accepting the need to use analogies, it criticizes borrowing them from inapplicable sciences. This borrowing creates the problem of trying to verify the "irreconcilable ambiguity" that arises from the application to men's social behavior of the notions of "system" drawn from biology or physics. It is urged that men, after all, are not corpuscles, nerve axions, or atomic particles because, *inter alia,* they have some degree of free will that enables them to break old, systemic patterns of social life. Although analogic thinking is useful, it is agreed, the use of inappropriate analogies forces research into doomed paths and develops findings that cannot speak intelligently about social man.[7]

Although this critique is compelling on its face, we have some reservations about its applicability to systems analysis and about its inarticulate value premise. It is not really so certain that the Eastonian framework presupposes much congruency with biological or physical models. Easton has declared the roots of his ideas to be not in these models but in communication sciences, but they diverge at important points even here.[8] Further, a demurrer might be appropriate here, to that effect that even if the two sets were similar, the consequences for understanding men's behavior in the social system are not so important. As Sroufe put it with a certain irreverence, "contemporary political systems analysts . . . know very well that Londoners do not in all instances behave as slime mold."

Part of this debate may stem from the semantic problem of the use of terms common to the social and biological models but having different connotations in each. Another part of this debate, however, may well rest on an unexpressed value premise, namely, that because human beings have free will (and we choose not to linger on the ambiguities of that phrase), it is not good to compare them with objects in experience that do not. This is a variant of a whole class of criticisms of systems analysis — its undesirability — on which we will comment later.

The Anti-Systems Model Critique. Yet another variant of the anti-model critique charges that because this approach focuses upon system operations in abstract terms, rather than upon behavioral patterns of individuals or groups, important aspects of political life are ignored. Thus, it is said, little is heard in such analyses about control and influence, disruption and breakdown of the political system, and such mass political behavior as voting or political socialization. These are certainly major aspects of political life, and any analytic framework that excluded them would be poverty-stricken. Yet it is possible that much of this general critique is premature. The development of Easton's ideas has been slow, but research employing them has recently developed a body of research knowledge which challenges this critique. Certainly this book, like a few others focusing upon the appropriation process of Congress or on the judicial process, as well as Easton's recent study of the origin of political perceptions among children, do not ignore what is claimed to be ignored.[9]

Part of this critique, too, is over differing views of what constitutes the "important" analytic questions to study in politics. We believe, however, that critics assume that an agreement exists on the priority of the primary inquiries shaping the discipline's work. Unfortunately, that assumption is not warranted, as witness the passionate turmoil among political scientists after World War II over the central thrust of the discipline. They cannot agree even that the proper focus is upon "power," for as March has noted in an important essay, "the power of power" as an analytical concept is quite limited.[10]

Easton believes the system's capacity to persist is the most important aspect to study, whereas some urge other aspects, charging that the persistence emphasis indicts the whole systems analysis. Yet the logic of the analysis does not require persistence to be any more basic or inclusive a focus than others, such as goal attainment. For that reason, our study of the subsystem of schools has not compelled us to use the persistence focus. Instead, we have followed Schubert in rejecting any assumption of homeostasis in this subsystem just as he rejected it for the subsystem of courts. Thus, "We shall, however, seek to discover the kinds of influences that both shape and lead to changes in judicial systems and the correlative kinds of influences that judicial systems bring to bear upon other systems, both public and private, with which they interact." [11] Substitute the word "American schools" for "judicial systems" and one has a brief statement of major concerns of the present volume.

On the other hand, we have provided examples of all those analytical concepts and data that, some have charged, were ignored in systems analysis — the behavior of individual actors vs. mass publics, the force of innovative demands, the specification of feedback processes that lead to recycling conversion, power, and influence, and so on. Wherever possible we have dealt only with aggregate data in order better to generalize about properties of School and State and their interactions. In the process, we have shown where much is still unknown and have called for substantive research; therefore we do not claim to have provided full information on the subject.

Had we felt the necessity of ordering our work by the notion of system persistence, it would have been possible at many places to cite our data as evidence of this concept in operation. But this was not a necessary feature dictated by the conditions of the systems framework. Instead, we preferred to use that framework only to organize our data in some sequential process for describing the interactions of State and School in policy making. As long as political scientists do not agree on this question of what is the most important — sometimes defined as most "inclusive" — inquiry to put to the subject, we are content to pass over the persistence inquiry as not clearly dictated by the systems framework. We shall return to this point shortly.

The Imitation Critique. Easton's emphasis upon system persistence as the most inclusive question for political analysis has been the basis for another general critique of systems analysis. It is that this analysis is really not new but is instead imitative of functional analysis. The latter has been the subject of far too much writing to be described here even in briefest form.[12] But considerable effort has been made to distinguish as well as to compare the two. Central here has been functional analysis's emphasis upon "system maintenance" as a critical function that motivates or shapes social institutions' behavior. For some this is indistinguishable from Easton's focus upon system persistence; for Easton, the persistence concept is clearly distinct because of the dynamic perspective it provides political analysis.[13] In part, all of this critique is what Spiro has termed the "Who Said It First?" question, that aspect of the sociology of knowledge that searches for antecedents and correlates in current ideas.[14]

This is a minor question for our purposes, as our attention has not been upon the origins and likenesses of this framework of analysis but upon its utility. That utility has been mainly to explain the interrelationship of schools with other subsystems of society and the process by which schools convert some demands into public policy, thereby allocating values and resources differentially. It may be, indeed, that others using a functional analytic framework may deal differently or similarly with the data of the political system as here conceived; indeed, some object to use of "political system" itself, sticking with its traditional meaning.[15] It is not clear to us how demonstrating that one framework is similar in some degree to another invalidates the utility of either for purposes of research and analysis. Given our earlier statement about the difficulty of validating the "whole truth" about an explanatory theory dealing with any set of social phenomena, this imitation critique seems to bear little fruit.

The Specificity Critique. But another set of arguments has more meaning. This is the criticism that systems analysis evades the need to resolve the technical problems of providing measures of its central concepts. Such technical problems are: if persistence is important in gauging a system's response to stress-generated demands, what is the range of adjustment within which persistence can be said to result and beyond which the system no longer persists? How does one specify a measurement of input demands so as to permit a comparison of different systems' abilities to cope with stress? If persistence is a function of support, how does one measure support so as to relate varying amounts of it to varying persistence capacities of different systems?

Much of Easton's own work has veered away from technical measurement devices as a matter of preference.[16] In a discipline where technical measurements and specific small studies abound, he has insisted on developing a general framework of analysis that would encompass a variety of research subjects and not on stopping to specify precisely all such concepts. It is also true, however, that he has not ignored the need to specify *indicators of his concepts,* generally stated though they are. For example:

> If we are to speak intelligibly about some minimal support, even though we cannot identify what this minimum may be except to recognize its presence, it is essential to know what kinds of variables would need to be taken into account to obtain an ordinal measure of support. We have seen that we would have to balance the number of members supporting and opposing a system, their power position, the intensity of their feelings in these respects, their capacity to express these feelings in action, and their readiness to do so under the circumstances.[17]

This critique complains, however, that more than indication of relevant variables is needed in the form of greater specification, e.g., measures of the range of persistence, intensity of demands and support, efficacy of the feedback process, etc.

In response, it seems we might be better served if students of political life would themselves turn to these tasks. Otherwise, this critique looks too much like the belief that because the manufacturer did not provide a totally detailed manual on the operation of the engine, one would not — because he could not — drive a car. Easton's point seems valid:

> Just as computer technology has today provided empirical research workers with techniques that in the social sciences have already outrun the theoretical capacity of these disciplines to utilize the machines fully, so at times theory itself may out-distance the current capabilities of empirical technology. In each case, efforts of the one to catch up with the other are not only unavoidable; they are an essential ingredient of scientific progress.[18]

The Inexplicability Critique. A final set of criticisms of the systems framework may be subsumed under the argument that it does not help explain or predict its subject matter — political life. The problem lies in the generality of its analytical scheme, which can make no truth claims about the real world it allegedly refers to. As Gregor has noted, such models of reality

> suggest *something* about the societal and political phenomena under scrutiny, the nature of the quasi-mechanical homeostatic processes, which relevant variables might influence each other, and so on. But explanatory and predictive power can only be the consequence of ver-ification studies conducted on the primary object of study itself. . . . They are, at best, "working hypotheses," always instrumental, but never explanations.[19]

The fit between model and reality, it is urged, is further blurred by the fact that, by definition, models have to simplify reality radically; but if the simplification is not done precisely or rigorously, the fit is accordingly reduced.

Involved here is a rich and intricate debate on how one can know reality. It sensibly warns us that the failure to test our ideas about phenomena against those phenomena can produce abstractions that tell us little about reality. But as that critique is applied to systems analysis, we suspect that it assumes more than its proponents would claim. Nowhere do they claim that they are working with a "theory" in the formal definition of theory; few claim that the framework can generate hypotheses.[20] More in keeping with our thinking on its utility in explaining the political world is Sroufe's brief statement after reviewing the limitations of the model.

> We may use the systems approach as a conceptual framework which provides a model, a definitional question, boundaries, and analytic con-cepts and questions. It can assist us in describing and comparing sys-tems that are important to us; it may help us to understand but it will not lead to a theory of politics of education. We will not be able to explain in the formal scientific sense; we will be able to tell what hap-pened, and [provide] informal speculation about why it happened.[21]

In most respects, systems analysis is a general method for analyzing the data of experience but not one for demonstrating or predicting "correct" reality alternatives for social problems. As Kaplan noted, "Advice to a political scientist to use systems theory to solve a problem, even when it is the appropriate methodology, would advance him as far but no farther than would advice to a physical scientist to use the methods of science." [22] It may be that this is thus no more than a method of explaining, where, in Stephens' phrase, "Explanation is here just an overlay on the events of the real world, and prediction is nothing more than the future-oriented use of explanation." [23] Implied in this is the tentative nature of the explanatory effort and an awareness of the complexity of that task.

It might help to explore further the question of the inexplicability of systems analysis if more — and more comparative — research were conducted under its aegis. Particularly useful would be studies over time of the consequences for systems of stress events, of the differential reaction to the same event by different subsystems within one society, or of changes in political-system support that may or may not arise from innovations in school subsystems. Only with results of research programs of this kind can we have sufficient empirical knowledge to see whether this framework of political analysis is successful as "attempted explanation," to use Stephens' term.

Some work of this kind has been undertaken during the 1960's with particular reference to the school subsystem. We have referred to it in earlier chapters in discussing the consequences of stress for the input of demands upon school boards and superintendents.[24] We have also seen it reflected in analysis of political culture as an intervening variable affecting state policy output. We have seen the uses of macroanalysis as a method of operationalizing concepts within systems analysis, with particular reference to school policy. All of these are comparative, aggregate, analytic techniques rooted explicitly in systems analysis and suggestive of the kinds of work that may yet be done. Some are cross-sectional and some longitudinal in the data they employ. But all move far beyond the case study in being nonepisodic and in proceeding from a conceptual framework that permits "explanations" of far greater generalization.

The major defense, then, against the variety of critiques that challenge the effectiveness of systems analysis is that opponents demand more of it than it claims to provide, and that it has not yet been sufficiently employed to sustain the charge. As this volume attests, however, particularly in its review of existing research under this intellectual aegis, its utility is not small. More can be explained, and the results — although far from the demands of formal theory — will probably increase our understanding of the politics of education more than any other conceptualization used to date. It is impossible to proceed to study political life without some a priori conceptualization, and it is useless to wait until a full-blown and testable theory arrives. Finite man in an infinite world must make do with partial theories and be satisfied with partial explanations. The only intellectual alternatives are a futile nihilism or a dilatory utopianism.

The Undesirability Critique

The preceding critiques overtly fastened upon limitations in the theoretical, conceptual, and methodological aspects of systems analysis, but another set of critiques rests upon another ground — that of value. This attack is partly diffused in general critique of behavioralism as an improper mode of investigating the political condition of men, but two charges seem particularly directed towards systems analysis.[25] Again, we simplify many extensive, sophisticated, and compelling arguments in this twofold scheme. The two main charges are that men are too varied to fit within the straitjacket of systems analysis and that emphasis upon system persistence operates to defend the *status quo* and hence to oppose desirable social change. That is, one criticism goes to a desired view of man and the other to a desired view of social change.

Critics complain that systems analysis in its abstract handling of only groups of men — not individuals — has no place for the special and varying human qualities that make men different if not unpredictable. This accounts for a purported amorality about such analysis, for it is not concerned with man's qualitative end values and how they may be achieved. Wolin puts the charge well:

> Political theories deal with structures which embody and exercise the most awesome powers of which man is capable of concentrating. On some occasions these powers are used violently and destructively; more often they are used to intimidate; and still more often they are used to reinforce a going system of distributive inequities. Much depends, therefore, on how meaningfully a theory deals with these basic features of any political society. The capabilities of a theory are determined by the nature and type of distortions it embodies. In the case of systems theory these distortions are crippling. It enables its exponents to talk about "outputs" but not about distributive justice or fairness; about "steering" but not about statecraft; about "messages" or "inputs" but not about the quality of the citizens or their lives.[26]

We agree that this lack of concern for the qualitative conditions in which systems may operate is an accurate analysis. In treating the question of persistence conditions, which is a system quality, Easton does not pass judgment on how well or poorly citizens live, clearly a human quality. He does, of course, pay central attention to how these individual qualities may affect system qualities. The authors, like Easton, are concerned with human qualities, to whose improvements we have dedicated much of our professional and personal lives, so it is not easy to accept the critique as valid.

To accept it would, moreover, run afoul of a familiar fallacy, the use of value concepts to prove or disprove empirical concepts. Much of this critique borders on the charge of using facts to "prove" one's values and using values to "disprove" disapproved empirical concepts. One need not accept persistence as the most inclusive question for political analysis, as we do not; yet one may still recognize that analyzing the conditions that maximize and minimize persistence is not a "bad" or "good" act but an intellectual one. Some of this humanist critique partakes of a *non sequitur* in its charge that systems analysis does not include what the critic would include.

Thus looking again at Wolin's preceding statement, we are told that "much depends, therefore, on how meaningfully a theory deals with these basic features of any political society." These "basic features" are earlier defined *empirically* by the destructive uses of the State's political power. However, this political vision sees only the life-inhibiting power of that institution, which certainly is a limited vew of reality. Clearly, the State does perform life-enhancing functions, as the history of national policy reform throughout our history would testify. The fallacy that stems from this criticism, then, is that a partial view of reality is offered as the total one, and thereafter the value judgment is made that any theory not so based is inaccurate empirically and, by implication, defective morally. But perceiving and conceiving reality are not the same order of thought as making moral judgments on what is perceived or conceived. One may do so, of course, but no intrinsic connection ties the two together in a valid judgment. It is all rather like the totalitarian requirement that all scholars judge in regime norms what they perceive in their scholarly tasks, or else be deemed moral delinquents. Like the confusion between the road map and the road, this critique condemns the mapmaker for not drawing a prettier design.

Another matter is the charge that systems analysis may have a social perspective that can, under certain usages, be directed toward ends that are capable of being valued. This is the second of the critiques of undesirability, namely, that preoccupation with system persistence (or maintenance, in functional terms) leads its adherents to adopt policy views supportive of the existing political authorities and opposed to desirable policy changes. In short, systems analysis produces a conservative viewpoint.[27]

In this view, as Goldschmidt has complained, functional and systems analysis tend "to see anything which exists, particularly if it has existed for a long time, as functional and system-sustaining and, hence, good." [28] That acceptance is said to arise from a view of American politics in which change is slow but improvements are incremental; the competition of interest groups over material advantages is the best mode of political action, whereas the presentation of sharp social differences by parties is injurious and "dirty"; the task of government is to regulate conflicting interests according to "rules of the game" but not to seek some "public interest"; and from this competition the best distribution of material goods will emerge as long as no single group dominates. The charge is that, having ostensibly found American politics to operate in this fashion, behavioral political scientists have looked upon the results and found them good.[29]

The inadequacy of this behavioralist perspective is said to lie in the emergence of problems unaccounted for — or ignored — by this view and in the resultant doubts about the ability of the system to solve them. As Wolin notes:

> Nowhere are these doubts more evident than in the field of education where there is widespread lack of confidence about the capability of existing educational institutions, practices, and values; deep scepticism about whether society can be persuaded to face up to the heavy financial, political, and psychic demands which radical change requires; and despair over whether the traditional methods of policy-making, supervision, accountability, and community involvement can cope with dimensions of the crisis. Meanwhile, our schools, like our cities, are streaked with lawlessness, violence, alienation, and incivility.[30]

What is needed, therefore, is a new theory about politics and education, i.e., a normative theory,

> which starts from the assumption that the society is in deep trouble, proceeds by searching for a formulation which identifies those troubles, and concludes with some sketch of the possibilities, necessities, and dangers for a better politics and a better education. . . .
> . . . the politics of education is most[ly] about deciding what kinds of individuals should be cherished and encouraged by education and what kinds of social tasks properly require educational support.[31]

Response to this critique is complicated by the mix of diagnosis, prescription, and prognosis that is presented, as well as by the possibility that one can agree, both empirically and normatively, with part but not all of the analysis. As to what systems analysis implies in the way of major assumptions, we again note that much of this criticism is not focused upon this framework particularly but upon behavioralism in general, so it is hard to see what, specifically, is being criticized. The criticism that systems analysis deals only with stability in its systems-persistence orientation can be met by noting, as we have above, that it is not essential that one focus upon persistence, and that Easton himself denies the stability orientation charged against him.[32] That systems analysis does not explicitly deal with normative questions about the ends of the political system, about the nature of the good society, is not only correct but obvious. The concept is not geared to that mode of analysis, so the charge is, again, something of a *non sequitur.*

We suggest that a larger problem raised by this critique is a confusion of value with reality, of belief *about* reality with that reality itself. Earlier we noted the difficult problem of developing and validating concepts about the operations of reality that "fit" that reality. Even more difficult is the problem that arises when beliefs about what reality should be are mixed with partial knowledge of what it is.

The critique of undesirability complains of a concept of reality that, allegedly, must necessarily lead to support of society and its policy structure; the complaint is against a purported view that "whatever society has become is right." This allegation, however, mixes normative and empirical judgments. For example, if Jones believes that condition X exists in society, we can say several things about his belief. First, we can judge that he is "wrong" empirically; the critique of undesirability against systems analysis does this in part and does so properly, as there are empirical criteria for judging what exists and — less certainly — what causes whatever exists. Second, we can say about Jones's view that it is "wrong" normatively; this employs value — not empirical — criteria for judging Jones's belief about what exists. It is appropriate, of course, to say that his view is not merely mistaken in fact but also unethical, immoral, or whatever term of value disapproval one chooses.

Next, however, occurs a step in the critique of undesirability that mixes the empirical and normative judgments. That is, the disapproved views are alleged to contribute to the conditions described. This is a blurring of the "is" and "ought" of existence. Somehow, behavioralists' views are thought to be so important that someone with political power not only listened to them, but acted upon them in a way that reinforced the current distribution of resources and values in society — a reinforcement and distribution that are condemned. We suggest that this (a) overestimates how much attention policy makers pay to learned journals and scholarly books and (b) fails to demonstrate the causal connection.

Moreover, much of this critique asserts that its normative judgment of reality — in this case American society — is truly what reality *is,* as the language of Wolin asserts above. Like mirror images of those they criticize, they believe that whatever society has become is wrong — and there is no doubt in this view that all functions of the political system are dysfunctional for its citizens.[33]

In the language of the common man, there is no reason why believing a thing makes it so — self-fulfilling and self-denying prophecies to the contrary notwithstanding. The current crises in education are great enough to provide room for disagreement with diagnosis, prescription, *and* prognosis, any one of these, or none. Men may differ with the diagnosis of these ills but agree on the prescription, or agree on diagnosis but not on prescription — and prognosis is certainly the most diverse and uncertain of all. In public policy struggles, the major contest is not over the desirable end to be attained but over the means of attaining it. Thus, a recent examination of educational ills agrees thoroughly on what the problems are in educating lower-status, urban children but differs on the alternative methods of curing this terrible social malady.[34] We have seen in the previous three chapters the swirl of disagreement over improvements in curriculum, finance, and integration. Here, too, agreement on diagnosis produced conflict, not agreement, on prescription.

We urge, therefore, that the critique of undesirability cannot demonstrate the unity of cause and effect it purports to find in the real world, nor can it validate the fit of its normative and empirical arguments. It probably imputes more influence to behavioralist writing than is demonstrated. The intensity of this critique probably ascribes even more accuracy to the behavioralists' presentation of the political world than its presenters do.[35]

The Utilities of Systems Analysis

In the foregoing we have taken so much space explaining what systems analysis is *not* that the reader may have lost sight of the utilities we believe it does have. A brief resume of these will close this debate.

At one level, this framework is, as the term implies, a useful device for integrating descriptive institutional data with data about events more powerfully than can be done in a case study. Integration explains how some demands put upon the political system cause it to satisfy them by an authoritative allocation of values and resources which, upon insertion into the environment, is designed to modify the stress that originated the demands. This orientation provides a dynamic view of the political system and not the static one found in earlier, traditional, legal-institutional analyses.

Moreover, this concept forces the student to see the political subsystem operating constantly in relation to other social subsystems. The weblike connectivity in this concept has at least two major consequences that can enrich our understanding of the political world. It maximizes the chances for interdisciplinary exchanges by focusing the attention of different disciplines upon a common object in experience (the political system) and upon a concept of "system" also common to other disciplines. Second, the concept's connectivity maximizes the chances for comparative research and analysis, a necessary step if we are to develop generalizations — much less predictions — of any power whatsoever. In that light, note macroanalytic studies, initiated by Dye, revised by others, and now the subject of an extensive research endeavor. This investigation not only was generated by, but has benefited from, the use of a systems framework; in the process it has expanded our knowledge of the policy structure of the American city and state.[36]

Yet for us, as for Sroufe,

> the most interesting opportunity provided by political systems analysis is that of analytically examining those areas previously considered outside the political sphere. . . . We may now consider questions that could not be analyzed usefully with traditional concepts of politics (meaning partisanship, elections, and legislation). It is now feasible to examine the "politics of instruction," as well as politics of curriculum,

the local board, or the PTA. . . . Many of our "apolitical" institutions may be examined as political systems or subsystems; may be examined with regard to their function in the larger political system, or as a system of functionally related components processing inputs into system outputs . . . and responding to modifications in their environment.[37]

It is clear that this utility, as well as the others, have provided the thrust to this book. In the process we have sought to answer two prime questions overtly drawn from systems analysis. In Sroufe's terms, they are: "How are values allocated in the educational system? How does the educational system relate to the larger political system?" While we have in the process made normative judgments on both the allocations and relationships we found to exist, our primary task has been to determine how the data of experience adapt to the systems conceptualization. Our hope is that our efforts will demonstrate the utilities mentioned above and encourage others to work this ground.

THE NEW POLITICIZATION OF AMERICAN SCHOOLS

Concluding a book that encompasses so many phases of the politics of education is not a simple task. But we thought it in keeping with the use of the systems framework, and with the debate shown earlier in this chapter, to move from diagnosis to prognosis. The ties of the schools with other subsystems is an old truism in American education, except as it applies to the partisan political subsystem. Yet, as we have shown, increasingly the American schools are caught up in forces that are — even though unacknowledged — political. It seemed appropriate, then, as we close this volume, to return to the myth of apolitical schools that opened it, and to show how these institutions are presently participating in a new politicization. We do not term it an "increasing" politicization, for that would imply that the political involvement of schools with society has changed in magnitude. Instead, we argue that the change has been one of quality, involving a new focus upon old demands. At the very least, we argue, what is occurring is making overt what in the past has been sublimely covert.

An analysis of school politics at the turn of the twentieth century leads to the rather startling conclusion that the themes of political reform from 1900 have a familiar ring in 1970. Thus we now hear:

Make schoolmen more accountable for the quality of education.

Adapt the structure and process of schools to new conditions and pupil needs.

Cut the administrative red tape that impedes wide-ranging reform.

Create a new, local, political leadership to replace the vested interests that control city schools.[38]

However, as Tyack emphasizes, in 1890–1920 both the context and implications of the above statements were quite different from the reform called for today. As described in Chapter 1, the earlier outcome of these slogans was centralization of control under a superintendent and nonpartisan board elected from the city as a whole. Issel concludes that

> modernization stripped the ward school boards of power, left them intact only as boards of visitors, and placed the control of the schools in the hands of cosmopolitan and efficiency-minded, upper-class businessmen and professionals, whose legislative decisions would be carried out by dispassionate, university trained, educational experts according to the impersonal criteria of bureaucratic social organization.[39]

This turn-of-the-century reform swept away the spoils system for teaching jobs, governance by subcommittees of ward-based school boards, and the decentralized school management.

In those days superintendents and professors of educational administration often exchanged jobs. They had special reasons for favoring the "nonpolitical," elite boards and the elevation of the expert. A civil service system based on merit and objective exams lessened the danger of losing jobs after elections. In addition, a hierarchy of specialized administrative offices provided a career ladder based in part on expertise symbolized in university credentials. Tyack observed:

> With but few exceptions, superintendents and professors of administration at the turn of the century admired businessmen and saw in the specialized forms of corporate bureaucracy new models for the control and organization of urban schools. Increasingly, school administrators became cosmopolitan in orientation and turned for guidance to their national professional associations.[40]

The 1890–1920 school reforms led to the myth that education and politics were and should be separate; we have stressed throughout this volume the outcome of this myth. The reforms also established the basic structural and procedural components for school policy making in operation to this day. Today, however, we see the same slogans of the 1890–1920 era being used to (1) increase the overt intersect of education and politics, (2) break down the central administrative structure of American schools, and (3) restrict the power of the school professionals and the cosmopolitan elites on the school boards. The policy outcomes are likely to be the reverse of the implications of the same slogans in 1890–1920. In short, the contemporary call is to return School-State connections to the conditions of yesteryear.

The New Politics

This new politics of public education deserves closer attention. Basically, the demands of community groups, students, ethnic minorities, and, to some extent, organized teachers reflect a central theme. This is some form of unwillingness to continue a policy-making pattern dominated by professional administrators operating under professionally "neutral" norms — all taking place within a closed system. This dissatisfaction is seen in the public unwillingness to accept professional educators' views on tax and expenditure needs, on accountability for output performance, on student discipline, and to a lesser extent, on curriculum.

We can only highlight the changes now sought. In New York City, the chief school administrator in early 1971 recommended bypassing the civil service exams for appointing school administrators. These exams were established, it will be recalled, to insulate staff selection from political pressure, but they are now the focus of minority discontent. In some localities, parent concern has focused on more neighborhood lay control with proposals similar to the 1900 ward-based election system. These proposals seek to break up large, central, school administrative units into smaller neighborhood (ward) districts with autonomy in most school policy areas. The professionals' usual response has been to decentralize or redistribute central administrative prerogatives down to the professional field administrators. However, such decentralization does not satisfy the agitation for neighborhood lay boards dominated by a different ethnic and class background than that of the present centralized board.

The intersect between education and politics is intensifying in large part because of teacher negotiations and the cost-revenue squeeze in urban public education. Major policies (class size, instructional materials, differentiated staffing, and compensatory programs) are now written into a few collective bargaining agreements. After securing a viable organizational base and bargaining rights, teacher organizations will be raising their negotiating sights in the next decade from wages and working conditions to curricular and instructional issues. This in turn has led to community and administrative enthusiasm for specifying standards for teacher performance in the contracts.

As the substantive scope of teacher bargaining has expanded, so has the locus of accommodation. The mayor in many cities is the crucial actor who must settle with the teachers on the same basis as other municipal unions. The 1890–1920 reforms had circumscribed the role of the mayors, but teacher bargaining strategy and reciprocal aid agreements among urban unions are now bringing city politicians into the middle of school financial and curricular decisions.[41]

The new politicization is also partly financial in origin. Over the past decade, expenditures for public elementary and secondary education have been increasing at a rate 43 percent higher than the rate for the economy as a whole.[42] The rising costs have caused constant increases in the property tax — on a per capita basis from $81.00 in 1958 to $138.83 in 1968. Public education relies for over 50 percent of its revenue on property taxes, which do not expand quickly enough to keep pace with school costs that grew 12 percent in 1968–69 and 10.4 percent in 1969–70. Voters have been increasingly reluctant to increase their property tax rates to meet these costs. In Ohio, for instance, only 29 percent of the property tax referenda were approved in 1970, compared to 84 percent in 1960; in Illinois, the figures were 44 percent, down from 72 percent.[43]

This bleak financial condition underlies several trends increasing the politicization of American education. It requires a new kind of aggressive communication and sales campaign to justify these spiraling tax increases. Consequently, schoolmen must increasingly adopt the campaign techniques of the elected politician from whom they wanted to be separate. But even this will not be enough. The cost-revenue squeeze portends a transfer of financial support and subsequent control to the state level where the tax base is more elastic and less sensitive politically than local property taxes. The increased state supervision and lack of local financial flexibility will further narrow the authority and prerogatives of local school boards — as will the mayor's role in teacher bargaining. It also means that state politicians will want more information and supervision with regard to costly school policies that they must justify to their constituents.[44]

All of these trends tend to erode the influence of the professional educator, who for so long had fostered an image of being "above politics." [45] Also, the emerging forms of school governance run counter to the outcomes of the 1890–1920 reforms discussed in Chapter 1. The forms of political behavior are changing from orderly school board debates to confrontation politics and demonstrations. The prerogatives of local school boards are increasingly reduced by financial pressures and federal-state controls.

It remains to be seen whether new forms and styles of governance will result in significant changes in the interaction between students and teachers in the classroom. We must be careful that apparent changes in the balance of power toward nonprofessionals setting more broad educational policy does not sidetrack us into believing substantive education has changed at the cutting edge — the classroom where teachers meet children. As one observes changes in superintendent–school board–lay community policy-making patterns, he could be seeing nothing more significant in an outcome sense than the revolving chairs of different Latin-American dictators. The names and official policy may change, but the public services and opportunities for the masses of citizens or students may remain basically the same. Public education is a "bottom-heavy" enterprise of over 19,300 school districts and 2 million classroom teachers. It takes a long time for the trends featured in the current newspaper headlines to permeate this massive public enterprise — if they ever do.

CONCLUSION

The new politicization of American schools should be understood as something more than just a contemporary reaction from dissatisfied citizens. This journalistic perception, which, like all such, requires "shooting history on the wing," ignores too much. It fails to place this trend within the historical dimension, or to see it as a part of contemporary social structures and processes. Thus this casual view portrays current demands for "community control" or "decentralization" as new ideas, when, as we have shown, they were once widely prevalent in school administration. It tells us nothing about the way current policy decisions reflect prevalent social structure and norms. Rather, we argue the need for student, citizen, administrator, and scholar — and even the journalist — to grasp the link of past to present and the connectivity of the social processes that operate in this new politicization.

Because for decades the politics of American schools have been little noted does not change the struggle of schoolmen and school constituencies for available resources during that time. Indeed, as we have seen, professionals during these decades successfully implemented their educational values in state institutions and laws — an overtly political action. It is certainly no less political that in the present period those groups with new educational values should seek to move school authorities to redefine standards of administrative controls, curriculum, and teaching — again, by an overt search for new law. In this perspective, then, there is similarity in the past and present efforts of distressed groups to demand of the political system that it meet their wants. There is similarity, too, in the concomitant efforts of authorities to convert these demands in a way they expect will best cope with the stress. There is further similarity, whether in the days of McKinley or Nixon, in the struggle to define authoritatively the regime norms that teachers must reflect — whether loyalty to the values of a ward boss, a "professional" school, or an ethnic subcommunity.

Our analysis is not that *everything* is the same, of course. New actors emerge, new issues arise, new channels for demand input are forged, new conversion processes are devised, and, clearly, new values are pursued. But what we do urge is the continuity of the process involved then and now, a process of the political system converting new demands arising from an environment under new stresses, and of transforming the system's outputs through the impact of these demands upon that environment.

In this sense, systems analysis serves its highest utility by making clear how things happen in a comparative fashion. The result is that we can see the past in the present without being chained to a historical determinism. The old educational battle cries have faded away to the murmurs of history books, the very buildings of the past are no more, the old actors are long in their graves, and only a few persons are alive from that era when school politics shifted from a partisan to a professional basis. Nevertheless, we see in the current protests against almost all conditions of American schools a process that shares many basic qualities with these long dead forces and agents.

All of this may be understood in an alternative but complementary framework, that of the clash between bureaucratic and participatory forces in American democracy.[46] Bureaucracy is the routinization of past policy decisions, resulting in a decisional structure testifying to past authoritative resource allocations favoring one set of interests. Thus, note the decisions made all across America decades ago that Progressives' wishes about the use of school resources would be directed in professional terms. A host of routine decisions were incorporated in this, giving substantive body to values about teacher training and credentialing, educational administration, curriculum preparation and instruction, and so on. In our day, however, this bureaucratic body of values is challenged by new values through the participatory thrust of those unsatisfied by the operations of such routinized decisions about school resources. The professionals' defensive reactions can impede if not kill this thrust, as noted by many current criticisms of American schools we have referred to throughout this book. But the outcome is not now known; we are witnessing merely the beginning of this effort.

Yet the mosaic of our schools already shows different conditions in this defensive-offensive struggle. Curricular changes about ethnic history are well advanced in the larger schools of inner-city and suburban America. Professionals' resistance to changing definitions of competence has often been compromised in the acceptance of paraprofessionals and teachers' aides. In California, ethnic protests against numerous credentials requirements for superintendents led the legislature to reduce them. But these changes have been made only after intense conflict, and in many other schools the effort has not even begun. Everywhere, though, the bureaucratic forces, as defined above, resist these attacks as dangerous to their definition of professionalism. Which they certainly are, for such attacks are the swinging edge of the participatory force of American democracy, working again at the structure of schools.

That force, in turn, reminds us that the new politicization may also be seen as merely the latest skirmish in the old American effort to work out the values of democracy noted in Chapter 3. As we said then, "The stress swirling today in our society still stems from this confrontation between individual and group pressures to define life." Each controversy now in the news is reflective of the tension between the majoritarian and individualist values of our democracy. Schoolmen claim they speak for a majority whose earlier decisions about the general direction of school policy are the authority for their *professional* decisions about the details of schooling. They are confronted, however, by minorities claiming that the democratic value structure has something to say about protecting the individualist values that they claim are not being met.

Clearly this clash of majoritarian and individualist justifications for resource allocation is highly visible in many current school fights. Those opposed to busing in desegregation, clearly a majority on national polls, try to shout down desegregationists on the ground of the moral and constitutional correctness of *vox populi*. Busing supporters, however, urge the old claim that majorities can be wrong in their tyranny over minorities and are so now. Ethnic leaders calling for their members to be accepted as teachers without the credentialing requirements imposed by a white, middle-class majority are making a claim to the special worth of individual abilities. Their opponents see only attacks on concepts of "competence" long cherished and accepted by the majority of professionals. The roles reverse in the current conflict over school financing. The majority of voters no longer support tax referenda put up by the minority professionals. The latter assert special claims for their views to be accommodated by the majority, which the majority denies.

Enough has been suggested here to indicate that the politics of education must be conceptualized in numerous frameworks. The use of one does not preclude but rather complements others and thus expands the scope of our understanding. Unlike analysis that looks at the American school system only as a set of structures and policies, those frameworks employed throughout these pages have sought to emphasize process — the continuous conflict between basic democratic values, the changing but continuous interaction of the values of professionals and their challengers, and the input-conversion-output-feedback concept of systems analysis. Against much of the perception and criticism of these schools as a social structure, that see it only as some monolith impervious to currents of change, we argue that this is only a partial perspective.

Rather, we suggest that congruent with the static elements are dynamic processes, working over time, interacting with subsystems within the schools, reciprocally influencing and influenced by the larger environment in which they are embedded — and that much of this is political. If schools are a part of society, as all educational scholars proclaim, the connection is not that of pieces of a painting to one another. Rather one is reminded of a kinesthetic sculpture. Here, moving parts interweave in always new but always constrained patterns, reflecting the composer's fragmentary percept of beauty, but based essentially upon mechanical tensions that must be released because they can never be avoided. Although one can go too far with analogies, one cannot go anywhere without them. We merely note in the past and the present of American schools these opposing tensions between the majority and minority claims to authority, the professional and lay claims to wisdom, and the demands upon resources in limited supply. The interactions of these forces, both normative and material, but always personal and human, make the schools' involvement in the political process intrinsic, not accidental, and permanent, not occasional.

This struggle makes a fascinating study for the scholar, as well as a continual source of gratification and frustration for the citizen. One can learn from the other, as long as neither deceives himself about the political quality of what he is viewing.

Notes

Chapter 1

1. See Thomas H. Eliot, "Toward an Understanding of Public School Politics," *American Political Science Review,* 52 (1959), 1032–51. See also Lesley H. Browder, "A Suburban School Superintendent Plays Politics," in Michael W. Kirst (ed.), *The Politics of Education at the Local, State, and Federal Levels* (Berkeley: McCutchan, 1970), 191–94.

2. See David B. Tyack, "Needed: The Reform of a Reform," in National School Boards Association, *New Dimensions of School Board Leadership* (Evanston, Ill.: N.S.B.A., 1969), 29–51.

3. *Ibid.,* 30–31.

4. *Ibid.,* 32.

5. David Tyack, "City Schools at the Turn of the Century," unpublished manuscript, 1970.

6. Charles W. Eliot, "Educational Reform and the Social Order," *The School Review,* 17 (April, 1909), 220.

7. Arthur H. Chamberlain, "The Growth and Power of the City School Superintendent," *University of California Publications,* 3 (May 15, 1913).

8. Samuel P. Hays, "The Politics of Reform in Municipal Government in the Progressive Era," *Pacific Northwest Quarterly,* 55 (1963), 163.

9. Tyack, "Needed: The Reform of a Reform," 35.

10. George S. Counts, *The Social Composition of Boards of Education* (Chicago: University of Chicago Press, July, 1927).

11. Elinor M. Gersman, "Progressive Reform of the St. Louis School Board, 1897," *History of Education Quarterly,* 10 (1970), 8–15.

12. Browder, 192.

13. Roscoe C. Martin, *Government and the Suburban School* (Syracuse: Syracuse University Press, 1962), 89.

14. For a discussion of this, see Irving Kristol, "Decentralization for What," *The Public Interest,* No. 11 (Spring, 1968), 18–25; and Herbert Kaufman, "Administrative Decentralization and Political Power," paper prepared for 1968 annual meeting of the American Political Science Association.

15. Thomas E. Cronin and Norman C. Thomas, "Educational Policy Advisors and the Great Society," *Public Policy,* 18 (1970), 659–86.

16. Fred N. Kerlinger, "The Mythology of Educational Research: The Descriptive Approach," *School and Society,* 93 (1965), 222–25.

17. Laurence Iannaccone, *Politics in Education* (New York: Center for Applied Research in Education, 1967).

18. Thomas H. Eliot.

19. Michael W. Kirst and Edith K. Mosher, "The Politics of Public Education: A

Research Review," *Review of Educational Research,* 39 (1969); Frederick M. Wirt, "Theory and Research Needs in the Study of American Educational Politics," *Journal of Educational Administration,* 8 (1970), 53–87.

20. A. James Gregor, "Political Science and the Uses of Functional Analysis," *American Political Science Review,* 62 (1968), 425.

21. David Easton, *A Systems Analysis of Political Life* (New York: Wiley, 1965), 490; hereafter referred to as *SAPL.*

22. David Easton, *A Framework for Political Analysis* (Englewood Cliffs, N.J.: Prentice-Hall, 1965).

23. Easton, *SAPL,* 32.

24. Citations for following unnoted quotations are *SAPL,* 22, 26, 27.

25. *SAPL,* 30.

26. *SAPL,* 479.

27. *SAPL,* 481.

28. *SAPL,* vii–viii.

29. *SAPL,* 368.

Chapter 2

1. This section has been informed by reflections on this question by Heinz Eulau, "Political Science and Education: The Long View and the Short," paper presented for C.O.B.R.E. Workshop on the Politics of Elementary and Secondary Education, September, 1970, Stanford University. This and other papers will appear in Michael W. Kirst (ed.), *State, School, and Politics: Research Directions* (Lexington, Mass.: Heath, 1972).

2. Charles Silberman, *Crisis in the Classroom* (New York: Random House, 1970), documents much of this contradiction and dissent.

3. These reflections are elaborated upon in T. Bentley Edwards and Frederick M. Wirt (eds.), *School Desegregation in the North,* chs. 1, 13; Frederick M. Wirt and Willis D. Hawley (eds.), *New Dimensions of Freedom in America* (San Francisco: Chandler, 1967, 1969).

4. For comparison with the U.S.S.R., see George Z. F. Bereday and Jaan Pennar (eds.), *The Politics of Soviet Education* (New York: Praeger, 1960), esp. chs. 3–4; George Z. F. Bereday and Bonnie B. Stretch, "Political Education in the U.S.A. and the U.S.S.R.," *Comparative Education Review,* 7 (1963), 1–16; and Jeremy R. Azrael, "Patterns of Polity-Directed Educational Development: The Soviet Union," in James S. Coleman (ed.), *Education and Political Development* (Princeton: Princeton University Press, 1965), 233–71.

5. The following was suggested by Kenneth Prewitt, "Social Selection and Social Citizenship," paper presented for the C.O.B.R.E. Research Workshop in the Politics of Elementary and Secondary Education, September, 1970, Stanford University. Prewitt leans on two earlier essays: Talcott Parsons, "The School Class as a Social System: Some of Its Function in American Society," *Social Structure and Personality* (New York: Free Press, 1964), 129–54; and T. H. Marshall, "Citizenship and Social Class," *Class, Citizenship and Social Development* (New York: Doubleday, Anchor, 1964). This paper will also appear in Kirst (ed.).

6. Parsons, 130.

7. For a summary statement of these notions and their origins in the clash between class realities and the American creed, see H. Lloyd Warner, *Democracy in Jonesville* (New York: Harper & Row, 1949); and A. B. Hollingshead, *Elmtown's Youth: The Impact of Social Classes on Adolescents* (New York: Wiley, 1949).

8. On these interrelationships, see David Easton, "The Function of Formal Education," *School Review,* 65 (1957), 304–16; and Byron G. Massialas, *Education and the Political System* (Reading, Mass.: Addison-Wesley, 1969), ch. 1; Dean Jaros and Bradley C. Canon, "Transmitting Basic Political Values: The Role of the Educational System," *School Review,* 77 (1969), 94–107.

9. David Easton, *A Systems Analysis of Political Life* (New York: Wiley, 1965), 273.

10. David Easton and Jack Dennis, *Children in the Political System* (New York: McGraw-Hill, 1969), 7. The definition is not as simple as it looks; see Fred I. Greenstein, "A Note on the Ambiguity of 'Political Socialization': Definitions, Criticisms and Strategies of Inquiry," *Journal of Politics,* 32 (1970), 969–78.

11. The contents of these orientations are usually conceptualized broadly as values, affect, and cognition, but role behaviors may be taught without such prior understanding. For a summary of scholars' agreement on this orientation content, see Jack Dennis, "Major Problems of Political Socialization Research," *Midwest Journal of Political Science,* 12 (1968), 91–98.

12. A fuller explanation of the theoretical and conceptual elements here is developed in Easton and Dennis, part 1, esp. ch. 3. Easton reminds us in private correspondence, however, that schools are not always successful in bolstering a system. In Quebec, he notes, many teachers are accused of fostering "separatist" sentiment among their students.

13. Edgar Litt, "Education and Political Enlightenment in America" *Annals of the American Academy of Political and Social Sciences,* 361 (1965), 35.

14. The first systematic examination of civic education was an eight-country study directed in the late 1920's by Charles E. Merriam; see his *The Making of Citizens: A Comparative Study of Methods of Civic Training* (Chicago: University of Chicago Press, 1931). Political science concern on the subject was dropped for another quarter-century until Easton's writing in the 1950's and Herbert H. Hyman's *Political Socialization* (New York: Free Press, 1959), although this ignored schools as a socializing agent in its focus upon the family. The first fully cross-national study in the mode indicated in the text was Gabriel A. Almond and Sidney Verba, *The Civic Culture: Political Attitudes and Democracy in Five Nations* (Princeton: Princeton University Press, 1963).

15. Litt, from where the following quotations are drawn.

16. Frederick R. Smith, "The Curriculum," in Byron G. Massialas and Frederick R. Smith (eds.), *New Challenges in the Social Studies* (Belmont, Calif.: Wadsworth, 1965).

17. M. Kent Jennings, "Correlates of the Social Studies Curriculum," in C. Benjamin Cox and Byron G. Massialas (eds.), *Social Studies in the United States* (New York: Harcourt Brace Jovanovich, 1967), 289–309.

18. Robert D. Hess and Judith V. Torney, *The Development of Political Attitudes in Children* (Chicago: Aldine, 1967), 105–15. For an extended analysis, see Hess and Torney, *The Development of Basic Attitudes and Values Toward Government and Citizenship During the Elementary School Years, Part 1* (Chicago: University of Chicago, Cooperative Research Project No. 1078, 1965).

19. John J. Patrick, "The Implications of Political Socialization Research for Curriculum Development and Instruction in the Social Studies," paper read at the 1968 American Political Science Association convention; the author is an associate of the High School Curriculum Center in Government, Indiana University, whose occasional papers illuminate this field and whose efforts are directed toward reforming this curriculum.

For specific content analysis, see Franklin Patterson, "Citizenship and the High School: Representative Current Practices," in Franklin Patterson *et al., The Adolescent Citizen* (New York: Free Press, 1960), 100–75; Frederick R. Smith and John J. Patrick, "Civics: Relating Social Study to Social Reality," in Cox and Massialas (eds.), 105–27; Byron G. Massialas, "American Government," in *ibid.,* 167–95.

For some curriculum reform suggestions, see Donald W. Oliver and James P. Shaver, *Teaching Public Issues in the High School* (Boston: Houghton Mifflin, 1966); Byron G. Massialas and C. Benjamin Cox, *Inquiry in Social Studies* (New York: McGraw-Hill. 1966), esp. ch. 2.

20. John P. Lunstrum, "The Treatment of Controversial Issues in Social Studies Instruction," *High School Journal,* 49 (1965), 13–21; for a fuller picture, see Mas-

sialas and Cox, esp. 158–60. A detailed study of right-wing pressures upon textbooks and curriculum is Jack Nelson and Gene Roberts, Jr., *The Censors and the Schools* (Boston: Little, Brown, 1963).

21. For a thorough historical study of these instruments in inculcating nationalism, see Gladys A. Wiggin, *Education and Nationalism* (New York: McGraw-Hill, 1962); the role of the textbook is examined in ch. 9. On the Southern perspective, see Bernard A. Weisberger, "Dark and Bloody Ground of Reconstruction Historiography," *Journal of Southern History*, 25 (1959), 427–47.

22. The earliest such analysis may have been Bessie L. Pierce, *Civic Attitudes in American Schools* (Chicago: University of Chicago Press, 1930). The study covering the most texts (93) is James P. Shaver, "Reflective Thinking Values and Social Studies Textbooks," *School Review*, 73 (1960), 226–57. See also Mark M. Krug, " 'Safe' Textbooks and Citizenship Education," *ibid.*, 68 (1960), 463–80; Edgar Litt, "Civic Education, Community Norms, and Political Indoctrination," *American Sociological Review*, 28 (1963), 71–72; Byron G. Massialas, "American Government: 'We Are the Greatest,' " Cox and Massialas (eds.), 167–95; Smith and Patrick; Stanley E. Ballinger, "The Social Studies and Social Controversy," *School Review*, 71 (1963), 97–111. For studies of alternatives, see Massialas and Cox, ch. 9.

23. Content analysis of the earlier omissions are found in sources cited in n. 22. For specialized studies, see U.S. Congress, House Committee on Education and Labor, Ad Hoc Subcommittee on De Facto School Segregation, *Books for Schools and the Treatment of Minorities* (1966); the foregoing is popularized in John Brademas, "Don't Censor Textbooks — But Let's Keep Out Biased or Inaccurate Information," *Nation's Schools*, 79 (1967), 38–52; for a study of a special distortion, see Virgil J. Vogel, "The Indian in American History," *Integrated Education*, 6 (1968), 16–32; For studies of changing content, see Lloyd Marcus, *The Treatment of Minorities in Secondary School Textbooks* (New York: Anti-Defamation League of B'nai B'rith, 1961); and Sol M. Elkin, "Minorities in Textbooks: The Latest Chapter," *Teachers College Record*, 66 (1965), 502–08.

24. National Education Association, *The Education of Teachers: Curriculum Programs* (Washington, D.C.: NEA, 1959), 173–92, as cited in Massialas and Cox, ch. 12.

25. *Ibid.*, 285; for elaboration see John R. Palmer, "The Problem of Historical Explanation," *Social Education*, 27 (1963).

26. The Kansas figure is cited in Harlan Hahn, "Teacher Preparation in Political Science," *Social Education*, 29 (1965), 86–89. Symptomatic of professional social scientist interest is the development in the American Political Science Association in 1970 of a Pre-Collegiate Education Committee, and earlier the work of the center mentioned in n. 19, to develop a model curriculum. Indicative of new thinking on such preparation is Massialas and Cox, ch. 12. It is striking how often this course is taught by an athletic coach.

27. Harmon Zeigler, *The Political Life of American Teachers* (Englewood Cliffs, N.J.: Prentice-Hall, 1967), ch. 4, quotation at 113.

28. Howard K. Beale, *Are American Teachers Free?* (New York: Scribner's, 1936).

29. For case studies see Joseph F. Maloney, *"The Lonesome Train" in Levittown* (University, Ala.: Inter-University Case Program, No. 39, 1958); Donald W. Robinson, "The Teachers Take a Birching," *Phi Delta Kappan* (1962), 182–88. For more systematic analysis of teacher constraints and sanctions, see Zeigler, ch. 5; and Howard S. Becker, "The Teacher in the Authority System of the Public School," *Journal of Educational Sociology*, 27 (1953).

30. For a review of research on this attitudinal dimension, see Merlyn M. Gubser, "Anti-Democratic Attitudes of American Educators," *School and Community*, 54 (1967), 14–16; see also John C. Weiser and James E. Hayes, "Democratic Attitudes of Teachers and Prospective Teachers," *Phi Delta Kappan*, 47 (1966), 476–81.

31. A full review is found in Richard E. Dawson and Kenneth Prewitt, *Political*

Socialization (Boston: Little, Brown, 1968); see also William R. Schonfeld, "The Focus of Political Socialization Research: An Evaluation," *World Politics*, 23 (April, 1971), 544–78.

32. Hyman.

33. Hess and Torney, *The Development of Political Attitudes in Children*, ch. 5; M. Kent Jennings and Richard G. Niemi, "The Transmission of Political Values from Parent to Child," *American Political Science Review*, 62 (1968), 169–84, involving a national sample of 1,669 seniors. Another study of these data shows that it is the mother, rather than the father, who is more influential in shaping partisan affiliation and attitudes on some public issues; see M. Kent Jennings and Kenneth P. Langton, "Mothers vs. Fathers: The Formation of Political Orientations Among Young Americans," *Journal of Politics*, 31 (1969), 329–58.

34. Dennis, 109. For a similar judgment drawn from a review of the literature, see Vernon M. Goetcheus and Harvey C. Mansfield, "Innovations and Trends in the Study of American Politics," *Annals of the American Academy of Political and Social Science*, 391 (1970), 178–81; and Dawson and Prewitt, 215–18.

35. See Litt, n. 22.

36. Earlier research with null findings includes Roy A. Price, "Citizenship Studies in Syracuse," *Phi Delta Kappan*, 33 (1951), 179–81; Earl E. Edgar, "Kansas Study of Education for Citizenship," *ibid.*, 175–78; Roy E. Horton, Jr., "American Freedom and the Values of Youth," in H. M. Remmers (ed.), *Anti-Democratic Attitudes in American Schools* (Evanston: Northwestern University Press, 1963), 18–60; Litt; Patterson, 71–73.

For similar results in college, see Albert Somit *et al.*, "The Effect of the Introductory Political Science Course on Student Attitudes Toward Political Participation," *American Political Science Review*, 52 (1958), 1129–32; James A. Robinson *et al.*, "Teaching with Inter-Nation Simulation and Case Studies," *ibid.*, 60 (1966), 53–65. The Langton-Jennings study is "Political Socialization and the High School Civics Curriculum in the United States," *ibid.*, 62 (1968), 852–67, with exchange following at *ibid.*, 63 (1969), 172–73. Curriculum revisions flowing from such findings have been suggested by *idem* and by Patrick.

37. Dennis; see also Dawson and Prewitt, 215–18.

38. Easton, *A Systems Analysis*, 157; the relationship between input support and these three objects is explored at *ibid.*, chs. 11–13.

39. Angus Campbell *et al.*, *The American Voter* (New York: Wiley, 1960), 160; Henry Lee Moon, *Balance of Power: The Negro Vote* (Garden City, N.Y.: Doubleday, 1948).

40. The findings grossly simplified here are drawn from Hess and Torney; Easton and Dennis; Fred I. Greenstein, *Children and Politics* (New Haven: Yale University Press, 1965). For some criticisms, see Goetcheus and Mansfield; Sheilah R. Koppen, "Children and Compliance: A Comparative Analysis of Socialization Studies," *Law and Society Review*, 4 (1970), 545–64; Dean Jaros *et al.*, "The Malevolent Leader: Political Socialization in an American Sub-Culture," *American Political Science Review*, 62 (1968), 564–75; Schonfeld.

41. In some places a more realistic civic learning model is encouraged, but even this is consonant with community expectations of their children who are viewed as potential leaders. See Litt, cited in n. 15 at 74; This well designed research demonstrated the differential civic content of texts, and of community leaders and teacher values which operate in communities having differential incomes and occupations. Similarly, see Martin L. Levin, "Social Climates and Political Socialization," *Public Opinion Quarterly*, 25 (1961), 596–606.

42. For several international surveys on this attitude, see V. O. Key, Jr., *Public Opinion and American Democracy* (New York: Knopf, 1961), 42–43; and Almond and Verba.

43. For a review also emphasizing the limits of present knowledge while drawing

heavily upon sociology of education studies, see Jaros and Canon. For a review emphasizing both what we know and what we still need to know, see Dawson and Prewitt, 201–18; Dennis; and Schonfeld.

Chapter 3

1. For analysis, see Willmoore Kendall, *John Locke and the Doctrine of Majority-Rule* (Urbana: University of Illinois Press, 1941); Henry Steele Commager, *Majority Rule and Minority Rights* (New York: Oxford University Press, 1943); Herbert McClosky, "The Fallacy of Absolute Majority Rule," *Journal of Politics,* 11 (1949), 637–54; J. Roland Pennock, "Responsiveness, Responsibility, and Majority Rule," *American Political Science Review,* 46 (1952), 791–96.
2. Evidence is found in Samuel A. Stouffer, *Communism, Conformity, and Civil Liberties* (New York: Doubleday, 1955); James W. Prothro and Charles M. Grigg, "Fundamental Principles of Democracy: Bases of Agreement and Disagreement," *Journal of Politics,* 22 (1960), 276–94; Herbert McClosky, "Consensus and Ideology in American Politics," *American Political Science Review,* 58 (1964), 361–82. For similar evidence about teachers, see Chapter 2, n. 30, above.
3. Hugh D. Graham and Robert Gurr, *The History of Violence in America* (New York: Bantam Books, 1969).
4. On impact of regionalism, compare Norval D. Glenn and J. L. Simmons, "Are Regional Cultural Differences Diminishing?" *Public Opinion Quarterly,* 31 (1967), 176–93; Samuel C. Patterson, "The Political Cultures of the American States," *Journal of Politics,* 30 (1968), 187–209; Daniel J. Elazar, *American Federalism: A View from the States* (New York: Crowell, 1966); and Ira Sharkansky, *Regionalism in American Politics* (Indianapolis: Bobbs-Merrill, 1969). On sex and income differentiation, see Lester W. Milbrath, *Political Participation* (Chicago: Rand McNally, 1965), ch. 5; V. O. Key, Jr., *Public Opinion and American Democracy* (New York: Knopf, 1961), ch. 6.
5. These combinations are explored in Oliver P. Williams *et al., Suburban Differences and Metropolitan Policies: A Philadelphia Story* (Philadelphia: University of Pennsylvania Press, 1965).
6. The following relies upon Currin Shields, "The American Tradition of Empirical Collectivism," *American Political Science Review,* 46 (1952), 104–20.
7. Louis Hartz, *The Liberal Tradition in America* (Chicago: University of Chicago Press, 1955).
8. Elazar.
9. H. G. Good, *A History of American Education* (New York: Macmillan, 1956), ch. 4.
10. *Ibid.,* ch. 5.
11. Although the themes of these two paragraphs are not usually put this bluntly, most history of education studies support them, e.g., in *ibid.* For a detailed study of this process, see Lawrence A. Cremin, *The Transformation of the School: Progressivism in American Education, 1876–1957* (New York: Vintage Books, 1964).
12. A historical catalog of this expansion includes Ordinance of 1785; Ordinance of 1787; 1862, First Morrill Act; 1887, Hatch Act; 1890, Second Morrill Act; 1914, Smith-Lever Agricultural Extension Act; 1917, Smith-Hughes Vocational Act; 1918, Vocational Rehabilitation Act; 1933, School Lunch Program; 1935, Bankhead Jones Act (amended Smith-Lever); 1936, George Dean Act (amended Smith-Hughes); 1937, First Public Health Fellowships granted; 1940, Vocational Education for National Defense Act; 1944, GI Bill of Rights; 1950, National Science Foundation Act; 1954, Cooperative Research Program; 1958, National Defense Education Act; 1963, Higher Educational Facilities Act; 1963, Manpower Defense Training Act; 1964, Economic Opportunities Act; 1965, Elementary & Secondary Education Act. For a review, see *Congressional Quarterly, Federal Role in Education,* 2d ed. (Washington: Congressional Quarterly Service, 1967).
13. Adolphe E. Meyer, *An Educational History of the American People,* 2d ed.

(New York: McGraw-Hill, 1967), ch. 2.; Meyer notes at 39 that the primer "bedecked its pages with pictures of Adam and Eve, without even a blush to clothe them, standing alongside the most costly tree in human annals."

14. *Ibid.,* chs. 9–10; Good, ch. 5.

15. Alan Rosenthal, *Pedagogues and Power* (Syracuse: Syracuse University Press, 1969), 6–10. For a full current history, see G. Howard Goold and Arvid J. Burke, "The Organized Teaching Profession," in Edgar Fuller and Jim B. Pearson (eds.), *Education in the States: Nationwide Development Since 1900* (Washington, D.C.: NEA, 1969), ch. 14.

16. James Koerner, *Who Controls American Education?* (Boston: Beacon Press, 1968), 26.

17. *Ibid.,* 27.

18. Harmon Zeigler, *The Political World of the High School Teacher* (Eugene: University of Oregon Press, 1966). For a special study of the Oregon affiliate, see Norman R. Luttbeg and Harmon Zeigler, "Attitude Consensus and Conflict in an Interest Group: An Assessment of Cohesion," *American Political Science Review,* 60 (1966) 655–65.

19. For a general background on the AFT, see Patrick W. Carlton and Harold I. Goodwin, *The Collective Dilemma: Negotiations in Education* (Columbus: Jones, 1969). AFT publishes a monthly newspaper, *American Teacher,* which provides current information on AFT policy directions.

20. Thomas H. Eliot, Nicholas A. Masters, and Robert Salisbury, *State Politics and Public Schools* (New York: Knopf, 1964).

21. James Sundquist, *Politics and Policy* (Washington, D.C.: Brookings Institution, 1968), 155–200. In 1969, the NEA was a crucial part of the Emergency Committee for Full Funding. This Committee was able to persuade Congress to increase the President's education budget by over $500 million.

22. For an elaboration on this view see Koerner, 32–33.

23. Roald I. Campbell *et al., The Organization and Control of American Schools* (Columbus: Merrill, 1970), 327–66; William T. Kvareceus, "PTA: The Irrelevant Giant," *The Nation,* 197, No. 10 (October 5, 1963), 200–01.

24. Koerner, 147–48.

25. "The Value of the PTA," *Today's Education,* 58 (1969), 31–33.

26. Neal Gross, *Who Runs Our Schools?* (New York: Wiley, 1958), 36–77. On the superintendent's use of the PTA for communications to improve school-home relations, see Carelton W. Washburne and Sidney P. Marland, Jr., *Winnetka* (Englewood Cliffs, N.J.: Prentice-Hall, 1963), 331.

27. Masters *et al.,* 14, 105, 200–01.

28. Descriptive leaflet, Council for Basic Education (Washington, D.C., n.d.), 3–4.

29. See M. Kent Jennings and Harmon Zeigler, "Interest Representation in School Governance," paper prepared for American Political Science Association meeting, 1970.

30. Gross, 23–24.

31. See sources cited in Chapter 9, n. 1.

32. See Richard LaPiere, *Social Change* (New York: McGraw-Hill, 1965), 197; Zeigler; Mary A. Raywid, *The Axe-Grinders* (New York: Macmillan, 1962); Jack Nelson and Gene Roberts, Jr., *The Censors and the Schools* (Boston: Little, Brown, 1963). The distinction offered here borders on that of the "sacred and secular communities" analyzed in Laurence Iannaccone and Frank W. Lutz, *Politics, Power and Policy: The Governing of Local School Districts* (Columbus: Merrill, 1970).

33. Bulletin for October, "The White Book of the John Birch Society for 1961," (Belmont, Mass.: The Society, 1961), 19.

34. Stanley Eames, "Schools Targets of Red's Enemy," *Boston Herald,* August 29, 1960. Evidence of such action is found in Donald W. Robinson, "The Teachers Take a Birching," *Phi Delta Kappan,* 43 (1962), 182–88.

35. Lesley H. Browder, "A Suburban School Superintendent Plays Politics," in Michael W. Kirst (ed.), *The Politics of Education at the Local, State, and Federal*

Levels (Berkeley: McCutchan, 1970), 199 ff.; Iannaccone and Lutz offer another excellent analysis.

36. For a theoretical treatment of interest group origins, see Robert H. Salisbury, "An Exchange Theory of Interest Groups," *Midwest Journal of Political Science,* 13 (1969), 1–32; and Maneur L. Olson, *The Logic of Collective Action* (Cambridge: Harvard University Press, 1965).

37. For an account of this accommodation process, see Ralph W. Tyler, "National Assessment: A History and Sociology," in James W. Guthrie and Edward Wynne (eds.), *New Models for American Education* (Englewood Cliffs, N.J.: Prentice-Hall, 1971), ch. 2.

38. For one view of Ford's role in this controversy, see Martin Meyer, *The Teachers Strike* (New York: Harper & Row, 1968).

39. Michael Lipsky, "Protest as a Political Resource," *American Political Science Review,* 62 (1968), 1145.

40. The "problem of the powerless" concept stems from James Q. Wilson, "The Strategy of Protest: Problems of Negro Civic Action," *Journal of Conflict Resolution,* 3 (1961), 291–303.

41. For the evidence of the reality, see U.S. Commission on Civil Rights, *Southern School Desegregation, 1966–67* (1967), ch. 8.

42. See John Birmingham (ed.), *Our Time Is Now: Notes from the High School Underground* (New York: Praeger, 1970).

43. See Jerome H. Skolnick, *The Politics of Protest* (New York: Ballantine Books, 1969).

44. Lipsky, 1154–57, notes at least six tactics of response by protest targets that do not provide protesters full satisfaction, and he is not very optimistic about the probability of success of protest strategy.

45. Jennings and Zeigler.

Chapter 4

1. David Easton, *A Framework for Political Analysis* (Englewood Cliffs, N.J.: Prentice-Hall, 1965), 122.

2. H. M. Hamlin, "Organized Citizen Participation in the Public Schools," *Review of Educational Research,* 23 (1953), 346–52. Compare this with the study fifteen years later by Otis A. Crosby, "How to Prepare Winning Bond Issues," *Nation's Schools,* 81 (1968), 81–84.

3. Richard J. Brown, "Party Platforms and Public Education," *Social Studies* (1961), 206–10. For a review of such linkage models and the data, see Norman R. Luttbeg (ed.), *Public Opinion and Public Policy* (Homewood, Ill.: Dorsey Press, 1968).

4. E. D. Hodgson, "Decision-Making and the Politics of Education," *Canadian Education and Research Digest,* 8 (1968), 19–33; John J. Hunt, "Politics in the Role of the Superintendent," *Phi Delta Kappan,* 49 (1968), 348–50. A major statement is Roald F. Campbell *et al., The Organization and Control of American Schools* (Columbus: Merrill, 1965).

5. Charles R. Adrian and Charles Press, *Governing Urban America,* 3d ed. (New York: McGraw-Hill, 1968), 434.

6. John C. Walden, "School Board Changes and Superintendent Turnover," *Administrator's Notebook,* 15 (1967). This is part of a several-dissertation project on the subject of community demands and board reactions, reported in Laurence Iannaccone and Frank W. Lutz, *Politics, Power and Policy: The Governing of Local School Districts* (Columbus: Merrill, 1970).

7. The Detroit reference is in Marilyn Gittell *et al.,* "Fiscal Status and School Policy Making in Six Large School Districts," in Michael W. Kirst (ed.), *The Politics of Education* (Berkeley: McCutchan, 1970), 63. The influence of partisan groups or affiliation is found in Oliver P. Williams and Charles E. Adrian, "The Insulation of Local Politics Under the Nonpartisan Ballot," *American Political Science Review,*

53 (1959), 1052–63; Charles R. Adrian, "A Typology for Nonpartisan Elections," *Western Political Quarterly,* 12 (1959), 449–58; and Willis D. Hawley, *Nonpartisan Urban Politics* (New York: Wiley, 1972).

8. Robert L. Crain *et al., The Politics of School Desegregation* (Garden City, N.Y.: Doubleday, Anchor, 1969).

9. M. Kent Jennings and Harmon Zeigler, "Response Styles and Politics: The Case of School Boards," *Midwest Journal of Political Science,* 15 (1971), 290–321.

10. Students interested in this subject might begin with James S. Coleman, *Community Conflict* (New York: Free Press, 1957).

11. Angus Campbell *et al., The American Voter* (New York: Wiley, 1960); Lester W. Milbrath, *Political Participation* (Chicago: Rand McNally, 1965).

12. M. Kent Jennings and Harmon Zeigler, "The Salience of American State Politics," *American Political Science Review,* 64 (1970), 524–27.

13. Herbert McClosky *et al.,* "Issue Conflict and Consensus Among Party Leaders and Followers," *ibid.,* 54 (1960), 413; Thomas A. Flinn and Frederick M. Wirt, "Local Party Leaders: Groups of Like Minded Men," *Midwest Journal of Political Science,* 9 (1965), 82.

14. William Gamson, *Power and Discontent* (Homewood, Ill.: Dorsey Press, 1968), although the focus here is not upon school issues.

15. For a review of this debate, see Willis D. Hawley and Frederick M. Wirt (eds.), *The Search for Community Power* (Englewood Cliffs, N.J.: Prentice-Hall, 1968). For illustrations of the level of analytical thinking, see Terry N. Clark (ed.), *Community Structure and Decision-Making: Comparative Analysis* (San Francisco: Chandler, 1968); for an illustration of comparative research, see Terry N. Clark, "Community Structure, Decision-Making, Budget Expenditures, and Urban Renewal in 51 American Communities," *American Sociological Review,* 33 (1968), 576–93. See also Frederick M. Wirt (ed.), *Future Directions in Community Power Research: A Colloquium* (Berkeley: University of California, Institute of Governmental Studies, 1971).

16. We have been informed on these queries by Willis D. Hawley from an unpublished paper. For a bibliography, see Hawley and Wirt, 367–79; Charles Press, *Main Street Politics* (East Lansing, Mich.: Institute for Community Development, 1962).

17. James G. March, "The Power of Power," in David Easton (ed.), *Varieties of Political Theory* (Englewood Cliffs, N.J.: Prentice-Hall, 1966), 39–70.

18. See the articles by John Walton, "Discipline, Method and Community Power: A Note on the Sociology of Knowledge," *American Sociological Review,* 31 (1966), 684–89; and "Substance and Artifact: The Current Status of Research on Community Power Structure," *American Journal of Sociology,* 71 (1966), 430–38. However, using a larger sample of studies and a more discriminating statistical technique, Walton's relationship between findings and the discipline, method of analysis, etc. does not hold up. See Terry Clark *et al.,* "Discipline, Method, Community Structure, and Decision-Making: The Role and Limitations of the Sociology of Knowledge," *American Sociologist,* 3 (1968), 214–17.

19. The first approach is illustrated in Robert E. Agger *et al., The Rulers and the Ruled* (New York: Wiley, 1964); and William V. D'Antonio and William H Form, *Influentials in Two Border Cities* (South Bend, Ind.: University of Notre Dame Press, 1965). The second is illustrated in Walton and in Claire W. Gilbert, "Some Trends in Community Politics: A Secondary Analysis of Power Structure Data from 166 Communities," *Southwestern Social Science Quarterly,* 48 (1967), 373–81. The third approach is seen in Clark, *Community Structure and Decision Making.* The "sample" is reported in Peter H. Rossi and Robert Crain, "The NORC Permanent Community Sample," *Public Opinion Quarterly,* 32 (1968), 261–72.

20. Peter Bachrach, *The Theory of Democratic Elitism* (Boston: Little, Brown, 1967).

21. Nicholas Masters *et al., Politics, Poverty and Education: An Analysis of Decision-making Structures* (Washington, D.C.: Office of Economic Opportunity,

1968); Roland W. Warren (ed.), *Politics and the Ghettos* (New York: Atherton, 1969); and Paul E. Peterson, "Forms of Representation: Participation of the Poor in the Community Action Program," *American Political Science Review,* 64 (1970), 491–507.

22. Edgar L. Morphet, Roe L. Johns, and Theodore L. Reller, *Educational Organization and Administration,* 2d ed. (Englewood Cliffs, N.J.: Prentice-Hall, 1967), 194.

23. Robert S. and Helen M. Lynd, *Middletown,* part 2 (New York: Harcourt Brace Jovanovich, 1929); and *Middletown in Transition* (New York: Harcourt Brace Jovanovich, 1937), ch. 6. For a more thorough critique of the Lynds for imputing power to this family, see Nelson W. Polsby, *Community Power and Political Theory* (New Haven: Yale University Press, 1963), 14–24; Floyd Hunter, *Community Power Structure* (Chapel Hill: University of North Carolina Press, 1953), 214–15, 223; Robert A. Dahl, *Who Governs?* (New Haven: Yale University Press, 1960), ch. 11; Agger *et al.,* ch. 4.

24. For articles on this power and the policies of transportation, defense contracts, poverty programs, and Japanese communities — but none on schools — see the entire issue of *Southwestern Social Science Quarterly,* 48, No. 3 (December, 1967). An aggregate study omitting this is Terry Clark, "Community Structure, Decision-Making, Budget Expenditures."

25. Robert R. Alford, *Bureaucracy and Participation: Political Culture in Four Wisconsin Cities* (Chicago: Rand McNally, 1969).

26. See the Pellegrin bibliography in *Southwestern Social Science Quarterly,* 48 (1967), and especially the reference to Agger, Bloomberg *et al.*

27. See Leland C. Wilson, "Community Power Controls Related to the Administration of Education," Ph.D. dissertation, Peabody College, 1952; Theodore J. Jensen, "Identification and Utilization of Opinion Leaders in School District Reorganization," Ph.D. dissertation, University of Wisconsin, 1952; Keith Goldhammer, "The Roles of School District Officials in Policy-Determination in an Oregon Community," Ph.D. dissertation, University of Oregon, 1954; Keith Goldhammer, "Community Power Structure and School Board Membership," *American School Board Journal,* 130 (1955), 23–25; Donald E. Tope, "Northwest C.P.E.A. — Aims and Results," *The School Executive,* 74 (1955), 74–76; Vincent Ostrom, "Who Forms School Policy?" *ibid.,* 77–79.

28. Harold V. Webb, *Community Power Structure Related to School Administration* (Laramie: Curriculum and Research Center, College of Education, University of Wyoming, 1956).

29. John M. Foskett, "A Comparative Study of Community Influence," in Donald Tope *et al., The Social Sciences View School Administration* (Englewood Cliffs, N.J.: Prentice-Hall, 1965), 115–30.

30. Warner Bloomberg *et al., Suburban Power Structures and Public Education* (Syracuse: Syracuse University Press, 1963), 88 ff., 168; In a related study from the same series, see Jesse Burkhead, *Public School Finance: Economics and Politics.*

31. Ralph B. Kimbrough, *Political Power and Educational Decision-Making* (Chicago: Rand McNally, 1964), esp. chs. 4–5, 10–11.

32. This interest has stimulated a number of dissertations at the University of Florida. Compare *ibid.;* Kimbrough, "Development of a Concept of Social Power," in Robert S. Cahill and Stephen P. Hencley (eds.), *The Politics of Education in the Local Community* (Danville, Ill.: Interstate Printers & Publishers, 1964), ch. 5; and Appendix H in n. 36 *infra.*

33. Donald J. McCarty, "How Community Power Structures Influence Administrative Tenure," *American School Board Journal,* 148 (1964), 11–13, offers some hypotheses in a highly researchable area.

34. Cahill and Hencley, 75.

35. Crain.

36. Roe L. Johns and Ralph B. Kimbrough, *The Relationship of Socio-economic Factors, Educational Leadership Patterns, and Elements of Community Power Structure to Local School Fiscal Policy* (Washington, D.C.: Bureau of Research, Office of Education, HEW, 1968).

37. This phenomenon has been reported for many other kinds of expenditures, that is, what has been spent in the past determines current expenditures more than other potential explanatory variables. See Ira Sharkansky, "Economic and Political Correlates of State Government Expenditures: General Tendencies and Deviant Cases," *Midwest Journal of Political Science,* 11 (1967), 173–92; and Ira Sharkansky, *Spending in the American States* (Chicago: Rand McNally, 1968). This research found this explanation was true most for general government and then for education among numerous state expenditures.

38. A clear signal in an important training journal is Russell T. Gregg, "Political Dimensions of Educational Leadership," *Teachers College Record,* 67 (1965), 118–28. Illustrative of texts' use of the concept is Morphet *et al., 75–76.*

39. John H. Bunzel, "Pressure Groups in Politics and Education," *National Elementary Principal,* 43 (1964), 12–16, is typical of the political science approval, while Neal Gross, *Who Runs Our Schools?* (New York: Wiley, 1958), typifies the educational scholar's disapproval.

40. For example, see Fred D. Carver and Donald O. Crowe, "An Interdisciplinary Framework for the Study of Community Power," *Educational Administration Quarterly,* 5 (1969), 50–64; and the still-valuable Cahill and Hencley.

41. Gilbert, 381.

42. John Walton, "The Vertical Axis of Community Organization and the Structure of Power," *Southwestern Social Science Quarterly,* 48 (1967), 353–68.

Chapter 5

1. David Easton, *A Framework for Political Analysis* (Englewood Cliffs, N.J.: Prentice-Hall, 1965), 114.

2. Why this change came may be understood from Heinz Eulau, *The Behavioral Persuasion in Politics* (New York: Random House, 1963), chs. 2–3; and Albert Somit and Joseph Tanenhaus, *The Development of American Political Science* (Boston: Allyn & Bacon, 1967).

3. Easton, 132–33.

4. Alpheus L. White, *Local School Boards: Organization and Practices* (U.S. Office of Education, HEW, 1962).

5. Donald J. McCarty, "School Board Membership: Why Do Citizens Serve?" *Administrators Notebook,* 8 (September, 1959).

6. See Fred D. Carver, "Social Class and School Board Role Expectations," *Urban Education,* 3 (1968), 143–54.

7. David Minar, "Community Basis of Conflict in School System Politics," *American Sociological Review,* 31 (1966), 822–35.

8. M. Kent Jennings and Harmon Zeigler, "Interest Representation in School Governance," paper presented at the American Political Science Association meeting, September, 1970, 11–20.

9. David W. Minar, "Educational Decision Making in Suburban Communities," in Michael W. Kirst (ed.), *The Politics of Education* (Berkeley: McCutchan, 1970), 167–83.

10. Robert Salisbury, "Schools and Politics in the Big City," *Harvard Education Review,* 37 (1967), 408–24.

11. Norman D. Kerr, "The School Board as an Agency of Legitimation," *Sociology of Education,* 38 (1964), 34–59.

12. Keith Goldhammer, *The School Board* (New York: Center for Applied Research, 1964). For a number of viewpoints on school board performance, see William Dickinson (ed.), *New Dimensions in School Board Leadership* (Evanston: National School Boards Association, 1969). For a comprehensive review of school board research, see H. Thomas James, *School Board Bibliography* (Stanford: School of Education, 1967).

13. See Robert Crain, *The Politics of School Desegregation* (Chicago: Aldine, 1968).

14. Robert Bendiner, *The Politics of Schools* (New York: Harper & Row, 1969),

165. For a full study of the limits on the local school system, see Frederick M. Wirt, "The Slender Reed: Limits on the Local School Agency in Expanding Equal Educational Opportunity," report to U.S. Senate Subcommittee on Equal Educational Opportunities, July, 1971.

15. Richard F. Carter and John Sutthoff, *Communities and Their Schools* (Stanford: Institute for Communication Research, 1960), ch. 2.

16. Richard F. Carter, *Voters and Their Schools* (Stanford: Institute for Communication Research, 1960), 73–76.

17. Roscoe Martin, *Government and the Suburban School* (Syracuse: Syracuse University Press, 1962), 55.

18. For a discussion of the topic, see Luvern L. Cunningham and Raphael O. Nystrand, *Citizen Participation In School Affairs* (Washington, D.C.: Urban Coalition, 1969).

19. Marilyn Gittell and T. Edward Hollander, *Six Urban School Districts* (New York: Praeger, 1969), 51.

20. Minar, ns. 7 and 9 above. For another dimension of suburban behavior, see Benjamin Walter and Frederick M. Wirt, "Social and Political Dimensions of American Suburbs," in Brian Berry (ed.), *Classification of Cities: New Methods and Alternative Uses* (New York: Wiley, 1972).

21. Jennings and Zeigler.

22. See for instance, M. Kent Jennings and Harmon Zeigler, "Response Styles and Politics: The Case of School Boards," *Midwest Journal of Political Science,* 15 (1971), 290–321.

23. See Laurence Iannaccone and Frank W. Lutz, *Politics, Power and Policy: The Governing of Local School Districts* (Columbus: Merrill, 1970); John C. Walden, "School Board Changes and Superintendent Turnover," *Administrator's Notebook,* 15 (1967).

24. See Keith Goldhammer, *The Jackson County Story* (Eugene: Center for Advanced Study of Educational Administration, 1964); Herbert J. Gans, *The Levittowners* (New York: Pantheon, 1967), 86–103; and Iannaccone and Lutz.

25. For an analysis of politics and school facilities, see Louis H. Masotti, *Education and Politics in Suburbia* (Cleveland: Western Reserve University Press, 1967).

26. Martin, 61.

27. Interview with Professor William O'Dell, May, 1971, by the Stanford University Faculty Committee.

28. For the evidence on the vital matter of money, see H. Thomas James, James Kelly, and Walter Ganns, *Determinants of Educational Expenditures in Large Cities of the United States* (Stanford: School of Education, 1966), 55–80.

29. *Ibid.* and Gittell and Hollander.

30. Gittell and Hollander.

31. David Rogers, *110 Livingston Street* (New York: Random House, 1969).

32. David Rogers, "The Failure of Inner City Schools: A Crisis of Management and Service Delivery," in *Educational Technology* (September 1970), 28–29.

33. See Robert Lyke, "Political Issues in School Decentralization" in Kirst (ed.), 111–33.

34. See for instance Mario Fantini, Marilyn Gittell, and Richard Magat, *Community Control and the Urban School* (New York: Praeger, 1970). For a discussion of community control in areas other than education see Alan Altshuler, *Community Control* (New York: Pegasus, 1970).

35. Lyke, 124–25. See also, Henry Levin (ed.), *Community Control of Schools* (Washington, D.C.: Brookings Institution, 1970).

36. For a review of decentralization and politics in six cities see George R. LaNoue, "The Politics of School Decentralization," a paper presented at the American Political Science Association Convention, 1970. This will appear in George R. LaNoue and Bruce Smith, *The Politics of School Decentralization* (Lexington, Mass.: Heath, in press). A complete bibliography on this topic is by Margot Melrood, *A Bibliography on Decentralization* (Milwaukee: Institute of Governmental Affairs, University of Wisconsin, 1970).

37. LaNoue, 26–52.

38. M. Kent Jennings, "Paternal Grievances and School Politics," *Public Opinion Quarterly,* 32 (1968), 363–78.

39. Salisbury.

40. Alan Rosenthal, *Pedagogues and Power* (Syracuse: Syracuse University Press, 1969).

41. Gittell and Hollander.

42. See Richard Saxe, "Mayors and Schools," *Urban Education,* 4 (1969), 243–52.

43. For a more comprehensive discussion, see John Birmingham (ed.), *Our Time Is Now* (New York: Praeger, 1970); and Marc Lebarle and Tom Schyson, *The High School Revolutionaries* (New York: Random House, 1970). The following are community organizations in New York City that encourage student use: Project Justice, Bronx; Queens Coalition of Concern, Jamaica; United Bronx Parents, Bronx; West Side Parent Union, Columbus Ave.

44. See Raphael O. Nystrand, "High School Students as Policy Advocates," *Theory Into Practice,* 8 (1969), 273–76.

45. For a review of these phenomena, see Raphael O. Nystrand (ed.), *Student Unrest in Public Schools* (Worthington, Ohio: Jones, 1969).

46. For a comparative urban review of this tension, see Robert R. Alford, *Bureaucracy and Participation* (Chicago: Rand McNally, 1969).

Chapter 6

1. The best analysis of Populism and Progressivism is Eric F. Goldman, *Rendezvous with Destiny* (New York: Vintage Books, 1956); the quotation is at 338. For the early arguments, see William Munro (ed.), *The Initiative, Referendum and Recall* (New York: Macmillan, 1913). For a midcentury review of the results, see Joseph G. LaPalombara and Charles B. Hagan, "Direct Legislation: An Appraisal and a Suggestion," *American Political Science Review,* 45 (1951), 400–21.

2. *Book of States, 1970–1971* (Lexington, Ky.: Council of State Governments, 1970), 304.

3. U.S. National Center for Educational Statistics, Office of Education, "Bonds Sales for Public School Purposes," annual reports.

4. Richard F. Carter and John Sutthoff, *Communities and Their Schools* (Stanford: Institute for Communication Research, 1960), chs. 4–5.

5. *Ibid.,* 107.

6. A smaller study, six referenda in Akron, found that turnout and support were *positively* correlated. Areas of least support show signs of what we infer were Catholic working class. See Charles L. Willis, "Analysis of Voter Response to School Financial Proposals," *Public Opinion Quarterly,* 31 (1967–1968), 648–51.

7. Richard F. Carter, *Voters and Their Schools* (Stanford: Institute for Communication Research, 1960), 3.

8. *Ibid.,* 5.

9. *Ibid.,* chs. 2–3.

10. A smaller but confirming study of the differentiating function of this outlook concludes that voting "no" stems from a sense of powerlessness. While this is found particularly heavily in the lower class, it is not a class phenomenon but an aspect of "phobic" politics, whereby one's fears and suspicions are transferred into the political world. See John Wayne Horton and W. E. Thompson, "Powerlessness and Political Negativism: A Study of Defeated Local Referendums," *American Journal of Sociology,* 67 (1962), 485–93.

11. For a review of the evidence on the political aspects, see Lester Milbrath, *Political Participation* (Chicago: Rand McNally, 1965), ch. 3; on the schooling variable, see James Coleman *et al., Equality of Educational Opportunity* (Washington, D.C.: Government Printing Office, 1967).

12. Carter, ch. 4.

13. *Ibid.,* ch. 5.

14. On the methodological problem involved and a solution, see W. Phillips

Shively, " 'Ecological' Inference: The Use of Aggregate Data to Study Individuals," *American Political Science Review*, 63 (1969), 1183–96. For an illustrative study pairing these data sets, see Robert E. Agger, "The Politics of Local Education: A Comparative Study of Community Decision-Making," in Donald E. Tope (ed.), *A Forward Look — The Preparation of School Administration 1970* (Eugene: Bureau of Educational Research, University of Oregon, 1960), 131–72.

15. James Q. Wilson and Edward C. Banfield, "Public-Regardingness as a Value Premise in Voting Behavior," *American Political Science Review*, 58 (1964), 876–87; for additional evidence see their fn. 5 and Eugene S. Uyeki, "Patterns of Voting in a Metropolitan Area," *Urban Affairs Quarterly*, 1 (1966), 65–77.

16. Nathan Glazer and Daniel P. Moynihan, *Beyond the Melting Pot* (Cambridge: MIT Press, 1963), 290.

17. The New Jersey study is Gerald Pomper, "Ethnic and Group Voting in Non-partisan Municipal Elections," *Public Opinion Quarterly*, 30 (1966); see also J. Leiper Freeman, "Local Party Systems: Theoretical Considerations and a Case Analysis," *American Journal of Sociology*, 64 (1958), 282–89. On ethnic attitudes toward schools, see Glazer and Moynihan.

The non–political scientist may be interested in the dispute over the persistence and impact of ethnic voting in the pages of the *American Political Science Review* during the mid-1960's; the Banfield and Wilson article was followed by Raymond E. Wolfinger, "The Development and Persistence of Ethnic Voting," *ibid.*, 59 (1965), 896–908; Raymond E. Wolfinger and John O. Field, "Political Ethos and the Structure of City Government," *ibid.*, 60 (1966), 306–26; Robert L. Lineberry and Edmund P. Fowler, "Reformism and Public Policies in American Cities," and Michael Parenti, "Ethnic Politics and the Persistence of Ethnic Identification," in *ibid.*, 61 (1967), 701–16, 717–26. A sharply critical analysis, using Wisconsin city data, runs against this thesis; see Roger E. Durand, "Ethnicity, Political Culture, and Urban Conflict," paper presented at the annual meeting of the American Political Science Association, 1970.

It is characteristic of the neglect of school referenda that this policy output is not analyzed in any of these studies.

18. For Cleveland data, see James A. Norton, "Referenda Voting in a Metropolitan Area," *Western Political Quarterly*, 16 (1963), 195–212; James A. Norton, *Referenda Voting in Metropolitan Cleveland: Statistical Section* (Cleveland: Metropolitan Services Commission, 1960); and Uyeki.

19. Beginning with 1961–1962, the total percentages of successful elections in these twelve states were: 70.9, 67.0, 70.7, 70.6, 67.2, 66.0, 59.5, 49.6, and overall 67.1. Data calculated from source in n. 3, *supra*.

20. Carter and Sutthoff, 110, provided the data for our calculations.

21. For a review of such literature long before the current interest in community control, see H. M. Hamlin, "Organized Citizen Participation in the Public Schools," *Review of Educational Research*, 23 (1953), 346–52.

22. Neal Gross *et al.*, *Explorations in Role Analysis: Studies of the School Superintendency Role* (New York: Wiley, 1958).

23. David W. Minar, "Community Basis of Conflict in School System Politics," *American Sociological Review*, 31 (1966), 822–35.

24. *Ibid.*, 825.

25. Charles Silberman, *Crisis in the Classroom* (New York: Random House, 1970).

Chapter 7

1. For an overview of state organization for education see Edgar L. Morphet and David Jesser, *Emerging State Responsibilities for Education* (Denver: Improving State Leadership in Education, 1970). For encyclopedic detail on the states' role in developing and shaping local schools' organization and power, see Edgar Fuller and

Jim B. Pearson (eds.), *Education in the States,* 2 vols. (Washington, D.C.: NEA, 1969).

2. See Michael D. Usdan, David Minar, and Emanuel Hurwitz, *Education and State Politics* (New York: Teachers College Press, Columbia University, 1969).

3. For an overview of the processes and programs of state finance, see Charles Benson, *Economics of Public Education* (Boston: Houghton Mifflin, 1967); and Dick Netzer, *Economics of the Property Tax* (Washington, D.C.: Brookings Institution, 1966).

4. For a critique of financial minimums and state aid formulas, see James Guthrie *et al., Schools and Inequality* (Cambridge: MIT Press, 1971). A listing of required courses for each state, illustrating the minimums, can be found in George D. Marconnit, "State Legislatures and the School Curriculum," *Phi Delta Kappan,* 49 (1968), 269–72.

5. Stephen K. Bailey *et al., Schoolmen and Politics* (Syracuse: Syracuse Press, 1962), 47.

6. *Ibid.,* 8.

7. Clyde B. Moore, *Educational Growth and the New York State Constitution* (Albany: New York State Educational Conference Board, February, 1958), as cited in Bailey, 9.

8. Frederick C. Mosher and Orville F. Poland, *The Costs of American Governments: Facts, Trends, Myths* (New York: Dodd, Mead, 1964), 116. For evidence of the dominant weight of schools in state expenditures since 1902, see *ibid.,* 43.

9. See Nicholas Masters *et al., State Politics and Public Schools* (New York: Knopf, 1964).

10. Governor's Committee on Public Education, *Public Education in Texas* (Austin: Texas Education Agency, 1969). For a comparative perceptual study, see Leroy Ferguson, "How State Legislators View the Problem of School Needs," in Robert C. Crew (ed.), *State Politics* (Belmont: Wadsworth, 1968), 481. For a close examination of California, see Paul Collins, "Legislative Influence and the Changing Relationships of the California Educational Associations, 1960–1969," unpublished Ph.D. dissertation, University of California, Berkeley, 1971.

11. Masters *et al.,* 265.

12. There is no recent comparative state study of the governor's role and staff for education policy. For a discussion of the governor's office, see Coleman P. Ransone, Jr., *The Office of the Governor in the United States* (University, Ala.: University of Alabama Press, 1956); and Duane Lockhard, *The Politics of State and Local Government* (New York: Macmillan, 1969), ch. 13.

13. Gerald E. Sroufe, "Recruitment Processes and Composition of State Boards of Education," paper presented at 1969 meeting of the American Educational Research Association.

14. In all but one of the states using the appointment model of selection, the governor is responsible for making the appointment.

15. Sroufe, 22.

16. James Koerner, *Who Controls American Education?* (Boston: Beacon Press, 1968), 85. The activities and influence of state boards of education is a dark continent in view of the paucity of research.

17. *Ibid.*

18. Many observations in this section have been drawn from a Ford Foundation study of state distribution of federal aid, including consideration of state boards in six states. See Joel S. Berke and Michael W. Kirst, *Federal Aid to Education: Who Benefits? Who Governs?* (Lexington, Mass.: Heath, 1972).

19. For the perceptions of local superintendents of SDE's, see Keith Goldhammer *et al., Issues and Problems in Contemporary Educational Administration* (Eugene: University of Oregon, 1967), ch. 4.

20. See n. 18 above.

21. See also Roald I. Campbell and Donald H. Layton, *Policy Making for Amer-*

ican Education (Chicago: Midwest Administration Center, 1969), ch. 3. A full treatment of this process is Jay D. Scribner, "Impacts of Federal Programs on State Departments of Education," in Fuller and Pearson, vol. 2, ch. 11.

22. James B. Conant, *Shaping Educational Policy* (New York: McGraw-Hill, 1964), 37–38.

23. An exploratory analysis on this topic is David L. Colton, "State Power and Local Decision Making in Education," paper presented to the American Educational Research Association meeting, 1969, and indirectly the studies cited in n. 52 *infra*. The SDE is headed in six states by an appointed official, in twenty-three by an independent board, and in twenty-one by an elected official; see *Book of the States, 1964–1965* (Chicago: Council of State Governments, 1965).

24. B. Dean Bowles, "The Power Structure in State Education Politics," *Phi Delta Kappan*, 49 (1968), 337–40.

25. See source in Table 7.3, at 15. The annual reports of this Advisory Council provide good longitudinal data on personnel changes in state education agencies.

26. Campbell and Layton, 55.

27. *Ibid.*, 56.

28. See Michael D. Usdan, "The Role and Future of State Educational Coalitions," *Educational Administration Quarterly*, 5 (1969), 26–42; and Allan M. Carter, "The Shaping of the Compact for Education," *Educational Record* (Washington, D.C.: American Council on Education, 1966).

29. For empirical evidence, See U.S. Senate Committee on Government Operations, Intergovernmental Relations Subcommittee, *The Federal System as Seen by State and Local Officials* (1963).

30. Masters *et al.*, 268–69.

31. For a categorization of influence patterns, see Laurence Iannaccone, *Politics in Education* (New York: Center for Applied Research in Education, 1967). For a good case study of such tactics, see Michael D. Usdan, *The Political Power of Education in New York State* (New York: Teachers College Press, Columbia University, 1963).

32. See Alan Rosenthal, *Pedagogues and Power* (Syracuse: Syracuse University Press, 1969), ch. 1.

33. Masters *et al.*, 187–90.

34. *Ibid.*, 189.

35. For a perspective on this rivalry from the standpoint of big cities, see Alan K. Campbell, "Socio-Economic, Political, and Fiscal Environment of Educational Policy Making in Large Cities," in Michael W. Kirst (ed.), *The Politics of Education* (Berkeley: McCutchan, 1970), 300–17. For contrast, see Tom Wiley, *Politics and Purse Strings in New Mexico's Public Schools* (Albuquerque: University of New Mexico Press, 1968).

36. Discussions of state political coalitions are included in the previously cited works by Iannaccone, Bailey, Masters *et al.*, and more recently by Laurence Iannaccone, "Norms Governing Urban-State Politics of Education," in Frank Lutz (ed.), *Toward Improved Urban Education* (Worthington, Ohio: Charles Jones, 1970), 233–53.

37. For an elaboration of this concept, see Iannaccone, *Politics in Education*, ch. 3.

38. See Bailey, 47–50.

39. Masters *et al.*

40. Lucian W. Pye and Sidney Verba (eds.), *Political Culture and Political Development* (Princeton: Princeton University Press, 1965), 513.

41. Samuel Patterson, "The Political Culture of the American States," *Journal of Politics*, 30 (1968), 187–209; the divergence is shown in Norval D. Glenn and J. L. Simmons, "Are Regional Cultural Differences Diminishing," *Public Opinion Quarterly*, 31 (1967), 176–93. This variety thesis is developed more fully in Daniel J. Elazar, *American Federalism: A View from the States* (New York: Crowell, 1966)

42. For a review of this literature, see Ira Sharkansky, *Regionalism in American Politics* (Indianapolis: Bobbs-Merrill, 1970), appendix A. As we shall shortly see, Sharkansky does direct himself to certain aspects of school politics in its policy aspects.

43. See Bailey *et al.*, 241–44.

44. Laurence Iannaccone, "A First Step on Making Sense Out of Massachusetts," from a study noted in n. 18.

45. See Elazar, 188–99.

46. *Ibid.*, 184. For general treatment of intergovernmental politics see W. Brooke Graves, *American Intergovernmental Relations* (New York: Scribner's, 1964).

47. Masters *et al.*, 263–64.

48. See source in n. 18 for study of this noncoalition.

49. See, for instance, Pearson and Fuller.

50. The Ford study, cited in n. 18, provided a preliminary report of these data; see Joel S. Berke *et al.*, *Federal Aid to Public Education: Who Benefits?* (Syracuse: Policy Institute, Syracuse University Research Corporation, January 31, 1971). On the 1960 data, see Seymour C. Sacks and David C. Ranney, "Suburban Education: A Fiscal Analysis," *Urban Affairs Quarterly*, 2 (1966), 107.

51. Masters *et al.*, 271.

52. On the variations, see Joseph M. Schlesinger, "The Politics of the Executive," in Herbert Jacob and Kenneth Vines (eds.), *Politics in the American States* (Boston: Little, Brown, 1965).

53. For the first set of findings below, see Thomas R. Dye, *Politics, Economics, and the Public* (Chicago: Rand McNally, 1966); "Politics, Economics, and Educational Outcomes in the States," *Educational Administration Quarterly*, 3 (1967), 28–48; "Governmental Structure, Urban Environment, and Educational Policy," *Midwest Journal of Political Science*, 11 (1967) 353–80; and "Executive Power and Public Policy in the States," *Western Political Quarterly*, 22 (1969), 926–39. Dye was not the first with these findings, it should be noted.

For the second set of findings below, see Charles F. Cnudde and Donald J. Mc-Crone, "Party Competition and Welfare Policies in the American States," *American Political Science Review*, 63 (1969), 858–66; and Ira Sharkansky and Richard I. Hofferbert, "Dimensions of State Politics, Economics, and Public Policy," *ibid.*, 867–79; Brian R. Fry and Richard F. Winters, "The Politics of Redistribution," *ibid.*, 64 (1970), 508–22; and Ira Sharkansky, "Economic Development, Representative Mechanisms, Administrative Professionalism and Public Policies: A Comparative Analysis of Within-State Distributions of Economic and Political Traits," *Journal of Politics*, 33 (1971), 112–32. For a review through 1968, see Herbert Jacob and Michael Lipsky, "Outputs, Structure and Power: An Assessment of Changes in the Study of State and Local Politics," *ibid.*, 30 (1968), 510–38.

One policy output amenable to macroanalysis, but not used on 1970 data, is desegregation. Thus, Dan W. Dodson, "School Administration, Control, and Public Policy Concerning Integration," *Journal of Negro Education*, 34 (1965), 249–57; Thomas R. Dye, "Urban School Segregation: A Comparative Analysis," *Urban Affairs Quarterly*, 4 (1968), 141–65; and B. E. Vanfossen, "Variables Related to Resistance to Desegregation in the South," *Social Forces*, 47 (1968), 39–44.

Variables neither political nor economic have been applied here. See Marvin C. Aklin, "Religious Factors in the Determination of Educational Expenditures," *Educational Administration Quarterly*, 2 (1966), 123–32; David C. Ranney, "The Impact of Metropolitanism on Central City Education," *ibid.*, 4 (1968), 24–36; and Thomas R. Dye, "City-Suburban Social Distance and Public Policy," *Social Forces*, 44 (1965), 100–06.

54. Jack L. Walker, "The Diffusion of Innovations Among the American States, *ibid.*, 63 (1969), 880–99. See also Harmon Zeigler and Karl Johnson, "Educational Innovation and Political-Economic Systems," *Education and Urban Society*, 1 (1969), 161–76.

55. Masters *et al.*, 25.

56. *Ibid.*, 21.

57. Sharkansky, *Regionalism in American Politics,* 140–41; see especially chs. 5–6.

58. Stanley Kelley, Jr., *et al.*, "Registration and Voting; Putting First Things First," *American Political Science Review,* 61 (1967), 359–79; V. O. Key, Jr., *Southern Politics in State and Nation* (New York: Knopf, 1948); Eugene C. Lee, *The Politics of Nonpartisanship* (Berkeley: University of California Press, 1960).

59. The Institute of Governmental Studies, University of California, Berkeley, has published several influential studies of the constraints of the two-thirds rule in their Public Affairs Reports series; for example, Stanley Scott and Frank Marini, "Local Bond Elections in California: The Two-Thirds Majority Requirement," 3 (1962), No. 3; and Scott and Randy Hamilton, "Extraordinary Majority Voting Requirements v. Equal Representation: A Constitutional Challenge," 10 (1969), No. 4, and their bibliographies.

60. *Ibid.*, 4.

61. The total percentage of all bond issues approved over these years are, beginning with 1961–1962: 72.2, 72.4, 72.5, 74.7, 72.5, 66.6, 67.6, and 56.8. If the measure is percentage of all monies approved in these years, the figures are: 68.9, 69.6, 71.1, 79.4, 74.5, 69.2, 62.5, and 43.6.

62. A review of these new forces, with application to Michigan, is found in Guthrie *et al.* In late 1970, the United States Supreme Court declared that one aspect of such unequal allocation in Virginia violated equal protection of the laws. In Michigan, the governor was calling for the state to take over all financing of local schools. In August, 1971, the California Supreme Court overturned the constitutionality of the local property tax when it creates unequal educational opportunities (*Serrano v. Priest*). In October, 1971, a federal district court came to the same decision about Minnesota taxes. In both California and Minnesota, the courts found these taxes did create such inequalities.

Part Two: Introduction

1. We are grateful to Eugene Eidenberg and Roy D. Morey for bringing this statement to our attention in the preface to their *An Act of Congress* (New York: Norton, 1969).

2. William J. Russell, "Occupational Choice: An Analysis of the National Defense Student Loan Program," Ph.D. dissertation, University of California, Berkeley, 1971.

3. David Easton, *A Framework for Political Analysis* (Englewood Cliffs, N.J.: Prentice-Hall, 1965), 130.

Chapter 8

1. For an analysis of the passage and first two years of ESEA, see Stephen K. Bailey and Edith K. Mosher, *ESEA: The Office of Education Administers A Law* (Syracuse: Syracuse University Press, 1968). Numerous books and articles have been written about ESEA's passage, including Eugene Eidenberg and Roy D. Morey, *An Act of Congress* (New York: Norton, 1969).

2. Samuel Halperin, "ESEA: Five Years Later," a speech reprinted in *Congressional Record,* September 9, 1970, H8492–H8494.

3. See, for example, Ruby Martin and Phyllis McClure, *Title I of ESEA: Is It Helping Poor Children?* (Washington, D.C.: Washington Research Project, 1969).

4. U.S. Office of Education, *History of Title I, ESEA* (1965).

5. See Michael W. Kirst, "Federalism and Urban Education," *Education and Urban Society,* 39 (1970), 623–40; and Jerome T. Murphy, "Title I of ESEA: The Politics of Implementing Federal Education Reform," *Harvard Education Review,* 41 (1971), 35–63.

6. Robert Bendiner, *Obstacle Course on Capitol Hill* (New York: McGraw-Hill,

1964). See also Richard Fenno, *National Politics and Federal Aid to Education* (Syracuse: Syracuse University Press, 1962).

7. As quoted by Halperin, H8492.

8. James Sundquist, *Politics and Policy* (Washington, D.C.: Brookings Institution, 1968), ch. 5, analyses these political considerations.

9. See Eidenberg and Morey, 151–52.

10. For a comprehensive discussion, see David K. Cohen, "Politics and Research," *Review of Educational Research* (April, 1970), 213–239.

11. See Harry Picarriello, "Evaluation of Title I," unpublished paper, U.S. Office of Education. See also a study by G. E. Tempo, *Survey and Analysis of Title I Funding for Compensatory Education* (Santa Barbara, 1968).

12. Morton Grodzins, *The American System* (Chicago: Rand McNally, 1966).

13. Elizabeth Drew, "Education's Billion Dollar Baby," *Atlantic* (July, 1966), 37–43.

14. The subsequent analysis is based on a Ford Foundation–supported study of six states; see Joel S. Berke and Michael W. Kirst (eds.), *Federal Aid to Education: Who Benefits? Who Governs?* (Lexington, Mass.: Heath, 1972).

15. Myron Millstein, "Functions of the California State Department of Education as They Relate to Two Federally Funded Educational Programs," Ph.D. dissertation, University of California, Berkeley, 1967, 113.

16. See Berke and Kirst.

17. Francis Galbraith, "The California State Superintendent of Instruction: His Uses of Power, 1963–1965," Ph.D. dissertation, University of California, Berkeley, 1966.

18. See Jim B. Pearson and Edgar Fuller, *Education in The States: Historical Development and Outlooks* (Washington, D.C.: NEA, 1969), 1203. For a general treatment of Texas politics, see Stuart A. MacCorkle and Dick Smith, *Texas Government* (New York: McGraw-Hill, 1968).

19. For a comprehensive review of education policy in Texas, see the five-volume study of the Governor's Committee on Public Education, *The Challenge and the Change* (Austin: Texas Education Agency, 1968).

20. See Fred Gantt, Jr., *The Chief Executive of Texas* (Austin: University of Texas Press, 1964), ch. 5.

21. Martin and McClure.

22. "School Comparability Guidelines," *National Journal* (June 13, 1970), 1233–34.

23. *Ibid.*, 1234.

24. The following is based on interviews with Washington officials, particularly Samuel Halperin, former deputy assistant secretary of HEW for legislative relations.

25. Empirical evidence of the rural, poor-state orientation of this program is found in the studies of James W. Guthrie, "City Schools in a Federal Vise: The Political Dynamics of Federal Aid to Urban Schools," *Education and Urban Society,* 2 (1970), 199–218; and James W. Guthrie and Stephen B. Lawton, "The Distribution of Federal School Aid Funds; Who Wins? Who Loses? *Educational Administration Quarterly,* 5 (1969), 47–61.

26. For the tangled origins of this program, see John C. Donovan, *The Politics of Poverty* (New York: Pegasus, 1967); and Sundquist, ch. 4.

27. See, for example, Harvard Center for Law and Education, *Inequality in Education,* No. 2 (Cambridge, December 5, 1969).

28. *Ibid.*, No. 5 (June 30, 1970).

29. Even the effort to bring nonprofessionals in as consultants and advisory members at the national level has resulted in their cooptation. See Thomas E. Cronin and Norman C. Thomas, "Educational Policy Advisors and the Great Society," *Public Policy,* 18 (1970), 659–86.

30. National Advisory Council on the Education of Disadvantaged Children, first annual report, Washington, D.C., March 31, 1966.

31. Information supplied through interview with Edward Costa, Title I coordinator

for Rhode Island, other federal and state officials, and the staff of the NAACP Legal Defense Fund.

32. USOE policies such as this one are disseminated to chief state school officers as "program guides."

Chapter 9

1. For review of these cases, see Milton R. Konvitz, *First Amendment Freedoms* (Ithaca: Cornell University Press, 1963), part 1. For reactions to these decisions, see Frank J. Souraf, "Zorach v. Clauson: The Impact of a Supreme Court Decision," *American Political Science Review,* 53 (1959), 777–91; Robert H. Birkby, "The Supreme Court and the Bible Belt: Tennessee Reaction to the 'Schempp' Decision," *Midwest Journal of Political Science,* 10 (1966), 304–15; H. Frank Way, Jr., "Survey Research on Judicial Decisions: The Prayer and Bible Reading Cases," *Western Political Quarterly,* 21 (1968), 189–205; Kenneth M. Dolbeare and Phillip E. Hammond, "Local Elites, the Impact of Judicial Decisions, and the Process of Change," paper read at the 1969 convention of the American Political Science Association; Donald R. Reich, "Schoolhouse Religion and the Supreme Court: A Report on Attitudes of Teachers and Principals and on School Practices in Wisconsin and Ohio," paper read at the 1969 convention of the Association of American Law Schools; and William K. Muir, Jr., *Prayer in the Public Schools* (Chicago: University of Chicago Press, 1967). For discussion of the principles in conflict, see Dallin H. Oaks (ed.), *The Wall Between Church and State* (Chicago: University of Chicago Press, 1963).

2. Seminal statements of the thesis are Benjamin Cardozo, *The Nature of the Judicial Process* (New Haven: Yale University Press, 1921); and, in the contemporary period, Jack W. Peltason, *Federal Courts in the Political Process* (New York: Random House, 1955). For more recent analysis in this mode, see Samuel Krislov, *The Supreme Court in the Political Process* (New York: Macmillan, 1965); and Glendon Schubert, *Judicial Policy-Making* (Chicago: Scott, Foresman, 1965), esp. ch. 7; For empirical studies, see Herbert Jacob (ed.), *Law, Politics, and the Federal Courts* (Boston: Little, Brown, 1967).

3. Schubert, 7. Much of the following reflects this author's use of systems analysis of the judicial process.

4. David J. Danelski, *A Supreme Court Justice Is Appointed* (New York: Random House, 1964); for a bibliography, see Loren P. Beth, *Politics, the Constitution, and the Supreme Court* (Evanston: Row Peterson, 1962), 108–10.

5. Wallace Mendelson, *Capitalism, Democracy, and the Supreme Court* (New York: Appleton-Century-Crofts, 1960).

6. Clement R. Vose, *Caucasians Only* (Berkeley: University of California Press, 1959); and "Litigation as a Form of Pressure Group Activity," *Annals of the American Academy of Political and Social Science,* 319 (1958), 22–25.

7. The behavioral school embodying this concept of values is illustrated in Glendon Schubert, *Constitutional Politics* (New York: Holt, Rinehart & Winston, 1960); and Glendon Schubert (ed.), *Judicial Decision-Making* (New York: Free Press, 1963).

8. *Brown v. Board of Education,* 347 U.S. 483 (1954). This section summarizes the details found in Daniel M. Berman, *It Is So Ordered* (New York: Norton, 1966).

9. The thesis is developed in V. O. Key, Jr., *Southern Politics in State and Nation* (New York: Knopf, 1949); and C. Vann Woodward, *The Strange Career of Jim Crow* (New York: Oxford University Press, 1957).

10. See *Missouri ex rel. Gaines v. Canada,* 305 U.S. 337 (1938); *Sipuel v. Board of Regents of the University of Oklahoma,* 332 U.S. 631 (1948); *Sweatt v. Painter,* 339 U.S. 629 (1950); and *McLaurin v. Oklahoma State Regents,* 339 U.S. 637 (1950).

11. On the strategies involved, see Berman, ch. 3; and Alfred H. Kelly, "The School Desegregation Case," in John A. Garraty (ed.), *Quarrels That Have Shaped the Constitution* (New York: Harper & Row, 1964).

12. On such "law-office history," see Alfred H. Kelly, "Clio and the Court: An

Illicit Love Affair," in Philip B. Kurland (ed.), *The Supreme Court Review, 1965* (Chicago: University of Chicago Press, 1965).

13. A further complication was the sudden death of the chief justice a month before reargument and the recess appointment of Earl Warren, followed by a protracted senatorial struggle over his nomination.

14. See Berman, 114; and Kelly, "The School Desegregation Case."

15. *Brown v. Board of Education*, 349 U.S. 294 (1955).

16. The argument is developed fully in Schubert, *Judicial Policy-Making*, 149–53.

17. Benjamin Muse, *Ten Years of Prelude* (New York: Viking Press, 1964), ch. 2, gives the initial reaction; quotation is at 20.

18. Warren Breed, "Group Structure and Resistance to Desegregation in the Deep South," *Social Problems*, 10 (1962), 84–94.

19. Reed Sarratt, *The Ordeal of Desegregation: The First Decade* (New York: Harper & Row, 1966), chs. 1–2, portrays the reactions of governors and legislators. See also Samuel Krislov, "Constituency and Constitutionalism: The Desegregation Issue and Tensions and Aspirations of Southern Attorneys General," *Midwest Journal of Political Science*, 3 (1959), 75–92.

20. Seminal studies of this phenomenon are Walter F. Murphy, "Lower Court Checks on Supreme Court Power," *American Political Science Review*, 53 (1959), 1017–31; and Jack W. Peltason, *Fifty-Eight Lonely Men: Southern Federal Judges and School Desegregation* (New York: Harcourt Brace Jovanovich, 1962). See also Charles V. Hamilton, "Southern Judges and Negro Voting Rights: The Judicial Approach to the Solution of Controversial Social Problems," *Wisconsin Law Review*, 72 (1965), 72–102; Kenneth N. Vines, "Federal District Judges and Race Relations Cases in the South," *Journal of Politics*, 26 (1964), 337–57; and Leon Friedman (ed.), *Southern Justice* (Cleveland: World, 1963; New York: Random House, 1965).

21. Sarratt, chs. 4–11.

22. Muse, 50, provides the tally and sources. See also Sheldon Hackney, "Southern Violence," *American Historical Review*, 74 (1969), 906–25.

23. The major exception was Prince Edward County, Va.; see Bob Smith, *They Closed Their Schools* (Chapel Hill: University of North Carolina Press, 1965).

24. Muse, 62–65.

25. Stuart S. Nagel, "Court-Curbing Periods in American History," *Vanderbilt Law Review*, 18 (1965), 925–44.

26. For cases studies, see Howard E. Shuman, "Senate Rules and the Civil Rights Bill [1957]: A Case Study," *American Political Science Review*, 51 (1957), 955–75; Daniel M. Berman, *A Bill Becomes a Law*, 2d ed. (New York: Macmillan, 1966); John W. Anderson, *Eisenhower, Brownell and the Congress* (University, Ala.: University of Alabama Press, 1964); and James L. Sundquist, *Politics and Policy* (Washington, D.C.: Brookings Institution, 1968), ch. 6. For history of litigation over discrimination, see Loren Miller, *The Petitioners* (New York: Random House, 1966).

27. For a local case study of such resistance, see Frederick M. Wirt, *Politics of Southern Equality: Law and Social Change in a Mississippi County* (Chicago: Aldine, 1970), part 3.

28. For documentation of these data, see U.S. Commission on Civil Rights annual reports from 1959 to 1964, as well as transcripts of its several hearings on Negro school complaints.

29. *Cooper v. Aaron*, 358 U.S. 1 (1958). For listing of cases that the Court declined to review, see Jack Greenberg, "The Supreme Court, Civil Rights and Civil Dissonance," *Yale Law Journal*, 77 (1968), 1524–25, fn. 10.

30. *Goss v. Board of Education*, 373 U.S. 683 (1963). For post-1958 refusals to review, see Greenberg, 1525–26, fn. 15.

31. For this thesis, see Peltason, *Fifty-Eight Lonely Men*.

32. For this thesis, see Greenberg.

33. For direct evidence of these relationships to tolerance, see Paul B. Sheatsley, "White Attitudes Toward the Negro," *Daedalus*, 95 (1966), 224–29. For a more extensive analysis of polls on this subject, see William Brink and Louis Harris, *The*

Negro Revolution in America (New York: Simon & Schuster, 1964); and William Brink and Louis Harris, *Black and White* (New York: Simon & Schuster, 1967).

34. Thomas R. Dye, "Urban School Segregation: A Comparative Analysis," *Urban Affairs Quarterly,* 4 (1968), 141–66.

35. Tom P. Brady, *Black Monday* (Winona, Miss.: Association of Citizens' Councils, 1955).

36. Besides sources on these events cited in n. 26, see also *Revolution in Civil Rights* (Washington, D.C.: Congressional Quarterly), 4th ed. 1968. A more impressionistic account is Anthony Lewis, *The New York Times, Portrait of a Decade* (New York: Random House, 1964).

37. Gary Orfield, *The Reconstruction of Southern Education* (New York: Wiley-Interscience, 1969) provides detailed insight into these administrative problems in the early years.

38. *U.S. v. Jefferson County Board of Education,* 372 F.2d 836 (5 Cir. 1966), affirmed *en banc* 380 F.2d 385 (1967). See also *Alexander v. Holmes County Board of Education,* 90 S.C. 29 (1969); *Lee v. Macon County Board of Education,* 267 F. Supp. 458 (M.D.Ala 1967); *Green v. School Board of New Kent County,* 391 U.S. 430 (1968). For a review of some of these, see U.S. Commission on Civil Rights, *Southern School Desegregation, 1966–67* (1967), Appendix VI.

39. See Holmes County case cited in n. 38. On the changing role of the Supreme Court from *Brown I* to the late 1960's, see Greenberg.

40. For one such signal reported by an able political analyst, see Theodore H. White, *The Making of the President, 1968* (New York: Atheneum, 1969), 137–38.

41. On this exception, see Wirt, ch. 10.

42. For a summary of these events, see *New York Times,* March 8, 1970, 1.

43. Text of speech in *ibid.,* March 25, 1970, 26–27.

44. A HEW report in March, 1970, claimed that only 7 of 300 Deep South school districts had to increase busing in order to desegregate, that most districts regularly bus anyhow (often all the children are bused), and that about 17 million are bused daily.

45. *Lawlessness and Disorder* and *The Federal Retreat in School Desegregation* (Atlanta: Southern Regional Council, 1968, 1969).

46. See US-CCR report in n. 38 and *Federal Enforcement of School Desegregation* (1969).

47. See HEW reports in *New York Times,* February 23, 1969, 51; and March 15, 1970, 70; in *Integrated Education,* 9 (1971), 50–51. The figures for students, school systems, and schools must be kept distinct in this evaluation.

48. The Mississippi reactions are found in contemporary press accounts. On attitude changes, see HEW report, August 24, 1969, a survey of 1,230 persons in 13 school districts desegregated for two years. For impressionistic views by those involved in the process, see Betsy Fancher, *Voices from the South* (Atlanta: Southern Regional Council, 1970). On private schools, see press during 1970 and US-CCR report in n. 38.

49. See HEW report, August 24, 1969, and Gallup poll in *New York Times,* September 2, 1969; a similar Gallup poll in spring of 1971 showed even greater change. For listing and summary of the extensive literature on influence of school desegregation in changing basic racial attitudes, see U.S. Commission on Civil Rights, *Racial Isolation in the Public Schools* (1967). See also Jon P. Alston and Melvin J. Knapp, "Acceptance of School Integration, 1965–1969," *Integrated Education,* 9 (1971), 11–15; and Donal E. Muir, "Six-Year Trends in Integration Attitudes of Deep-South University Students," *ibid.,* 21–27.

50. See Harris polls for March and June, 1970, and Gallup poll, December, 1970. On the combined hopeful and evasive picture, see *The South and Her Children: School Desegregation 1970–1971* (Atlanta: Southern Regional Council, 1971).

51. Orfield, 3; the following two paragraphs are drawn from *ibid.,* ch. 1.

52. Compare the actions of the two in *Revolution in Civil Rights* (Washington, D.C.: Congressional Quarterly, 1968), 4th ed., 36–52, and Sundquist.

53. Orfield, 312. These pressures, among others, moved enforcement to the HEW secretary's office; see *ibid., 320–48.*

54. Krislov, *The Supreme Court in the Political Process,* 145–46.

55. Walter F. Murphy and Joseph Tanenhaus, "Public Opinion and the United States Supreme Court: A Preliminary Mapping of Some Prerequisites for Court Legitimation of Regime Changes," *Law & Society Review,* 11 (1968), 357–84.

56. For data, see *ibid., 377–80.* For a study that supports much in this section, see Kenneth M. Dolbeare, "The Public Views the Supreme Court," in Jacob, 194–212.

57. The tie between knowledge and action in politics is well documented; for a summary of the research, see Lester W. Milbrath, *Political Participation* (Chicago: Rand McNally, 1965).

58. For evidence of partisan followers' differences of view on Court's role, see Kenneth M. Dolbeare and Phillip E. Hammond, "The Political Party Basis of Attitudes Toward the Supreme Court," *Public Opinion Quarterly,* 32 (1968), 16–30.

59. See Krislov, *The Supreme Court in the Political Process,* ch. 6, for factors affecting compliance with Court decisions. For a theoretical framework on law and social change, see Wirt, chs. 1, 14–15.

60. See Murphy and Tanenhaus, 362–63; and Dolbeare, "The Public Views the Supreme Court," 200.

61. For references to research on reaction to these decisions, see n. 1.

Chapter 10

1. William F. Pilder, "The Concept of Utility in Curriculum Discourse: 1918–1967," Ph.D. dissertation, Ohio State University, 1968.

2. H. D. Werle, "Lay Participation in Curriculum Improvement Program," *Dissertation Abstracts,* 25 (1964), 5081.

3. Herbert Spencer, *Education: Intellectual, Moral, and Physical* (New York: Appleton, 1870).

4. Algo D. Henderson, "Innovations in Medical Education," *Journal of Higher Education,* 40 (1969), 7.

5. Patricia Pine, "Where Education Begins," *American Education,* 4 (1968), 14; and Carl Bereiter and Siegfried Engelman, *Teaching Disadvantaged Children in the Preschool* (Englewood Cliffs, N.J.: Prentice-Hall, 1966).

6. Bonnie B. Stretch, "The Rise of the Free School," *Saturday Review,* June 20, 1970.

7. Charles Lindbloom and David Braybrooke, *A Strategy of Decision* (New York: Free Press, 1963).

8. See for instance, R. M. Gagne, "The Analysis of Instructional Objectives for the Design of Instruction," in Robert Glaser (ed.), *Teaching Machines and Programmed Learning,* II (Washington, D.C.: 1965), 21–65; and Brian N. Lewis and Gordon Park, "The Theory and Practice of Adaptive Teaching Systems," *ibid.,* 213–66. An earlier work was Robert B. Miller, "Analysis and Specification for Behavior Training," in Robert Glaser (ed.), *Training Research and Education* (Pittsburgh: University of Pittsburgh, 1962), 31–62.

9. For example, see Wilford Aikin, *The Story of the Eight Year Study* (New York: Harper & Row, 1942); E. W. Eisner, "Educational Objectives: Help or Hindrance?" *School Review,* 75 (1967), 3; and James Moffet, "Misbehavioral English: A Position Paper," in National Council of Teachers of English, *On Writing Behavioral Objectives for English* (Champaign: NCTE, 1970), 111–16.

10. James Sundquist, *Politics and Policy* (Washington, D.C.: Brookings Institution, 1969), ch. 5.

11. Western Association of Schools and Colleges, *Visiting Handbook: 1965.*

12. James Koerner, *Who Controls American Education?* (Boston: Beacon Press, 1968).

13. See Aikin; and Charles Chamberlin, *Did They Succeed in College?* (New York: Harper & Row, 1942).

14. Daniel Elazar, *American Federalism: A View from the States* (New York: Crowell, 1965).

15. James B. Conant, *The Comprehensive High School* (New York: McGraw-Hill, 1967).

16. *Ibid.*

17. Koerner, 126–127.

18. Hillel Black, *The American Schoolbook* (New York: Morrow, 1967).

19. Koerner, 65.

20. Arnold Grobman, *The Changing Classroom* (Garden City, N.Y.: Doubleday, 1969); and Paul Marsh, "The Physical Science Study Committee," Ph.D. dissertation, Harvard University, 1963.

21. See Black.

22. Koerner, 62.

23. See Grobman; Black.

24. Gordon B. Turner, "The American Council of Learned Societies and Curriculum Revision," in Heath (ed.), *New Curricula* (New York: Harper & Row, 1964), 136–60.

25. Roland J. Pellegrin, "An Analysis of Sources and Processes of Innovation in Education" (Eugene: Center for the Advanced Study of Educational Administration, University of Oregon), 15.

26. George Gallup, *How the Nation Views the Public Schools* (Princeton: Gallup International, 1969), 9.

27. Roscoe Martin, *Government and the Suburban School* (Syracuse: Syracuse University Press, 1962), 55.

28. Marilyn Gittel *et al.*, "Investigation of Fiscally Independent and Dependent School Districts" (Washington, D.C.: U.S. Office of Education Research, Project No. 3237, 1967), 115.

29. Richard W. Saxe, "Mayors and Schools," *Urban Education,* 4 (1969), 3.

30. *Ibid.,* 250.

31. Robert H. Salisbury, "Schools and Politics in the Big City," *Harvard Educational Review,* 37 (1967), 3.

32. Martin, 61. See also Gordon M. Mackenzie, "Curricular Change," in Mathew Miles (ed.), *Innovation in Education* (New York: Teachers College Press, 1964), 399–424.

33. Richard O. Carlson, *Adoption of Educational Innovations* (Eugene: Center for the Advanced Study of Educational Administration, University of Oregon, 1965).

34. *Ibid.,* 64.

35. For a more recent study in the San Francisco Bay Area, see Gerald Hamrin, "An Analysis of Factors Influencing Educational Change," Ph.D. dissertation, Stanford University, 1970.

36. See Carlson; Hamrin.

37. Pellegrin, 9.

38. Mark Chester *et al.*, "The Principals' Role in Facilitating Innovation," *Theory into Practice,* 1 (1963), 2. See also Henry M. Brichell, "State Organization for Educational Change," in Miles.

39. H. Thomas James *et al.*, *Determinants of Educational Expenditures in Large Cities* (Stanford: School of Education, 1966), 60.

40. Saxe, 251.

41. See Charles Silberman, *Crisis in the Classroom* (New York: Random House, 1970).

Part Three

1. Sheldon S. Wolin, "Politics, Education, and Theory," 1, paper presented at COBRE Workshop on Politics of Elementary and Secondary Education, September, 1970, to appear in Michael W. Kirst (ed.), *State, School, and Politics: Research Directions* (Lexington, Mass.: Heath, 1972).

2. A clear presentation of the problems involved are David H. Fischer, *Historians' Fallacies: Toward a Logic of Historical Thought* (New York: Harper & Row, 1970). This work looks at far more than historians' efforts, as witness its numerous critiques of political science research.

3. This section draws its main critical themes from the following: Herbert J. Spiro, "An Evaluation of Systems Theory," in James C. Charlesworth (ed.), *Contemporary Political Analysis* (New York: Free Press, 1967), ch. 9; A. James Gregor, "Political Science and the Uses of Functional Analysis," *American Political Science Review*, 62 (1968), 425–39; Gerald E. Sroufe, "Political Systems Analysis and Research in Educational Administration: Can the Emperor Be Clothed?" paper presented at the meeting of the American Educational Research Association, 1969; Jerome Stephens, "The Logic of Functional and Systems Analysis in Political Science," *Midwest Journal of Political Science*, 13 (1969), 367–94; James L. Grant, "Systems Theory Is Not Empirically Relevant — What Is?" paper presented at the Western Political Science Association meeting, 1970. These works are distinct from criticisms of functionalism or of behavioralism, with which criticism of systems analysis is often mixed.

4. Grant, 14–15. Grant is more sanguine about the problem than this statement suggests. For a fuller and typical criticism of model thinking, see H. Goldhamer, "Fashion in Social Science," *World Politics*, 6 (1954), 394–404.

5. Martin Landau, "On the Use of Metaphor in Political Analysis," *Social Research* 28 (1961), 353, 343; see also T. Kuhn, *The Structure of Scientific Revolutions* (Chicago: University of Chicago Press, 1962).

6. Fischer, 4–5.

7. See R. C. Buck, "Logic of General Systems Theory," in H. Feigl and M. Scriven (eds.), *Minnesota Studies in the Philosophy of Sciences,* (Minneapolis: University of Minnesota Press, 1956), vol. 1, 223–39; and John G. Gunnell, "Social Science and Political Reality: The Problem of Explanation," *Social Research*, 35 (1968), 159–81.

8. David Easton, *A Framework for Political Analysis* (Englewood Cliffs, N.J.: Prentice-Hall, 1965), xi. Note the avoidance of the physical-biological models and the divergence from the communication model itself in Easton's discussion of the feedback loop in *A Systems Analysis of Political Life* (New York: Wiley, 1965), ch. 23, especially 367, n. 1.

9. Richard F. Fenno, Jr., *The Power of the Purse: Appropriation Politics in Congress* (Boston: Little, Brown, 1966); Glendon Schubert, *Judicial Policy-Making* (Chicago: Scott, Foresman, 1965); David Easton and Jack Dennis, *Children in the Political System* (New York: McGraw-Hill, 1969). For earlier usage, see Easton, *A Framework*, xi, note. In education, there have been Eugene Eidenberg and Roy D. Morey, *An Act of Congress* (New York: Norton, 1969); Philip Meranto, *The Politics of Federal Aid to Education in 1965* (Syracuse: Syracuse University Press, 1967); Philip H. Coombs, *The World Educational Crisis: A System Analysis* (New York: Oxford University Press, 1968); Jay D. Scribner, "A Functional-Systems Framework for Analyzing School Board Action," *Educational Administration Quarterly*, 11 (1966), 204–16; Jay D. Scribner, "The Politics of Educational Reform: Analyses of Political Demand," *Urban Education*, 4 (1970), 348–74; Nancy Bordier, "An Eastonian Systems Approach to Analysis of Education Politics," Ph.D. dissertation, 1971. Easton has a several-page bibliography utilizing this framework of analysis.

10. Two contrasting views of this controversy appear side by side in David Easton, "The New Revolution in Political Science," and Sheldon S. Wolin, "Political Theory as a Vocation," in *American Political Science Review*, 63 (1969), 1051–61, 1062–82. See also James G. March, "The Power of Power," in David Easton (ed.), *Varieties of Political Theory* (Englewood Cliffs, N.J.: Prentice-Hall, 1966), 39–70.

11. Schubert, 4.

12. A useful review is H. V. Wiseman, *Political Systems: Some Sociological Approaches* (New York: Praeger, 1966).

13. On the similarity, see Gregor; Stephens; and their bibliography. On this distinction, see Easton and Dennis, *Children in the Political System*, chs. 2–3.

14. Spiro, 164. The purported origins, in chronological order, are functionalism; a modern study of the brain's operations (W. R. Ashby, *Design for a Brain* [New York: Wiley, 1952], cited in Morton A. Kaplan, *Macropolitics* [Chicago: Aldine, 1969], 75–76); Arthur Bentley (in Myron Q. Hale, "The Cosmology of Arthur F. Bentley," in William E. Connolly [ed.], *The Bias of Pluralism* [New York: Atherton, 1969], 46–47); Hobbes (Spiro, 164); and — as with most political scientists — Aristotle (*ibid.*, 165). For the most intriguing parlay of origins, see William T. Bluhm, *Theories of the Political System* (Englewood Cliffs, N.J.: Prentice-Hall, 1965), 290–91.

15. For example, Henry Kariel, *Promise of Politics* (Englewood Cliffs, N.J.: Prentice-Hall, 1966).

16. This is not so, however, for his most recent study; see Easton and Dennis.

17. Easton, *A Systems Analysis,* 169.

18. *Ibid.,* 169–70.

19. Gregor, 431–32.

20. On Easton's denial that he has a "theory," see his *A Systems Analysis,* 12. On possibilities for hypotheses, see Kaplan, 58.

21. Sroufe, 21.

22. Kaplan, 71.

23. Grant, 13.

24. See Laurence Iannaccone and Frank W. Lutz, *Politics, Power and Policy: The Governing of Local School Districts* (Columbus: Merrill, 1970), and the dissertation research cited therein; see also Scribner, "The Politics of Educational Reform."

25. These criticisms are abstracted from the two Wolin articles cited in notes 1 and 10; Charles A. McCoy and John Playford (eds.), *Apolitical Politics: A Critique of Behaviorism* (New York: Crowell, 1967); Kariel.

26. Wolin, "Politics, Education, and Theory," 3–4.

27. A similar charge is made against Talcott Parsons' functional analysis for its purported emphasis upon stability rather than change. This criticism focuses only upon his earlier writing and ignores the dynamic focus of his later work; see William C. Mitchell, *Sociological Analysis and Politics: The Theories of Talcott Parsons* (Englewood Cliffs, N.J.: Prentice-Hall, 1967), 140–63.

28. M. L. Goldschmidt, "Democratic Theory and Contemporary Political Science," *Western Political Science Quarterly,* 19 (1966 supplement), 7.

29. This critique is extensive in the sources cited in n. 25. Wolin, "Politics, Education, and Theory," 4–5, finds these principles laid out in Robert A. Dahl and Charles E. Lindblom, *Politics, Economics, and Welfare* (New York: Harper & Row, 1953), 228–40; and in Charles E. Lindblom, *The Intelligence of Democracy* (New York: Free Press, 1965), 3–17, 117 ff., 274 ff.

30. Wolin, "Politics, Education, and Theory," 6.

31. *Ibid.,* 6, 9.

32. Among other rebuttals, see Easton and Dennis, chs. 2–3; and Easton, *A Framework,* 88.

33. Both seem to be forms of the genetic fallacy termed "fallacy of ethical historicism" by Fischer, 155–57.

34. James W. Guthrie and Edward Wynne (eds.), *New Models for American Education* (Englewood Cliffs, N.J.: Prentice-Hall, 1971).

35. We do not deal with another aspect of this controversy — that behavioralism is not value-free as it claims — because we regard it as a strawman; our view is reflected briefly in Ithiel de Sola Pool, "Some Facts about Values," *PS,* 3 (1970), 102–06.

36. For a review of this research, see Ch. 7, n. 53.

37. Sroufe, 19.

38. See David Tyack, "City Schools at the Turn of the Century: Centralization and Social Control," unpublished paper, Stanford University.

39. William H. Issel, "Modernization in Philadelphia School Reform, 1882–1905," *The Pennsylvania Magazine of History and Biography,* 94, No. 3 (July, 1970), 381–82.

40. Tyack, 13.

41. The recent San Francisco teachers strike is a good illustration of this trend. See articles in *San Francisco Chronicle* for week of April 5–12, 1971.

42. See National Education Association, *Financial Status of the Public Schools — 1970* (Washington, D.C., 1970). In August, 1971, the California Supreme Court voided California's use of local property taxes if it resulted in unequal educational opportunities (*Serrano v. Priest*); a federal district court did the same for Minnesota in October, 1971.

43. For an overview of the financial conditions of public education, see Advisory Commission on Intergovernmental Relations, *State and Local Finances — 1967 to 1970* (1969).

44. For an example of a proposal for increased state funding, see the proposals of Michigan's Governor Milliken in 1970.

45. For some interesting viewpoints on this trend, see National Committee, *The Struggle for Power in the Public Schools* (Conference Proceedings, Washington, D.C., March 17–19, 1968).

46. Robert R. Alford, *Bureaucracy and Participation* (Chicago: Rand McNally, 1969), chs. 1, 11 have an unsuspected relevance to our discussion.

Subject Index

Author Index